YEARNING TO BREATHE FREE

My Parents' Fight to Reunite during the Holocaust

Scripture quotations are modified from *The Holy Scriptures According to the Masoretic Text*, published by the Jewish Publication Society in 1917.

Cover image of Statue of Liberty: UbjsP /Shutterstock.com.
Preface image of Statue of Liberty: Luciano Mortula/Shutterstock.com.
Chapter 11 image of memorial candle: Pixel Embargo/Shutterstock.com.

Cover design: Peter Weisz
Cover Layout: Benjie Herskowitz, Etc. Studios
Typesetting: Renana Typesetting

ISBN: 978-965-229-864-5

1 3 5 7 9 8 6 4 2

Gefen Publishing House Ltd.
6 Hatzvi Street
Jerusalem 94386, Israel
972-2-538-0247
orders@gefenpublishing.com

Gefen Books
11 Edison Place
Springfield, NJ 07081
516-593-1234
orders@gefenpublishing.com

www.gefenpublishing.com

Printed in Israel

Send for our free catalog

Library of Congress Cataloging-in-Publication Data

Laulicht, Murray, author.
  Yearning to breathe free : my parents' fight to reunite during the Holocaust / Murray Jack Laulicht with Peter Weisz.
    pages cm
  Includes bibliographical references and index.
  ISBN 978-965-229-864-5
  1. Goldwasser, Abraham Chaskel, 1908-1944 – Correspondence. 2. Goldwasser, Ernestyna, 1906-1987 – Correspondence. 3. Jews – Poland – Krak?w – Biography. 4. Holocaust, Jewish (1939-1945) – Poland – Krak?w – Personal narratives. 5. Jews, Polish – United States – Biography. 6. Krak?w (Poland) – Biography. I. Goldwasser, Abraham Chaskel, 1908-1944. Correspondence. Selections. II. Goldwasser, Ernestyna, 1906-1987. Correspondence. Selections. III. Title.
  DS134.72.G67L38 2016
  940.53'18092243862--dc23
                                    2015032346

Yearning to Breathe Free

My Parents' Fight to Reunite during the Holocaust

Murray Jack Laulicht

with Peter Weisz

gefen
publishing house
JERUSALEM ◆ NEW YORK   Est. 1981

To the cherished memories of

Abraham and Ernestyna Goldwasser, my parents,
Philip Laulicht, my second father,
Rae and Joseph Kushner, my in-laws,

who all experienced the Holocaust firsthand

And to my children and grandchildren
who are perpetuating their magnificent legacies

*Then Jacob was greatly afraid and was distressed. And he divided the people
with him…into two camps. And he said, "If Esau comes to the one camp
and smites it, then the remaining camp shall escape."*

– Genesis 32:8–9

If men of the temperament and philosophy of [Assistant US Secretary of State Breckinridge] Long continue in control of immigration administration, we may as well take down that plaque from the Statue of Liberty and black out the "lamp beside the golden door."

– Josiah E. DuBois, Jr.

"Report to the Secretary on the Acquiescence of [the United States] Government in the Murder of the Jews,"
January 13, 1944

CONTENTS

Foreword

This book above all is a love story. It is the story of an extraordinary woman – the author's mother – as she desperately tries to bring her trapped husband to America during the 1940s. The travails of her experiences in America are well documented and serve to provide the reader with a unique first-person glimpse of what it was like to face the insurmountable obstacles placed in her way by a US State Department committed to barring entry through America's "golden door" to endangered European Jews.

These continuous delays and frustrations are at the heart of this story. But it is also a story of a son's searching for the truth of his father's ultimate fate during the waning days of the Holocaust. Now, after many years of searching, the author is still seeking answers to the mysteries of his father's final resting place and of the exact circumstances of his murder.

Beyond the personal drama recounted here, this book raises the greater question "Why did this happen?" Not the Holocaust per se, but what was behind the government officials who constantly erected road blocks to rescue? Via carefully reproduced archival correspondence, you will read of the author's mother's many attempts to unearth the truth and to seek answers and solutions. All to no avail.

Questions about the final fate of the author's father remain unanswered to this day. This not knowing has haunted the author for many years and caused him to track down rumors, interview witnesses, and pore through thousands of documents in search of information about the father he lost. The father he never met.

The stirring words of Emma Lazarus that grace the Statue of Liberty, "Give me your tired, your poor, your huddled masses, yearning to breathe free," form the backdrop for this powerful story. You will learn how at that particular time, and for this Jewish family, and many others like them, America's vaunted promise of liberty and sanctuary to the outcast – a promise that forms the very foundation of the American Dream – was completely and utterly betrayed.

I have known the author, Murray Laulicht, for more than twenty years, and I have witnessed his lifelong commitment to the importance of Holocaust education. As the chairman of the New Jersey Commission on Holocaust Education, he provided energy, direction, and commitment toward establishing a New Jersey Holocaust/anti-genocide educational mandate. He added to and supported the development of public and private school Holocaust curricula that are still in use today in New Jersey and around the country. Murray and his wife Linda support, through the Laulicht Foundation, many vital Holocaust educational programs.

Murray Laulicht's efforts in writing this book have resulted in a work that provides all of us with a means to examine the role America played in allowing thousands of Jewish victims to become stranded in Europe, and marked for annihilation. Ultimately, this love story – chronicling the tragic and heroic love shared by the author's parents as well as the author's love and hunger for the truth – will enlighten all of us about the grave mistakes made in the past. Hopefully, by learning from those mistakes, we will be able to provide a better future for others "yearning to breathe free."

Dr. Paul B. Winkler
Executive Director
New Jersey Commission on Holocaust Education

Dr. Paul B. Winkler, who has been leading the New Jersey Commission on Holocaust Education and its predecessors since their inception more than forty years ago

Introduction

Murray Laulicht has written a most unique, page-turning, and breathtaking memoir from the Holocaust. It is the story of a passionately devoted husband and wife-with-child, cruelly and tragically forced apart by Hitler's satanic hordes. A father desperately "yearning to breathe free" and to reunite via the "golden door" guarded by the "mighty woman with the torch." We read of their struggle, largely by means of their own words, in letters that traversed continents from Ernestyna, his mother, to Chaskel, his father, and from Chaskel to Ernestyna. The letters enable us to actually feel and experience the living and loving human beings whose only wish is to live together as a family and whose only sin is that they were Jews.

It is also the story of a courageous heroine, Ernestyna Goldwasser, an educated and resourceful woman who, as the inheritor of American citizenship from her father, Jakob Grunfeld, is able to flee Krakow and the Nazi inferno for America in January 1940. For the sake of the unborn child in her womb and in the hope that from the backdrop of a free America it will be easier for her to bring out her beloved Chaskel, she arrives alone, ready for the frustrating challenges and bitter disappointments that lie ahead.

It is also the story of a son (the author) in search of his biological father, whom he never met. The author knows very well that he owes his life to his father's selfless encouragement of his beloved wife to leave him and the fiery furnace that would soon engulf Poland for the sake of the life of their unborn child. Understandably, the author desperately strove to piece together a picture of his father with as many details of his life and death as could be discovered.

It is also the story of Ernestyna's struggle for Chaskel's permit into the United States against the bureaucratic delay purposefully effectuated by Assistant Secretary of State Breckinridge Long, close friend of President Roosevelt, obsessed with preventing a Jewish onslaught of immigrants. Murray Laulicht even cites a confidential memo from Long to all executive bureau chiefs to "delay and effectively stop for a temporary period of indefinite length, the number of immigrants into the United States. We could…put every obstacle in the way…which would postpone and postpone and postpone the granting of the visas." Murray Laulicht writes: "It is my desire to honor the sacred memory of those Holocaust victims denied entry [into America] that prompted me to write this book."

But most important of all, it is also the story of the eventual triumph of the Goldwasser-Laulicht families as well as the Jewish people worldwide against the Nazis and even against a complicit American State Department that I believe to be the most important message of this book. On the most fundamental level, Hitler waged a war against the Jews, against the Jewish people and against what he hoped would be the last Jew. He wanted to stamp "no exit" upon the entire Jewish people; he wanted to close off any door of egress, to see to it that the last Jew would be gunned down, suffocated, or incinerated.

I have just read the epilogue to the book. The author, the ember plucked from the fire, has produced, together with his beloved life's partner, Linda, a magnificent family of four daughters (and their husbands) and many grandchildren. All are dedicated to Torah learning and secular knowledge. All are extremely active in Jewish community building and the building of Jewish institutions. All are active supporters and defenders of the State of Israel.

The State of Israel was established in 1948 with its historic Law of Return, guaranteeing every Jew (and anyone who was Jewish enough to have been sent to Auschwitz is considered Jewish under the Law of Return) automatic citizenship and free haven in the Jewish state. This is the most effective response to Breckinridge Long and his loathsome ilk: Never Again!

Yes, Hitler set out to murder the last Jew, to destroy the last Jewish sacred text, to obliterate the Jewish people as a nation and Torah teaching as the heart of their religion. But Hitler perished at his own hands in a Berlin bunker, and the Nazi movement he thought would conquer the world is hardly a force within a global village now threatened by extremist Islam.

Judaism, on the other hand, is very much alive and kicking, with Israel now the most powerful nation in the Middle East, with the world Jewish population today nearing where it was before Hitler destroyed six million. And the Torah that Hitler attempted to obliterate is stronger than ever, with educational institutions for women like Stern College and Midreshet Lindenbaum, far outdistancing Ernestyna's Bais Yaakov in Krakow. And with Israel, the start-up nation, with advanced *yeshivat hesder* university programs, major hospitals such as Shaare Zedek with groundbreaking scientific breakthroughs in research as well as top-notch medical care, and development towns like Ofakim, which now boasts of a youth center for children and teens who, in addition to sports and culture, are also taught proper nutrition. And all of the above institutions are being funded and developed by Murray and Linda Laulicht, two exemplary embers snatched from the fiery furnace of Nazi Poland and Belarus.

Our God is not a God of death camps. He is a God of redemption. And Israel is not a nation of victims. We are a nation of victors. You see, we won the war against Hitler!

Alas, it was an exceedingly painful war in which we were forced to sacrifice six million of our people, all sacred and innocent. But in every war there are winners and there are losers. Indeed, there is only one winner. We won the war! Hitler is buried in his bunker and Murray and Linda Laulicht are developing Torah and medical and communal institutions in our eternal Holy Land and the United States. We may now sing a new song of Jewish victory:

In every generation they have stood up against us to annihilate us.
But the Holy One, Blessed be He, saves us and our eternal Torah from their hands.
Am Yisrael hai! Ohr Torah yigal ve'yiga'el.
The Jewish people lives! The light of Torah redeems and is redeemed.

– Shlomo Riskin

Rabbi Shlomo Riskin is the founding rabbi of Lincoln Square Synagogue on the Upper West Side of New York City, which he led for twenty years. He is the founding chief rabbi of the Israeli settlement of Efrat in the West Bank; the dean of Manhattan Day School in New York City; and the founder and chancellor of the Ohr Torah Stone Institutions, a network of high schools, colleges, and graduate programs in the United States and Israel. He belongs to the Modern Orthodox stream of Judaism.

Preface

On February 1, 1940, a thirty-three-year-old Jewish woman arrived alone in New York Harbor bearing, in her womb, the person who would eventually become me. Ernestyna Goldwasser had left behind her family, steeped in the rich Jewish culture of Krakow, to seek sanctuary from the marauding Germans who had viciously invaded Poland the previous September.

Through a twist of circumstance, Ernestyna's father, my grandfather, Jakob Grunfeld, had, as a young man, sojourned in the USA and succeeded in obtaining citizenship status before returning to Krakow, where he took a wife and raised a family. Jakob's youngest daughter was my mother, Ernestyna. As the child of a father who held US citizenship, Ernestyna enjoyed a special status that became priceless when the war broke out. She, too, was deemed a US citizen and thereby eligible to emigrate out of Poland. Unfortunately, Ernestyna's husband, my father, Chaskel Goldwasser, enjoyed no such status. As his wife, pregnant with their first child, embarked on her journey, Chaskel was forced to remain behind, trapped in the inferno that was soon to incinerate one-third of the world's Jewish population.

The decision to separate was clearly a heartrending affair. My parents were deeply in love and had recently received the good news that the child they had been trying for about three years to conceive would be arriving in May. But as the family observed, with ever-growing dread, the Nazi noose tightening around their lives, it became painfully clear that any Jew who could escape should do so quickly.

Photo taken at the wedding of my parents, Ernestyna and Chaskel Goldwasser, 1936.
Seated, from left: my grandmother, Leah Grunfeld; my cousin Ruzunya Hirschprung; my
mother and father; my cousin Yankush Hirschprung; my grandmother's sister Manya
Rosehandler; my mother's sister, Gusta Hirschprung.
Second row: my grandmother's brother, Shlomo Hirsch (*third from left*) and his wife (*first
left*) and two daughters (*second from left and second from right*); unidentified rabbi (*third
from right*); my mother's cousin Dita Kaye (*far right*).

My mother, Ernestyna, had received a special dispensation from the
German occupying authorities. This bit of *"protekzia"* allowed her, by
virtue of her US citizenship, to be exempt from the fiat that required all
Jews in Krakow to wear a white identifying armband bearing a blue Star
of David. But of course, given the arbitrary nature of the German authorities, there was no way for my mother to know how long her exalted status
could be counted on to protect her from the ever-widening list of oppres-
sive decrees that were being imposed daily on her fellow Jews.

Since Ernestyna, unlike her older sister Gusta, was at this point child-
less, it made sense for her to venture out first – even though it meant
leaving her dear husband Chaskel behind. The plan was for my mother to
connect in New York with her uncle Baruch (Bernard Greenfield), who
had immigrated to the US and settled in Brooklyn during the 1920s. Following a pattern that had been repeated countless times during the waves
of Jewish immigration to the US over the prior six decades, Ernestyna

would establish a beachhead in America and immediately set to work bringing her husband, mother, and sister over to join her. At least, that was the plan.

My mother entered the US through the "golden door" mentioned in the final words of the Emma Lazarus poem that graces the Statue of Liberty in New York harbor:

The New Colossus

Not like the brazen giant of Greek fame,
With conquering limbs astride from land to land;
Here at our sea-washed, sunset gates shall stand
A mighty woman with a torch, whose flame
Is the imprisoned lightning, and her name
Mother of Exiles. From her beacon-hand
Glows world-wide welcome; her mild eyes command
The air-bridged harbor that twin cities frame.
"Keep, ancient lands, your storied pomp!" cries she
With silent lips. "Give me your tired, your poor,
Your huddled masses yearning to breathe free,
The wretched refuse of your teeming shore.
Send these, the homeless, tempest-tost to me,
I lift my lamp beside the golden door!"

My mother took comfort in the words that identified America as the Mother of Exiles, a welcoming place of refuge for all "your huddled masses, yearning to breathe free." "Soon," she thought, as her vessel steamed by the lady with the lamp, "Chaskel will be able to join me. If I start working right away, he may be here by the time the baby arrives."

What my mother did not know – and what thousands of other Jews with ties to the US and in similar circumstances, also did not know – was that she now faced a powerful new adversary, intent on placing insurmountable obstacles in her path. Obstacles intended to ensure that no significant number of Jewish refugees would ever arrive on American soil. That adversary was the government of the United States and, in particular, the US Department of State, whose shameful and treacherous policies during the Holocaust succeeded in turning the words on the Statue of Liberty into nothing more than a cynical and hollow sham.

Using tactics less brutal, but every bit as antisemitic as those employed by the enemy my mother's family faced in Poland, these new adversaries employed subtle and insidious methods – obfuscation, bureaucratic red tape, heartless roadblocks, and sub-rosa "gentlemen's agreements" – to accomplish their objectives. These top-ranking officials made sure that European Jews were afforded no opportunity to escape their doom by fleeing to the US.

During my mother's valiant struggle to reunite with my father – a process that stretched well over two years – they were able to maintain an intimate and highly emotional correspondence. Many of their letters have been preserved and are presented in this volume as a first-person account of their desperate struggle. In addition, I have included letters written by my mother to various government agencies, embassies, politicians, and others as she sought to find the key that would unlock my father's imprisonment . . . before it was too late.

At times, when I think back to my mother's efforts during those desperate years, I picture her as a little girl standing on the sidewalk in front of her burning home, trying mightily to flag down one of the steady stream of fire engines barreling down the street that uniformly ignore her time and again. It is to her enduring memory, as well as to the memory of the man she strove to save, that this book is dedicated.

This is the story of my mother's valiant fight to reunite her beloved husband with the son he had wanted so desperately to see. But it is not merely my family's story. Documented cases of families in similar circumstances cropped up throughout the US during the war years – each one bearing a legitimate link to US citizenship, each one denied entry and abandoned to a doomed fate as Europe turned into an inferno and the American government turned its back to the flames.

It is my desire to honor the sacred memory of those denied Holocaust victims that prompted me to write this book. Those who, but for the intransigent culture of antisemitism that pervaded the US State Department during those years, would have found refuge from their "teeming shores" beneath the lady with the lamp, beside America's "golden door."

In the following chapters I have presented actual excerpted correspondence between my parents and between my mother and various government agencies written during those tumultuous years. These letters, when read in chronological order, document her truly heroic struggle in a unique and intimate fashion. I feel that this is the most compelling and approachable method of telling their amazing story.

My notes of introduction serve to place each letter into its appropriate context and to explain and clarify references found in the text. Taken together, these letters form a cohesive chronicle of how the antisemitic attitudes that pervaded the highest echelons of the US government during this period contributed to the slaughter of thousands of European Jews. Men, women, and children – "the homeless, tempest-tost" – who, had America offered a true golden door, as Emma Lazarus proclaimed – would have then been able to elude their cruel fate and find safe haven here in the land of the free.

Acknowledgments

The author wishes to extend his deep gratitude to the following individuals, without whose assistance this book could not have been produced:

- Mala Sperling, one of my few surviving cousins, whose voice-recorded translations of numerous Polish and German documents are an essential component of this book.
- Laurie Hasten, my daughter, who diligently transcribed Mala Sperling's translations of the correspondence between my parents and others.
- Professor Dan Hirschberg, Computer Science Department, the University of California, Irvine, and creator of the Krakow Genealogy website, for his invaluable assistance in researching my family's history in Poland.
- Shaya Ben Yehuda, Mark Shraberman, and Lital Beer of Yad Vashem Holocaust Martyrs' and Heroes' Remembrance Authority, Jerusalem, Israel, for their invaluable assistance in providing documents and information concerning my father's whereabouts during the Holocaust.
- Ilan Greenfield, Lynn Douek, and Kezia Raffel Pride of Gefen Publishing House for their magnificent work in publishing, designing, and editing this book.
- Peter Weisz, my literary collaborator, whose free-flowing writing style and assiduous research are evident throughout this book.
- Linda Laulicht, my loving wife and partner, for her constant encouragement and advice and for enabling me to live the life described in this book.

CHAPTER ONE

A World between the Walls

Our family tree – like the family trees of many American Jews – flourished in eastern Europe until it was cruelly cut down during the Holocaust. Its roots were embedded deeply in the rich, verdant soil along the fast-flowing Vistula River, at the point where it races through Krakow – today Poland's second largest city. Krakow's history stretches back to the eleventh century CE, and archival records reveal that Jews lived there even then – from its very beginnings – living through alternating periods of persecution and toleration by the Polish Catholic population.

In 1335, Casimir the Great – the father of the Polish nation – established the town of Kazimierz, near Krakow, specifically as a community to house its burgeoning Jewish population. This apparent act of benevolence toward the Jews was, according to the folk myth, based on Casimir's love for Esther, a comely Jewish girl who begged him to protect her from the antisemitic decrees that had severely curtailed Jewish life in Krakow.

From the fourteenth through the eighteenth centuries, Jewish life thrived in the area inside the main city defensive wall and a second wall that served as the demarcation line for the town's Christian residents. This zone was dubbed the Oppidum Iudeorum by the church, and it became the main cultural and spiritual center of Jewish Poland.

Kazimierz was originally a separate, independent city, but during the lifetime of my earliest known ancestor in the late eighteenth century, it was incorporated into Krakow proper. Its Oppidum Iudeorum remained the Jewish district, however, and became known by its German name: der Judenstadt (the Jewish city).

It was within this world between the walls that our family took root and its destiny took shape.

In tracing my family history back to the mid-eighteenth century – the earliest period I was able to document – it became clear that my biological parents, Ernestyna and Abraham (Chaskel) Goldwasser, held a unique status among the forebears who populate our family tree. Both of my biological parents could trace their lineage back to a common ancestor. Mozes Haskiel Goldwasser, born in or about 1766,* was both my mother's great-great-grandfather and my father's great-great-great grandfather. A look at the family tree chart illustrates this blood relationship.

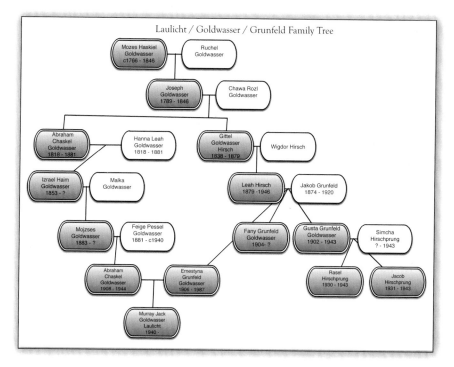

---

* This date, and the other dates pertaining to family members, were drawn from the genealogical records maintained by the Mormon Church, which have been compiled and updated online by Professor Dan Hirschberg of the University of California, Irvine. See "Goldwasser Familes" at http://www.ics.uci.edu/~dan/genealogy/Krakow/Families/Goldwasser.html. These dates are typically dates when a life-cycle event (i.e., birth, marriage, death) was recorded with the authorities and may or may not correspond to the actual dates on which they occurred. Reporting was often delayed in order to

If we consider Mozes to be the trunk of our family tree, then my parents' marriage in 1936 represents the conjoining of two of its upper branches into a single bough – from which my descendants and I would eventually blossom (see diagram).

Our family tree was destined to emerge in an area that was soaked with centuries of Jewish blood. Despite King Casimir's efforts in the fourteenth century to protect the Jews by segregating them into areas such as Kazimierz, church-inspired bloodshed against Poland's Jews continued to scar its history. In 1454, for example, antisemitic riots erupted in Silesia thanks to the inflamed rhetoric of the papal envoy and Franciscan friar, John of Capistrano, whose ruthless campaign against the Jews – whom he accused of profaning Christianity – resulted in the death or exile of thousands. Based on his success at ridding Lower Silesia of its "Jewish problem," John was invited to conduct a similar campaign in Krakow.

Ironically, this period was characterized in the history books as Poland's "Golden Age" or the Polish Renaissance. It saw the construction in 1492 of Krakow's Old Synagogue, which stands today as one of the world's oldest Jewish houses of worship. It is likely that my earliest known ancestor, Mozes Goldwasser, davened (prayed) there some three hundred years

later. Sadly, it serves today merely as a museum memorializing the vibrant and vanished Jewish culture that it once anchored.

Or he may have davened at the Rema Synagogue, built in 1553 in the Oppidum Iudeorum and named for the famous Talmudist the Rema (Rabbi Moshe Isserles), considered to be the "Maimonides of Polish Jewry."

The Old Synagogue in Krakow, Poland, today

Mozes Goldwasser lived during a particularly turbulent period. Shortly after his birth in the 1760s, the Polish parliament in Warsaw, known as the

avoid or postpone taxation and to avoid the attention of the government. The recording of civil dates was of little concern to members of the observant Jewish community.

Sejm, once again took up and debated the "Jewish question." They implemented a series of stringent measures that abolished the Jews' ability to own land or to hold jobs without first obtaining specific permission from the Christian town burghers. When Mozes was a youngster – around the time of the American Revolution – the Sejm passed legislation that sought to force Jews out of the cities into the countryside. It also voted to gravely restrict the civil authority of Poland's rabbis.

Those familiar with Poland's history understand its chimerical nature. The Polish nation has, over the centuries, disappeared entirely from the map, only to reascend like the Phoenix. At the time that Mozes Goldwasser entered the world, Poland was divided between Prussian and Austrian sovereignty. Krakow found itself under the Hapsburg flag, where conditions for Jews were only modestly more tolerable than for their brethren living in the Prussian zone. Mozes, no doubt, witnessed the demise of Krakow's Oppidum Iudeorum, which took place in 1782 when Austrian emperor Joseph II disbanded the *kahal* (the governing Jewish community council). The walls that defined the Jewish quarter came down forty years later.

In 1789, six years after the official end of the Oppidum Iudeorum's role as Krakow's Jewish sector, Mozes and his wife, Ruchel, became the proud parents of their first child, Joseph – my ancestor on both my mother and my father's side. Joseph was born during the year of the French Revolution and into the era of the European Enlightenment that led to increasing levels of civil liberties being extended to Jews. Of course, such expanded rights came at a price. Taxation, regulation, and military conscription now began to plague Europe's Jews. Joseph's father, Mozes, probably served in the emperor's army. He likely did not see combat, however, since the edict ordering Jewish conscription, issued the year before, did not initially assign Jews to combat duty.

The year of Joseph's birth was also marked by the adoption of the Jewish Ordinance of 1789. This had to be a pivotal event in the lives of Mozes and his family as well as all the Polish Jews living under Austrian rule. The ordinance attempted to bring about social and political equality between Jews and non-Jews. Forced expulsions were discontinued in favor of alternative policies of assimilation and absorption. There was a dark side to this seemingly benign new attitude toward the Jews. Jewish courts (*batei din*) along with the entire Jewish judiciary system, were summarily abolished. Jewish self-government was outlawed. Jews were to be governed just as the burghers were. The ordinance required that Jews dress in the same fashion as their Christian neighbors and send their children to proper German-speaking schools.

Jews were not to be treated equally in all areas, however. Mozes was still required to pay a special "Jewish tax," that non-Jews were not forced to pay. This just for the privilege of living as a Jew in a Christian society.

In 1791, when little Joseph Goldwasser, Mozes' son, was two years old, Kazimierz lost its status as a separate city and became a district of Krakow. It is likely that his family joined the many others and quickly moved out of the Oppidum Iudeorum's overcrowded streets into newer neighborhoods like Podgorze. The Jewish district maintained its ethnic character, however, even after this mass exodus, as Jews stayed within walking distance of the "old neighborhood" due to the halachic restrictions against traveling on the Sabbath. It is likely, therefore, that as Joseph grew into manhood during the dawn of the nineteenth century, he prayed at one of the 120 synagogues and prayer houses located in the Kazimierz Oppidum Iudeorum section.

The close of the eighteenth century saw Krakow swallowed up into the expanding Austro-Hungarian Empire. In 1799 all Jewish businesses were ordered closed down by the authorities in Vienna. In the face of dire economic hardship, intentionally brought on by the Jew-hating regime, the Goldwasser family did as European Jews had done for centuries. They hunkered down and waited for times to get better. They did not have long to wait.

The new century saw fresh breezes of reform sweeping through eastern Europe as citizens of Krakow sought to shake off the yoke of feudalism. In 1809, when Joseph was twenty years old and his father, Mozes, was in his mid-forties, Krakow again changed hands and became part of the Grand Duchy of Warsaw. This change led to the formation, six years later, of the Krakow Republic. Jews like the Goldwassers were again allowed to live in the Jewish section of Kazimierz while "cultured," that is assimilated, Jews were permitted to live in the Christian sections.

By the 1830s Krakow's Jewish population numbered nearly eleven thousand, enough to sustain an elementary school. It is eminently possible that some of the children of Joseph Goldwasser and his wife, Chawa Rozl, attended this school. It was within this next generation of Goldwassers that my lineage bifurcated, with the line of one of Joseph and Chawa Rozl's older children, Abraham Chaskel, born in 1818, leading to my father – who became his namesake – and with the line of another of Joseph and Chawa Rozl's younger children, Gittel, born in 1838, leading to my mother.

Tragedy struck when my mother's grandmother, Gittel Goldwasser, was eight years old and her older brother, my father's great-grandfather, Abraham Chaskel, was twenty-eight. They, and their siblings, lost both their father and grandfather at the same time. Their father, Joseph, was fifty-seven, and their grandfather, family patriarch Mozes, was nearly eighty at the time the Krakow Revolution broke out in 1846. This historic uprising was certainly connected to the deaths of both men during that pivotal year.

While the Krakow Republic was afforded a high degree of autonomy, it still remained part of the Austrian realm and was forced to conform to the monarchy's feudal system. In an alliance between the Krakow military and a secret pro-civil rights group known as the Polish Democratic Society, a revolt against the Austrian regime was planned for February 20, 1846. Led by several hundred peasants and miners, the rebels were soon joined by the urban proletariat and artisans. The violence spread beyond its initial target, Krakow's Austrian civil servants, as the insurgency directed its wrath against the local aristocracy and wealthy bourgeoisie.

Within a few days, as the revolution gained steam, it succeeded in driving a large Austrian battalion out of Krakow. The revolt's leaders thereupon issued a Manifesto to the Polish Nation that was widely circulated and succeeded in swelling the revolutionary forces to more than six thousand troops. A large contingent of Krakow Jews, inspired by the manifesto's powerful rhetoric promoting personal liberty and political freedom, reported for active duty. It is conceivable that Joseph was among them. A series of power struggles within the revolution's leadership soon took its toll. By early March, and after two pitched battles between the insurgents and the Austrian military, the revolt had been crushed. In its wake, Austrian culture was imposed on Krakow with a vengeance as by November,

Krakow was absorbed fully into the Austrian realm. Living conditions for the Jews became deplorable as plagues and disease ravaged the city during this post-revolt period.

Given that both Goldwassers, père and fils, succumbed in the pivotal year of 1846, we may assume that their demise was related to the ill-fated revolt. It is possible that Joseph was killed fighting for liberty against the tyrannical Austrian regime and that his father, Mozes, succumbed due to one of the many diseases that followed in the wake of the revolt.

The 1846 Krakow Revolution, merging the struggle for national independence with the struggle for social reforms, was highly honored by the European left. Marx and Engels referred to the Krakow Revolution in the Communist Manifesto. The quest for social justice, long a cherished Judaic value, and an ideal for which Joseph Goldwasser probably gave his life, was no doubt passed on to his heirs and descendants.

The Jewish world in which Mozes Goldwasser's grandchildren found themselves was one undergoing tectonic shifts as the effects of the European Enlightenment, as well as the Jewish response to this movement (known among the Jews as the Haskalah), swept eastward across Europe. The city of Krakow was emancipated from feudal rule in 1867. Gittel Goldwasser was twenty-nine and her brother, Abraham Chaskel, was forty-nine. They and their families were now permitted to settle in Krakow proper as one traditional Jewish institution after another faded from sight. The new leaders of the Jewish Religious Council were assimilationists and called themselves the Maskilim or the Enlightened Ones. They were responsible for the opening of the first secular Hebrew public library in Krakow in 1876.

It is safe to assume that Abraham Chaskel Goldwasser and his wife, Hanna Leah, sent their son, my great-grandfather, Izrael Haim Goldwasser, born in 1853, to an elementary school that was part of a diverse and growing number of schools that included traditional Yiddish-language *chadarim* (small single-classroom schools usually located in the rabbi's home) as well as secondary schools taught in Polish and German. As Izrael was growing up in the second half of the nineteenth century, the Jews were enjoying increasing acceptance and hence becoming part of Krakow's Polish-German cultural life. By the end of the century, Krakow's Jewish population had swelled to more than twenty-five thousand out of a total population of ninety-one thousand.

As was common throughout Europe, a growing Jewish nationalism movement was afoot in Krakow during the waning years of the nineteenth century. Not surprisingly, the calls for a Jewish homeland coincided with virulent antisemitism exemplified by the Dreyfus case in France in 1894, the Hilsner case in Czechoslovakia in 1899, and the Beylis case in Russia in 1913. This growing anti-Jewish sentiment was personified in Poland by Roman Dmowski under the banner of the right-wing National Democratic Party he created. Dmowski's party is considered to be a genuine precursor of Germany's National Socialist (Nazi) Party.

As in many parts of Europe, Jewish assimilation into mainstream society was halted in its tracks by the efforts of such nationalist movements that targeted Jews in order to promote their own ascendency through the use of political and economic power. Throughout Poland, during the 1890s, Dmowski's followers urged citizens to boycott Jewish shops. This won them the support of the petite bourgeoisie and Christian shopkeepers who competed against Jewish merchants.

We know from archival records that my paternal grandfather, Mojzesz Goldwasser, son of Izrael Haim, born in 1883, listed his occupation as merchant. As shops were typically handed down from father to son, it is likely that his father, Izrael Haim (whose name can be loosely translated as "Israel lives" and whose wife's name, Malka Kluger, means "wise queen"), was also a shopkeeper and therefore, no doubt harshly affected by the boycott and other onerous anti-Jewish measures.

But it was the future son-in-law of Izrael's aunt, Gittel Goldwasser, and her unregistered husband Wigdor Hirsch, who would be most deeply affected by the rising tide of European antisemitism. Gittel and Wigdor's youngest daughter, Leah, was born in 1879. Gittel's death followed less than three months later. Leah would one day become my grandmother, but not before marrying an adventurous and ambitious young man named Jakob Grunfeld, born in 1874. It was the perseverance and courage of Jakob Grunfeld, my maternal grandfather, that would make all the events that followed possible. For Jakob was a unique and singularly tenacious character. Faced with diminishing economic opportunities and increasing political repression in his home country, Jakob, as an unmarried and unemployed free spirit, joined the massive wave of eastern European immigration flowing across the Atlantic to America during the 1890s. He remained in the US just long enough to obtain his well-documented American citizenship before returning to Krakow to marry and raise a family.

Had Jakob not taken that journey, his daughter, my mother Ernestyna, would not have been able to escape the engulfing flames of the Holocaust, and our entire clan would have perished as our once

My maternal grandfather, Jakob Grunfeld (b. 1874), circa 1910

proud family tree was cruelly cut down in Krakow. Jakob Grunfeld's story is an extraordinary one and keenly worthy of closer examination.

CHAPTER TWO

Jakob's Gift

In ancient Judea, the citizens developed a unique method of determining whether an arriving stranger was or was not a member of the Jewish people. The test consisted of handing the stranger an ear of corn and asking him to identify it. If he could produce the proper regional pronunciation of the word *shibboleth* (שבולת), then he was presumed to be "one of us." Today, the English word *shibboleth* has come to mean a custom or ritual observed by a specific group of people.

Like many families, ours had its fables, its customs, and its cherished shibboleths. As I was growing up, I had begun to question my parents about their own mothers and fathers. I started expressing curiosity about the fact that my classmates all seemed to have several grandparents while I had but one. I recall my mother passing on to me the story of how her own grandmother, Gittel Goldwasser, had died on the last day of Passover. Her death was connected with the birth of her youngest child, my grandmother Leah. Through my genealogical research for this book I discovered that Gittel did, in fact, die on April 15, 1879, which was indeed the last day of Passover that year.*

Gittel Goldwasser (Hirsch), the true matriarch of my family, died from complications brought about by a difficult childbirth less than three

---

* Based on my mother's now-corroborated statements, I have for many years chanted the beautiful *haftarah* for the last day of Passover. Drawn from the book of Isaiah (11:6), the *haftarah* includes the well-known passage "The wolf shall dwell with the lamb, and the leopard shall lie down with the kid; and the calf and the young lion and the yearling together; and a little child shall lead them." Perhaps not coincidentally, the scene is depicted in a beautiful needlepoint made decades ago by my mother.

Needlepoint made by my mother, Ernestyna, depicting the words of the book of Isaiah that are chanted on the last day of Passover: "The wolf shall dwell with the lamb..."

months earlier. That child, Gittel's seventh, born on January 30, 1879, grew up to become my mother's mother, Leah Grunfeld (née Hirsch). Leah grew up and married my grandfather Jakob Grunfeld. It was Leah's husband Jakob and his singular actions that made it possible for me to sit here, comfortably in America, and write these words today. His amazing story begins a few years before my grandmother Leah's birth.

Born in Krakow on October 17, 1874 (according to Krakow genealogical records)* to Chaskel and his wife, Raizel (née Wiener) Grunfeld, Jakob was the sixth of ten children. Several of those children married and raised families that perished into ashes during the Holocaust. Some, like Jakob's younger brothers Izak and Baruch (Bernard), found sanctuary in America. And one – Jakob himself – died violently before the onslaught.

Poland, in the final decade of the nineteenth century, was a minefield of hazards for young Jewish men. Facing lifelong conscription into the Austro-Hungarian army, restricted in their schooling and professional opportunities as ever more severe anti-Jewish policies (such as onerous taxation aimed only at Jews) were being imposed, many young men joined the

---

* Documentation reveals some discrepancy about Jakob Grunfeld's date of birth. His US naturalization papers list his date of birth as November 4, 1874. His subsequent application for a US passport lists it as November 10, 1874.

widening flow of immigration from Russia's Pale of Settlement westward toward America's "streets of gold." Jakob Grunfeld was one such young man, determined to seek a better future by saying good-bye to his family and his culture and, like so many others – including two of his brothers – diving in to the massive wave of immigration breaking on America's shores. In August 1893, an eighteen-year-old Jakob booked passage in steerage on the SS *Gothia*, sailing from Hamburg and bound for New York harbor, arriving there on August 17, 1893.

The Jakob Grunfeld who stepped onto the pier in New York, after having surely saluted the welcoming Statue of Liberty – dedicated seven years earlier in 1886 – was not a particularly striking figure. At five foot six, his fair complexion and regular features allowed him to blend in with the tide of human cargo being disgorged that day. He found lodging near the Williamsburg Bridge, at 114 Lewis Street on New York's Lower East Side, the home of his brother, Izak.

The ensuing years were no doubt challenging ones for Jakob. Listing his occupation in various documents as "peddler" – a generic term for those who made their living day to day, *hondling* and scratching as best they could. Jakob hoped to find not only financial opportunities in America,

My great-grandfather, Chaskel Grunfeld (b. 1839), circa 1900

My great-grandmother, Raizel Grunfeld (b. 1840), circa 1900

but also social or even romantic ones. Sadly, he found none of these. Others, facing disappointment and disillusionment as they discovered that New York's streets were not actually paved with gold, often returned quickly to their home communities in Europe. The phenomenon was not particularly unusual. Hundreds of Jewish immigrants, mostly young men, decided America was not for them and abandoned their American adventures. Jakob, no doubt, gave serious thought to becoming one of them. Yet, he persevered in New York's hostile streets, scuffling along as well as he could, for one reason only. He understood that America had something of value to offer him if he could only stick it out for five years. It was this decision, made almost 120 years ago by my grandfather Jakob – this courageous choice to persevere long enough to become a citizen of the United States of America – that made all the difference. It was this decision that resulted in the future course of our family saga, and it must be regarded as our family's critical inflection point for all that was to ensue.

On October 6, 1898 – five years and seven weeks after setting foot on American soil – Jakob Grunfeld renounced his allegiance to the emperor of Austria-Hungary and became a legal citizen of the United States. For several months, Jakob attempted to leverage his newly minted and duly certified US citizenship into more lucrative employment opportunities. He soon found that his new status did not gain him much in the overcrowded job market that characterized the Jewish immigrant community of New York. He was still living with his brother, who now went by Isidor, at 613 East 11th Street, and had not been successful in any of his romantic initiatives to date. Finally Jakob, now twenty-four, threw in the towel. Just as he had initially found the fortitude to come to America's shores, he now summoned the same courage to leave them. But he would not be returning to Poland empty-handed. No, Jakob would carry home a prized imprimatur attested to by a precious green document in his pocket: an American passport.

So it was that in October 1899, one year after Jakob became a US citizen, he and his brother Isidor went to the US immigration office to request a US passport that would allow Jakob to leave the country "temporarily." Jakob stated he planned to go abroad for about two years before returning to the States. The application was signed by Jakob and witnessed by Isidor, and the permission was immediately granted. As they say, there is nothing more permanent than the temporary. My grandfather returned to Poland never to set foot in the United States again. Yet, his US citizenship endured and remained valid for the balance of his life … and beyond!

There is a possibility, given what happened soon after Jakob's return to Krakow, that he was enticed to come back for romantic reasons. Shortly after his return, Jakob married my future grandmother, Leah, in an initially unregistered ceremony. As noted earlier, Jews of that era often failed to record events such as births, deaths, and marriages with the Polish authorities, in order to avoid the required taxation and the unwelcome attention of the government. Leah and Jakob did finally record the marriage some years later in 1909 (see certificate).

Jakob found work in Krakow in what today would be termed the financial services industry. Actually he operated a small check-cashing service.

Leah and Jakob's first child, a daughter named Gusta, was born in 1902. Apparently another daughter, Fany, followed in 1904,* and finally, my mother, Ernestyna, in 1906. Thanks to the then-prevailing laws surrounding US citizenship, both Jakob's wife, Leah, as well as their daughters, Gusta and Ernestyna, were legal citizens of the United States – simply by virtue of their relationship to their husband and father.** This legal provision would eventually prove to be my mother's salvation during the inferno that was soon to ravage European Jewry.

As the girls were growing up, not much was made of their special citizenship status. There were much more important matters to attend to, such as putting bread on the table and getting an education. The latter was not as straightforward an affair as one might assume. Young Jewish women who came from traditional or observant families in those days typically received no formal schooling at all. But the winds of change were

---

* I only learned of the existence of Fany via the genealogical records maintained by Professor Hirschberg at the Krakow Genealogy website. I have no recollection of my mother, or anyone else in my family, ever mentioning her. As far as I knew, my mother had only one sibling, her older sister Gusta. There is no further mention of Fany in any of the correspondence or other documents I came across in my research for this book.
** The automatic citizenship for wives of American citizens was repealed in 1924 long after Jakob and Leah were married. Over the years, numerous residency and paperwork requirements have been added for alien wives to become citizens.

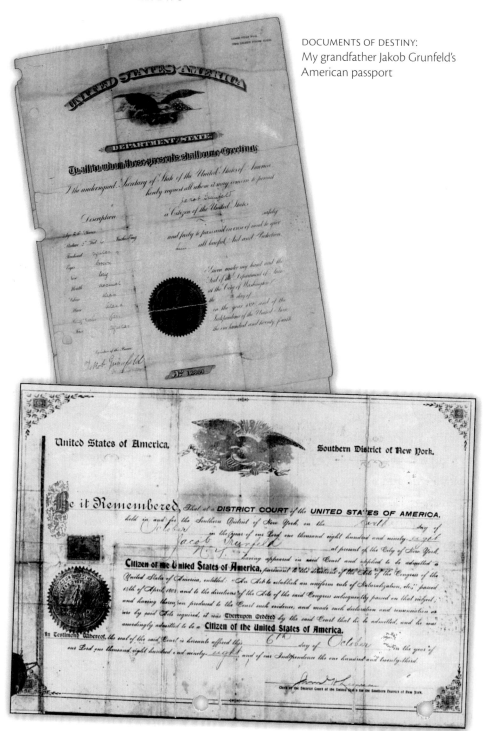

DOCUMENTS OF DESTINY:
My grandfather Jakob Grunfeld's
American passport

My grandfather Jakob Grunfeld's certificate of US citizenship:
the "golden ticket" that saved my mother

Leah and Jakob's marriage certificate, recorded on February 14, 1909, and certified on November 20, 1939. Note the address, Yosefa Street, where my family continued to live until the Holocaust.

sweeping through Torah communities in the 1920s and my grandmother Leah, a true visionary, was quick to embrace the whirlwind. By the time my mother, Ernestyna, was in her teens, those powerful new forces were beginning to exert themselves in the old Oppidum Iudeorum sector of Krakow. Foremost among the cultural shifts taking place was the role of women in Jewish life. Leading the charge and fanning those winds of change was a pioneering and far-sighted Jewish heroine from Krakow named Sarah Schenirer. And one of her devoted followers was my grandmother, Leah Grunfeld.

Sarah Schenirer was the unassuming and withdrawn daughter of Polish Chasidic parents. Working as a seamstress, she moved to Vienna at the outbreak of World War I. It was there that she organized her first Torah class for young Jewish women. The effort soon spread rapidly despite initial resistance. Propelling this growth was Sarah Schenirer's doggedly determined drive and forceful personality. She soon realized that in order

The only known
photograph of Sarah
Schenirer

to successfully elevate the educational level of Jewish girls, she would require the endorsement of respected European rabbis. She solicited and received the approval of Rabbi Avraham Mordechai Alter, known as the Gerrer Rebbe, and, most significantly, the blessing of Lithuanian rabbi Yisrael Meir Kagan Poupko, the venerated Chofetz Chaim ("desirer of life," named for his book) of the *musar* movement.

Armed with these stamps of approval, Schenirer was, in 1917, able to establish in Krakow the very first Jewish religious seminary for girls. She called it Bais Yaakov (house of Jacob), culled from a biblical verse in the book of Exodus (19:3) in which God instructs Moses to summon the women, prior to the men, at Mount Sinai to receive the Torah. My mother, Ernestyna, was one of Bais Yaakov's first enrollees. Sarah Schenirer was clearly mindful of the tenuous position shared by Jews in twentieth-century Europe when she penned the new school's mission statement: "to train Jewish daughters ... so they will know that they are the children of a people whose existence does not depend upon a territory of its own, as do other nations of the world whose existence is predicated upon a territory and similar racial background."

By the time of her death in 1935, more than two hundred Bais Yaakov schools were teaching Torah to approximately thirty-five thousand observant Jewish girls across Europe. Among them was another courageous young Jewish woman named Vichna Kaplan, who, as a respected rebbetzin, would export the concept to the new world and found the Bais Yaakov schools for girls in America.

My grandmother Leah's strong devotion to Jewish education resulted in her support of the Bais Yaakov movement and provided her daughter with a strong foundation of Jewish learning that my mother would eventually instill in me.

Unfortunately, Ernestyna's father Jakob never had the opportunity of seeing his daughters receive a formal Jewish education; he was struck down in the prime of his life. As mentioned, Jakob worked in the financial field and, at some point, opened a small check-cashing establishment in Krakow. The shop would meet the needs of local miners and factory workers who were paid weekly by check but needed cash to spend. Paying my grandfather a small fee, they would line up outside his shop on payday in order to turn their flimsy signed vouchers into hard zloty currency. Perhaps because he wished to somehow associate his business with the security of a local bank, Jakob chose a location right next door to a large bank in Krakow. He was in no way affiliated with the bank, but if his customers jumped to the contrary conclusion, that would only enhance the image of his establishment. Ironically, it was this same marketing ploy that resulted in his demise. For it was not only the miners and laborers of Krakow who assumed that the little check-cashing store was a part of the bank; this misconception also filtered into some of the town's criminal minds.

On one particularly wintry day in 1920, in the early morning before the paychecks were to be distributed, two young gunmen barged into Jakob's shop. Brandishing their weapons, they demanded that he hand over the money he surely had on hand in preparation for the coming payroll. Jakob acted without hesitation. He had been prepared for such a moment and had decided that if guns were shown, he would hand over everything without resistance. He gave the gunmen every bit of cash he had on hand, but this was not enough to satisfy the robbers.

"What is this?" they shouted, tossing his meager handful of zlotys on the floor. "This is a bank, isn't it? A bank has lots more than this. You're holding out on us. Now go get the rest of it. Move!"

"I-I-I am not a b-bank," my grandfather stammered. "Not a bank. Just a store. That's all I have. I swear. Now take it and leave me alone." His words went unheeded as one of the two armed intruders leveled his gun at Jakob's head and demanded more cash. When none was produced, the killer pulled the trigger and my grandfather, Jakob Grunfeld, age forty-five, fell to his death.

The story has an epilogue. Both robbers were eventually apprehended and prosecuted by the authorities. They were young men in their early twenties, and the mothers of both murderers together asked to meet with the wife of their victim, my grandmother Leah. Leah, a young widow at age forty-one, agreed. The mothers begged her to speak with the prosecutor and urge him to have mercy on their two wayward sons and not seek the death penalty. Did Leah agree to this request? The answer to this question – recounted to me by my mother many years ago – has sadly been lost in time. But in pondering the matter, I have concluded that Leah probably tempered her natural desire for revenge with compassion and agreed to do as she was asked.

My mother Ernestyna, now partially orphaned at age thirteen, continued in her educational endeavors. In addition to her firm belief that young Jewish women should receive the benefits of a Torah education, my grandmother Leah also believed in the then radical notion that women should be skilled in a trade. This belief became poignantly more profound after the tragic and sudden death of her husband Jakob. Leah never remarried yet was able to provide for her children throughout the 1920s and 1930s.

After attending Bais Yaakov, my mother, Ernestyna, was enrolled at a Krakow commercial academy to receive practical career training. She learned clerical work, such as bookkeeping, typing, and filing. She was also one of very few Jews admitted in the 1920s to Krakow's Jagiellonian University. At both the academy and the university, my mother repeatedly encountered the dark specter of antisemitism.

My mother, Ernestyna Grunfeld, circa 1930

Growing up in the insulated Jewish community of Krakow between the wars, a young girl could easily presume that Jews were, if not loved, at least tolerated by the larger Christian society. She soon learned otherwise. Though she was among the best students in both schools, she was regularly assigned a seat in the back of the classroom. On one occasion, when she returned to her seat at the academy, she discovered that someone had stuck a knife blade into her seat and scrawled an ominous message in Polish: "*Śmierć na wszystkich Żydów*" (Death to all Jews)!

On numerous other occasions, when she returned from the blackboard to her seat, she was taunted mercilessly by her classmates, who sneered at her Jewishness. These taunts were a harbinger of the days to come. Days that would see my mother wed my father, Abraham Chaskel Goldwasser, in August 1936, and nights that would result in her fleeing Krakow to the safety of American shores borne on the wings of eagles and an American passport made possible by the courage and pluck of her late father.

Jakob Grunfeld may have been regarded during his lifetime as something less than a success. He faced failure in America and was forced to return home. His business was based on collecting a few pennies for exchanging one piece of paper for another. His death was tragic, senseless, and hardly heroic. Yet he succeeded well beyond the scope of most men by virtue of the posthumous gift he bestowed on his beloved Leah and his daughter, Ernestyna. Had my mother not been blessed with this gift, she would certainly have perished in the Holocaust that killed 90 percent of the Jews of Poland. It was Jakob's gift, given from beyond the grave, that saved my mother's life, and thereby allowed her to enter the United States and me to enter the world.

The Grunfeld girls: my mother, Erna (*on the left*), and my aunt Gusta, circa 1930

CHAPTER THREE

A Ray of Hope

My father, Abraham (Chaskel) Goldwasser – like his father before him – married a woman two years his senior. While this was not unheard of among the Jews of Krakow in the 1930s, it certainly was not considered common. Chaskel was twenty-eight and my mother, Ernestyna, was thirty at the time of their marriage in August 1936. Growing up fatherless since her early teens, Ernestyna had developed an independent nature that bordered on toughness. Unlike her sister Gusta, who married a prosperous businessman at some point after their father Jakob was murdered, and immediately began raising a family, Ernestyna decided to pursue a career as a bookkeeper and became known for her resourcefulness and efficiency. It was undoubtedly these qualities, along with her beauty, that my father-to-be found attractive in his second cousin, Ernestyna, when he proposed marriage.

Chaskel, at the time of his marriage, was working as a furrier. One of the major attractions of the furrier trade was the portability of the inventory. Unlike lumber or livestock, which were difficult to conceal, pelts and hides could be easily stowed out of sight whenever thieves came to call. Quite simply, if the furs were not in sight, they could not be stolen.

Life in 1930s Poland has been described by some as a fool's paradise. Just as many in England were deluded into believing that Prime Minister Chamberlain had achieved a true "peace for our time" at Munich, the pervasive Polish false sense of security was the result of the faith placed by many Poles, such as my father, in similar paper peace agreements. A prime example was the Soviet-Polish Nonaggression Pact of 1932. This treaty called on both nations to resolve disputes via negotiation rather than violence. It was intended – along with the German-Polish Nonaggression Pact signed eighteen months later – to bolster Poland's position as an equidistant buffer between the two rising military powers on its eastern and western borders.

But it was in fact the secret and sinister provisions of a third treaty that would seal Poland's fate and demonstrate the true aggressive designs of both the Germans and the USSR. Known as the Molotov-Ribbentrop Pact and signed during the late hours of August 23, 1939, the pact provided Hitler with the assurances he needed to brazenly invade Poland without fear of Soviet intervention – effectively nullifying the earlier German-Polish agreement. Stalin, deeply concerned about the outcome of battles raging against Japan in the Nomonhan region, was lured into the Molotov-Ribbentrop Pact by assurances that Germany would not form a military alliance with the empire of Japan – assurances that several years later went up in smoke.

Once the Molotov-Ribbentrop Pact was in place, the dominos fell quickly. On September 1, 1939, Germany invaded Poland, meeting little resistance from the weak Polish military defenders. Japan, believing that Germany would not now open a second western front against the USSR, agreed to sign the Molotov-Togo agreement on September 15, thereby ending hostilities between Japan and the USSR. On the following day, Stalin, now confident that he would not be required to fight a two-front war, gave the order and on September 17 – a mere two and a half weeks after the German invasion – the Red Army marched into Poland from the East, ripping to shreds the 1932 Soviet-Polish nonaggression treaty.

The nation that once was Poland was summarily pulled apart between Germany and the USSR like a plump pullet. My family, along with all of Krakow, found itself in the German zone and, as hard as it is to fathom today, this fact brought them some relief. Despite the non-stop anti-Jewish rhetoric spouted by its leader, Germany was viewed by most Poles as the more civilized and cultured nation of the two. After all, Polish Jews and German Jews had fought side-by-side in the Kaiser's army during the Great War – many of them coming home decorated with German medals. Being well versed in the German tongue and *Kultur* was considered the hallmark of an educated Pole during the time my parents were growing up. But the Russians? Uneducated, antisemitic barbarians at best. Surely this misunderstanding of Nazism's true mission – to wit, the destruction of European, and eventually world, Judaism – contributed to my family's failure, as well as the failure of almost all of Krakow's Jews, to foresee, and thereupon flee, the coming onslaught.

In the end, of course, it was the USSR that emerged as the most naive of nations when, on June 22, 1941, Germany invaded Russia under the banner of Operation Barbarossa, effectively nullifying all of the provisions of the Molotov-Ribbentrop agreement.

During the years leading up to the German invasion of Poland, my father, too, lived in a world oblivious to the gathering catastrophe. By his late twenties he had achieved a sufficient level of prosperity to contemplate marriage. Chaskel's concept of married life was no doubt influenced by his own upbringing. His mother, Feige Pessel,* was something of a mother figure to her husband, Mojzesz, and that relationship surely colored Chaskel's choice when he finally elected to marry his thirty-year-old second cousin, Ernestyna. Such consanguineous marriages were not uncommon among the Jewish communities of eastern Europe, and in any case, one would need to go back three generations in order to find a true blood linkage between them.

My parents were wed in August 1936 with every intention of raising a family, but problems soon surfaced. Whether due to my mother's age or some other unknown factor, their efforts to conceive a child proved fruitless despite years of trying – years filled with disappointment and frustration.

My parents' wedding photo, August 1936

---

* Feige Pessel Honig's parents, my paternal great-grandparents, were Jakob and Ruchel Honig. Jacob and Rachel were probably the most romantic couple in the Bible. The word *honig* means "honey" or "sweet."

My mother could not imagine that her husband was the cause of the infertility. Chaskel was in the peak of health and an accomplished athlete. He loved soccer and showed no outward signs of any medical conditions. "It must be me," my mother reasoned. She decided to take matters into her own hands, but first, she would need to engage in a bit of well-intentioned deceit.

In the summer of 1939, Ernestyna told her husband that she was going on a vacation by herself to a nearby mountain resort. She needed some time to relieve the stress she had been experiencing on the job. But instead of heading to the mountain spa, my mother secretly traveled to Vienna to consult with a leading fertility specialist. The journey was a precarious one on several levels. Hitler had, just the year before, annexed Austria to the Reich under the bloodless invasion they dubbed the Anschluss (connection). A Jewish woman traveling alone, at a time when Jews were being increasingly persecuted, incurred an enormous risk. Despite the danger, my mother agreed to undergo a surgical procedure that was intended to unblock her fallopian tubes and allow the free passage of ova into her uterus. The operation proved successful, and within a few weeks Ernestyna announced to Chaskel that she was at long last pregnant. What she could not know at that moment, of course, is that Chaskel and the child would never set eyes on each other.

Within a few weeks, in a trumped-up response to alleged raids across the Polish/German border, the world once again stood as mute witness to the marching of German troops. An ocean of Panzer divisions flooded Poland, triggering the first volley of what would become known as World War II. It took only five days for the Germans to reach Krakow, which fell without a shot being fired. More than sixty thousand Krakow Jews – my entire family among them – out of a total population of 250,000, now found themselves trapped in the iron grip of German occupation. On October 26, 1939, Krakow was named the capital of the Generalgouvernement – the headquarters of the occupied "rump state" of Poland. As a result, the persecution of Krakow's Jews intensified; the authorities issued edict after anti-Jewish edict intended to identify, disenfranchise, isolate, humiliate, and eventually eliminate every last Jewish man, woman, and child in their grasp.

By early November, conditions became extreme as the Nazis turned up the pressure on Krakow's trapped Jewish population. For my parents, the dilemma was intensely personal: they had struggled to bring a baby into this world and now, just at the point when they had finally succeeded, the entire world had gone mad. It was clear that as Jews in Krakow, they were prisoners in an ever-tightening noose with little chance of escape or resistance. But there was one ray of hope. My mother, her sister Gusta, and their mother Leah each held a "magic ticket" – their United States citizenship. But could they use it? And if so, what was the best way?

My parents, Erna (*left*) and Chaskel (*center*) Goldwasser, with unidentified woman, 1937

These and other similar questions consumed my parents' attention during the weeks that followed the German occupation of Krakow. By this point conditions for Jews had gone from dire to draconian as the Germans and their collaborators embarked upon the systematic isolation and destruction of the city's Jewish population. The Hobson's choice facing my parents was a particularly horrid one. Remain together as a family and attempt to endure the nightmare together or use the "magic ticket" and split the family apart. As they weighed the pros and cons of their course, the deciding factor turned out to be me.

The American citizenship of Jakob Grunfeld's widow and daughters was a fact known to everyone in the family and was not something that had mattered very much to any of them over the years since Jakob's death. But now things had changed. Now that they found themselves trapped in the vise that was slowly crushing all Polish Jews – with Hitler on one side and Stalin on the other – this gift of transmitted US citizenship was suddenly transformed into a cherished birthright. It was a key that could unlock the cage into which the Germans had pushed them. How to employ that key was the topic of a critical conversation that my parents most likely held in mid-November 1939.

"You, and you alone, have the freedom to escape," my father must have advised. "God has given you the opportunity to have our baby in America. You should take it."

"It's not me alone," my mother surely pointed out. "Gusta and our mother also can establish US citizenship."*

"But Gusta has young children and a husband who would not be able to travel with her. If you go now, our baby will be born in America."

"But how can I leave you behind?" my mother implored.

"I will join you. Very soon," he replied. "Once you are in America with an American baby, you will be in a much better position to get me the papers I need to get out of Poland. The United States is a compassionate country. Americans are kind people. Once you explain the situation to them, they will grant you whatever you need to reunite our family."

My mother could not contest this argument. She realized that her chances of getting both my father and her baby to America would be greatly enhanced if she was already there – with an American-born child in her arms. She felt that Chaskel, who was healthy and a skilled trades-man, would be recognized by the US authorities as having much to offer and would therefore be a welcome immigrant. Yet the thought of tearing her family apart tormented my mother. Still she equivocated.

"This German nightmare will pass over soon, and I will arrive at your side before the baby does," my father whispered, embracing her. Buoyed by his optimistic posture – however tenuous it may have been – my mother began to relent.

"Go now and then I'll follow. You can get a passport right now. Don't waste the opportunity of a lifetime," my father pressed her. He cited the Torah story of how Jacob divided his estate into two parts in preparation for his brother Esau's feared attack. "As with Jacob, with the two of us

---

* Under the then prevailing law, United States citizenship was extended to those born abroad only when the father or husband was an American citizen. This made US cit-izens of my mother as well as her mother and her sister, Gusta (each of whom had an American father or husband) – but not my father or Gusta's husband or children. Parenthetically, children of American mothers became US citizens pursuant to a 1934 law that was not retroactive. Hence it did not protect Gusta's children, as they were born before 1934.

separated, the chances of at least one of us coming through this night-mare are doubled." Who could argue with such sage Torah-inspired logic? Finally, in what was surely the most difficult choice of her life, my mother agreed and began to make preparations.

On November 20, 1939, my mother started collecting the documents she needed to establish her US citizenship. She obtained a copy of her father's US passport and naturalization certificate. These, along with her parents' marriage certificate, her own birth certificate, and her and my father's marriage certificate, served to clearly establish Jakob's US citizen-ship and her blood connection to him.

A government-sanctioned raid on December 6 – similar to the state-sponsored terrorism known as Kristallnacht carried out the year before across Germany and Austria – resulted in scores of arrests, deaths, looted stores, and firebombed synagogues. My parents quickly recog-nized the nature of the impending threat to their safety and sprang into action. On the day after the *Aktion* against the Jews of Krakow, my mother marched into occupation headquarters with her papers, documenting her as a full-fledged citizen of the United States of America.

The papers were scrutinized by the German authorities, and my mother succeeded in walking out with a prized certificate, valid for sixty days, issued by *der Stadtkommissar* of Krakow. The document declared that "*Ernestyna Goldwasser ist Jude* [is a Jew]," and she is of United States nationality. Hence, the document went on to say, she is exempted from wearing "*der weisse Armbinde mit Davidstern*" (the white armband bearing the Star of David).

But what would happen when the sixty-day period was up and the certificate expired? What would happen to her *protekzia* (special dispen-sation)? How could she be sure it would be renewed? The only way to ensure her safety and protect the fragile life within her was to emigrate. It was decided. My mother soon obtained the passport that would allow her, and her alone, to leave Poland bound for the USA.

On the night of January 8, 1940, my parents spent the night together for the last time before my mother's departure. I doubt that they got much sleep at all as they peered into the inky darkness of the night and the vast sea of uncertainty that was their future. The following day, after a tearful

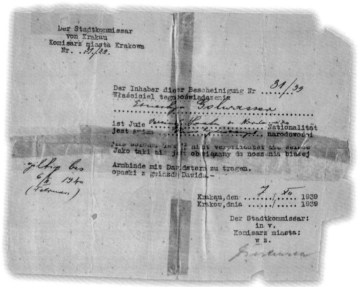

My mother's certificate – issued by the occupying German city
commissioner – exempting her from the requirement that she wear an
armband bearing the Star of David

farewell that saw my father stoop to give a tender kiss to his wife's abdomen, my mother, armed with her documents including a letter written in German by a Dr. Marja Glebocka of Krakow, certifying her pregnancy, climbed aboard a westbound train to Genoa, Italy, and rode off to meet her ship and her destiny.

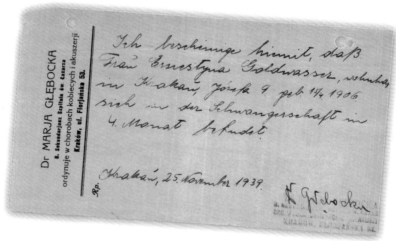

Note from Dr. Marja Glebocka attesting that my mother was in her
fourth month of pregnancy, November 25, 1939

The ss *Conte di Savoia*, the ship that carried my mother (who was carrying me) to America in January 1940

My father had booked passage for my mother aboard the Italian cruise ship *Conte di Savoia*, departing from Genoa on January 23, 1940. The ship was heavily advertised as offering the "smoothest crossings" of any Atlantic vessel due to the three huge gyroscopes it had been fitted with in the forward hold that purportedly reduced the ship's rolling action. This feature was no doubt a factor inasmuch as my father wished to make his wife, with her fragile pregnancy, as comfortable as possible during the Atlantic crossing. The ship ultimately met an ignoble end, however. Several years later, on September 11, 1943, the vessel, gyroscopes and all, was set ablaze and sunk by retreating German forces.

As the *Conte di Savoia* steamed into New York harbor on February 1, 1940, Ernestyna and the other passengers were summoned on deck for a look at the New Colossus, better known as the Statue of Liberty. What thoughts must have crossed my mother's mind as she listened to Emma Lazarus's stirring and immortal words inscribed on the base of the statue?

"Keep, ancient lands, your storied pomp!" cries she
With silent lips. "Give me your tired, your poor,
Your huddled masses yearning to breathe free,

The wretched refuse of your teeming shore.

Send these, the homeless, tempest-tost to me,

I lift my lamp beside the golden door!"

Beginning as soon as she entered the United States in February 1940, my mother spent the next several years pushing against that intractable and immovable "golden door" as she struggled to bring my father – trapped in Poland and most assuredly "yearning to breathe free" – to America. In so doing she encountered an adversary more subtly sinister and more devious than any enemy she had faced in Europe: the United States Department of State.

My father, Chaskel Goldwasser, taken after my mother's departure for the United States, 1940

My mother, Ernestyna Goldwasser, in 1939, shortly before her departure for the United States

CHAPTER FOUR

Mother of Exiles

February–March 1940

FEBRUARY 1, 1940
From My Father To My Mother

This letter was penned by my father, Chaskel, on the day my mother arrived in America. It was written in response to a letter and postcard sent to him by my mother from Vienna, en route to Genoa to set sail aboard the former Italian cruise ship *Conte di Savoia*, which would bring her to America. In this letter, my father urges my mother to try to "get us over as soon as possible." The plan was for Ernestyna to travel to America first and then secure entry for not only my father, but also for her mother, Leah, as well as her sister, Gusta, and, if possible, Gusta's family. Leah, my grandmother, and Gusta, my aunt, were also US citizens by virtue of their relationship to my grandfather, Jakob.

The letter closes with my father offering his regards to the baby (me), who was not due to be born for another three-plus months.

1 February, 1940

To my dearest in the entire world, Ernusha,

    Yesterday we received a postcard and a letter from you. They came together, and you can't imagine the happiness that it brought us. We danced from happiness. For twelve days we did not get anything from you. We could not imagine what had happened. As far as the regards,

33

I will send them on Monday. I would like you to try to get us over as soon as possible.

We have terrible frost here.

I can imagine how hard it is to manage all of your business. Thank God I am healthy and I have a good appetite. The only thing I'm missing is you. I want to see you as soon as possible. Mother bought a hearing aid for 350 zlotys in Krakow.

Gusta and the children are still with us but nobody sleeps in the house. Your quilt cover is wonderful. I use it because it is very, very cold here. I still work for Mr. Amand. I do not know for how much longer. Every evening we sit with Mrs. Feiler until 9:00 p.m. because we are lonely.

Darling, I miss you so much. I feel how I miss you so terribly and I need you. Hopefully, we will be together soon. Every Shabbos I go somewhere else; one time to Tesha and Franka and next time to Bronka.* I sit there for a half an hour but this is not for me.

Every Shabbos morning I go to Mother's. Lulusha and Bronka ask how long you will be over there in the United States. Everybody envies you and says that you are a courageous woman to go on such a long, long trip.

Your photograph from Vienna is wonderful. I put it into the mirror in the kitchen and we always look at it. Darling, you are so sweet. There is no other person in the world quite like you.

Regards to the baby from Daddy and tell him that he will come soon to be with him.

I am ending my letter. Next time I will write more. Stay healthy. I send you a thousand kisses.

Your loving husband, forever,
Chaskel

The letter goes on to include the following two postscripts. In the first, my father sends greetings to Ernestyna's uncle Baruch and his wife. Uncle Baruch was Bernard Greenfield, my grandfather Jakob's younger brother

---

* Bronka Klein, my mother's closest friend.

who had ventured to the United States, via France, in 1922. In addition to Uncle Baruch, who first provided housing for my mother in Brooklyn, my mother had another cousin, Leon Lachter, a highly successful business-man in Krakow, who had moved to the US with his family.

Dearest Ernunah,

Regards from me to Uncle Baruch and to your aunt, as well as Leon and his wife and children. Also, thank Uncle that he took you in so nicely.

Bye-bye, my dearest. See you soon.

Chaskel

Our American cousins, Lola and Leon Lachter, to whom my mother appealed for assistance after arriving to the United States, 1954

Finally, a post-postscript written by Ernestyna's sister Gusta mentions her husband Shimeck (Simcha Hirschprung) and speaks of sending him food and cigarette packages. At this point Shimeck had been conscripted into a Jewish labor camp as part of the German atrocities of December 6, 1939, referred to above. Gusta writes that Shimeck doesn't require any more food packages because he "has everything." Actually, conditions in the camps were deplorable with only minimum food available. It is any-one's guess if this reference was intended for the benefit of those eyes cen-soring Shimeck's letters or those monitoring Chaskel's correspondence.

My great-uncle Bernard (Baruch) Greenfield with his wife, Ernestine (*right*), and her sister, Fay Aron (*left*)

My great-uncle Bernard (Baruch) Greenfield and his wife, Ernestine

Gusta writes:

I received your letter and postcard and it made us very, very happy. Thank God all the bad times are behind you. Now we are only waiting for good news from you. I can let you know that Shimeck sent us a few letters last week and he writes that he received all the packages from me, but I should not send him more food, only cigarettes, because he has everything. Thank God for that.

How are you? How is it going? I am always with Mother because it is lonely here. Nothing new besides that. We kiss you and greet you heartily.

Yours,

Gusta

FEBRUARY 2, 1940

From My Grandmother to My Mother

On the following day, my grandmother, Leah, sends a letter to Ernestyna, her daughter, seeking word of her safe arrival in America. She mentions that my mother "went through a lot" before getting her ship ticket and describes the loneliness everyone feels after my mother's departure.

My dearest darling Ernusha,

Your wonderful letters from Milano gave us so much happiness. It is hard to describe. You went through a lot till you received a ticket for the ship. Thank God it is over and you are there. I hope that Bernard [Greenfield] and Leon [Lachter] will not let you remain alone.

Did you send a telegram to New York that you are coming? Was anyone there to greet you? You are probably still very tired from the trip. You cannot imagine how lonely it is here without you. But we live with good hope. Now I am awaiting a letter from you, my dearest child, from America.

Shimeck writes that he is okay. I will let Gusta add a few words to this letter. The whole family sends you regards.

Your mother

From My Aunt Gusta to My Mother

My aunt Gusta then adds her words of admiration and concern for her sister, from whom she finds herself separated for the first time. She apologizes for the fact that some sort of argument prevented her from writing in the letter sent the previous day. She goes on to make the sarcastic comment "Time is money." This is a humorous reference to the stereotypical American mindset and is intended to tease Ernestyna because she is an American now. The "Bronka" mentioned is Gusta and Ernestyna's best friend in Krakow.

My dearest darling Ernusha,

You cannot imagine the happiness it gave me to read your last letter. I am happy that you already boarded the ship. We have no doubt that you will arrive in good health. God should help that we should have the news already that you have landed and that you will not go through too much and that life will be good to you. You arranged everything so well. We wish you the best. Amen.

After you left everything seemed so empty. The apartment seemed so huge. Everybody walked around very sad. But your letters heal everything. Thank God that you are that far. Don't be angry that I did not write in the last letter. But I had a little argument here and I just could not write more. I know that you will not mind. But now I am writing to my sweet American sister.

Please write about the trip you had. Was it easy or very hard? Did you meet some people? I would like to write a lot, but I cannot take too much time. Time is money. I want to write to you about Bronka and about myself and so on. I promise the next letter will be a long one.

Regards and kisses,
Gusta

FEBRUARY 1940

Form 633 Instructions

Within days of her arrival in the United States, my mother had obtained these instruction sheets informing her how to go about completing Form

633, the questionnaire known as the "Petition for Issuance of Immigration Visa." Form 633 had to be completed by the petitioner, a US citizen who agrees to be financially responsible for the immigrant.

The instruction sheets required the applicant to attach a laundry list of sworn affidavits (in duplicate, which was no easy matter in those pre-photocopier days), including:

(a) list of petitioner's dependents

(b) net worth of petitioner and each dependent

(c) bank officer attesting to net worth

(d) employer attesting to salary

(e) credit rating from established credit bureau

(f) …and much more

Despite the grueling hurdles of completing the paperwork and assembling the necessary documents, my mother managed to accomplish this task within weeks.

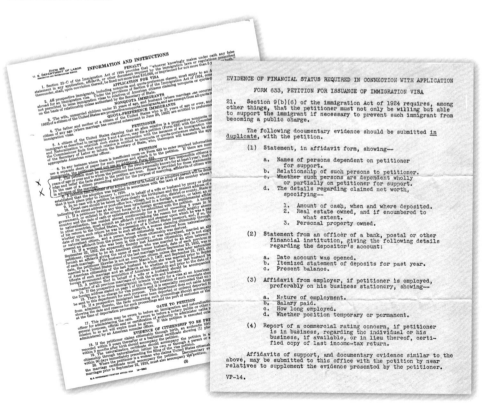

FEBRUARY 12, 1940
From My Father to My Mother

By February 12 no word had yet reached Krakow about my mother's fate. Had she reached America safely? Where was she living? What was the status of her pregnancy? These and other questions weighed heavily on my father and the other family members who remained trapped in Poland. In the following letter, one can feel my father's frustration and deep yearning to learn of his wife's welfare. In it, he refers to the fact that he sent my mother four postcards from Warsaw under the name of Rappaport. In all likelihood, the postcards were not actually sent from there. Rather my father used a false name and address to somehow increase the chances that my mother would receive them. Unfortunately, no February 1940 postcards from my father were found among the numerous letters preserved by my mother.

In the text, my father cryptically refers to my mother as "one American citizen" who sends regards to an "H. Wasser," – who, of course, is my father. This third-party syntax was probably used to instruct my mother to send her letters to the Warsaw address and also intended to throw off any authorities who might be monitoring his mail. It would be several weeks before he would finally receive any word from his wife in America.

The most important feature of this letter is the reference my father makes to his aunt Hermann. He advises Erna to contact her and his uncle Sigmund Hermann, for assistance in getting settled. The original letter bears the Hermanns' Camden, New Jersey, address written in the margin in my mother's hand.

Evidently, a favor was owed to my father's family by the Hermann family. In 1904, Sigmund had traveled ahead to America, leaving behind his wife and their children, including their son Saul. The family was finally reunited in the US, but not for some ten years. During this time, Saul resided with my father's parents. This contact becomes significant because it was Sigmund Hermann, and another son, Isadore Hermann (Saul's brother) who signed affidavits in which they agreed to serve as financial sponsors for my father as part of my mother's efforts to bring him to America (see February 28, 1940, entry below).

Despite my efforts to discover it, I was unable to find any genealogical support for the family relationship between Sigmund Hermann or his wife and my father. As my father's letter refers to "Aunt Hermann" and Sigmund's affidavit refers to my father as his nephew, it is likely that the relationship came through my father's mother, Feige Pessel (Honig) Goldwasser, about whom I know very little. "Aunt Hermann" may very well have been the sister of my paternal grandmother, Feige Pessel, whose family lived in Radomysl Wielki, a village about seventy miles from Krakow. Even my fortuitous discovery in 2012 of Saul's son, Dr. Allan Hermann, did not solve the mystery. Such are the ravages of time.

Finally, in this February 12 letter, Chaskel jokes a bit about whether the "baby" is asking for his father. At the time of this writing I was still three months from emerging from the womb.

February 12, 1940

My dearest in the whole world, Ernusha,

We received your last postcard on February 1. That is the same day that your ship was scheduled to depart Genoa. We are very worried because we haven't received any letters from you.

Did you arrive okay in New York? Who are you with? Where do you live? Do you think that we will be able to be together?

I sent three postcards under the name of G. Rappaport and one under the name of H. Rappaport from Warsaw. If you want to, you can write or go to my aunt Hermann. She also can help you. Her children were with us for a long time. Saul, my aunt's son, was with us for almost ten years....

One American citizen gave me regards from H. Wasser. I send the regards back under the address of W.R. Rappaport, Warsaw. And that is the way I find myself now.

Thank God I am not missing anything except you. You cannot imagine how sad it is here without you, my dearest. Thank God Gusta and the children are here, because I work and dearest Mother is busy. But they are very unruly sometimes. I can tell you that I feel well. Mother is okay. Only you are missing here, our dearest. How is the little baby? Has he asked where Daddy is? Tell him that I will be there soon.

Regards from the whole family and friends. I greet you and kiss you seven hundred times.

Loving you forever,
Chaskel

FEBRUARY 20, 1940
From My Father to My Mother

Another week drags by with no word from his wife. My father is clearly concerned. Did she arrive safely? Is she in good health? But his words do little to betray his anxiety as he keeps up a strong front. He writes that Ernestyna's brother-in-law, Shimeck, was released from the labor camp but looks very bad. Jews were subject to extreme deprivation in labor camps with many casualties. The fact that Shimeck was released was probably due to the fact that he was married with a family. The Germans felt that ghettoization was made easier if families were allowed to remain together.

My father's burning desire to reunite with my mother permeates every line of this impassioned epistle. He speaks of "things happening in the streets." At this point it was increasingly risky for Jews to be seen in public as Jews. Jewish-owned shops were being targeted for harassment in preparation for the massive deportations that would begin a few months hence.

My father expresses his well-founded fear that he will not be permitted to continue working much longer. His optimism about reaching America is expressed by his hope to learn to speak English.

He closes with the wish and prayer that he and my mother will be reunited in America in time for my birth in May.

February 20, 1940

My most beautiful in the whole world and dearest Ernusha,
Till today we did not receive any letters from you. But I hope that soon we will get something. Yesterday was a big happiness. Shimeck came back home in one piece. But he looks very bad. It is going to be an

even bigger happiness when we will get a letter from you, my dearest. My thoughts are always with you and I think about you all the time, my dearest. I feel very well. But I will feel even better when I will be together with you, and I hope it is going to be as soon as possible. Together-together.

Darling, write how you feel. How are you? How is the baby? And how do you like America? Is there any way that you think we will be together soon? Here it seems to me as if I haven't seen you for a whole year. Every minute I look at your photograph and I remind myself of our good-bye and how very brave you were when you left. God should grant us that times should be better. Because the first things are beginning to happen in the streets, but not at home, yet. At home it is okay.

I am still working, but I do not know for how much longer. I hope I am going to learn English. By us it's been a terrible winter this year. It is cold and long and I don't ever remember it ever being like that.

Stay healthy and happy. Regards for the little baby from his daddy. I hope I will be there when the time to give birth will come. I just pray to God that He should listen to me. Amen. I kiss you thousands of times. I love you very much and I always think of you.

Chaskel

Regards from the whole family that are here with me. Special regards from my family and all the friends.

Yours,
Chaskel

FEBRUARY 28, 1940
The Hermann Affidavits

Identifying himself as a "cousin of Abraham Jecheskel Goldwasser" of 9 Josefa Street, Krakow, Poland, Isadore Hermann (Uncle Sigmund's son) swore out this affidavit (abridged below) – on his letterhead denoting his position as chief counsel for the Tax Lien Bureau of the City of Camden, New Jersey. In it he delineates his financial position in detail and swears to provide support for his cousin (my father), whom he is seeking to bring to

ISADORE H. HERMANN
CHIEF COUNSEL

TAX LIEN BUREAU
CITY OF CAMDEN
NEW JERSEY

UNITED STATES OF AMERICA :
STATE OF NEW JERSEY   :SS.
COUNTY OF CAMDEN   :

     I, Isadore H. Hermann, age thirty-eight, being duly sworn, depose and say:

     I reside at 174 S. 27th Street, Camden, New Jersey. I am a naturalized citizen of the United States of America as evidenced by Naturalization Certificate Number 458447 issued on September 28, 1914, by Camden County Court of Common Pleas at Camden, New Jersey.

     I am married and dependent on me for support are my wife and one child, eight years of age.

     I am an Attorney and Counsellor at Law of the State of New Jersey and am actively engaged in the practice of law in the City of Camden and I am also employed by the City of Camden as Chief Counsel of the Tax Lien Bureau. I earn from the practice of law

(This excised portion of the Affidavit lists Isadore Hermann's income, assets, property and a detailed investment portfolio valued at $4300.)

     Attached hereto is copy of the 1938 income tax return with canceled check endorsed by the Collector of Internal Revenue attached.

     I am a cousin of Abraham Jecheskel Goldwasser now residing at Jozefa #9, Krakow, Poland, who desires to come to the United States.

     I do hereby promise and guarantee that I will receive and take care of my cousin who is applying for an immigration visa and will at no time allow him to become a public charge to any Community or Municipality.

     I am making this affidavit for the purpose of inducing the United States Consular authorities to grant the visa to my said relative and herewith submit coroborative proof as to my personal standing.

Sworn and subscribed to   :
before me this 28th day of   :
February   A.D. 1940   :

William Hermann

a Master in Chancery of New Jersey

the US. The affidavit concludes with these words: "I am making this affidavit for the purpose of inducing the United States Consular authorities to grant the visa to my said relative…"

In addition to this testimony, there exists a similar sworn statement of support from Isadore's father, Sigmund Hermann, plus another similar statement of support from a friend of Isadore's in Bayonne, New Jersey.

It appears, from other sources, that these affidavits were sworn to on or before February 28, 1940. Although no copy of it has been located, it is safe to assume that a Form 633 (Petition for Issuance…) was also filed alongside these statements. Hence the Form 633 my mother completed and filed on March 6 (see the relevant entry below) was a second such appeal for the granting of an entry visa for my father. Whether or not my mother was aware that the Hermanns had previously filed a similar petition in behalf of my father remains unclear.

MARCH 4, 1940
From My Father to My Mother

My father writes again expressing his concern that no word has yet reached him and reiterating his anguish over their separation. He talks of Shimeck's recovery after his ordeal in the labor camps. He informs my mother that my grandmother, Leah, has received permission from the US consul to obtain a cherished US passport and valiantly advises that she travel alone to join my mother in the US and not wait for my father to obtain his own visa.

Monday, March 4, 1940

My dearest darling Ernusha,

I want to let you know that we still did not get any letters from you. I hope every day that something will come. Our dear mother received a letter from the consul that she can get a passport. But she has to have a ticket for the ship. I would like to be as far along as Mother is. Shimeck eats with us together already the second week. He is very content from the food and he likes to come here. I still work by Mr. Amand. But I do not know for how long.

I would like you to take care of things as soon as you can. God should help us and help you that we should all be together. I am telling you, my dear, I miss you terribly. How do you feel? How is your pregnancy coming along? Where do you live? Did you write to my aunt and cousins [the Hermanns]?

...

Dearest, I think that mother should go by herself. She shouldn't wait for me the way you suggested she should. I am learning English. I've already had four lessons.

Regards. I love you. You are the dearest one in the world.

Yours, loving you forever,

The one who doesn't stop thinking of you.

Chaskel

P.S. Regards for the baby. Good-bye. My whole family sends you regards.

MARCH 6, 1940

From My Mother to the Commissioner of Immigration

Incredibly, within five weeks of setting foot on US soil, my mother had succeeded in the arduous task of completing and compiling the lengthy forms and detailed affidavits demanded by the US Immigration Service in order to obtain a visa for my father.

In this, her cover letter to the US Commissioner of Immigration and Naturalization, written in the flawless English that she had been taught by a childhood tutor in Krakow, my mother explains her circumstances and makes her appeal. In it, she states that she "returned" to the United States on February 1, 1940. This, of course, is not entirely accurate. My mother had never set foot in the US prior to that date. However, as a citizen of the United States who was now living here, she had repatriated herself and, in that sense, she had "returned" to the US. She may very well have believed that as an actual US repatriated resident, she would have a better chance of success in her quest.

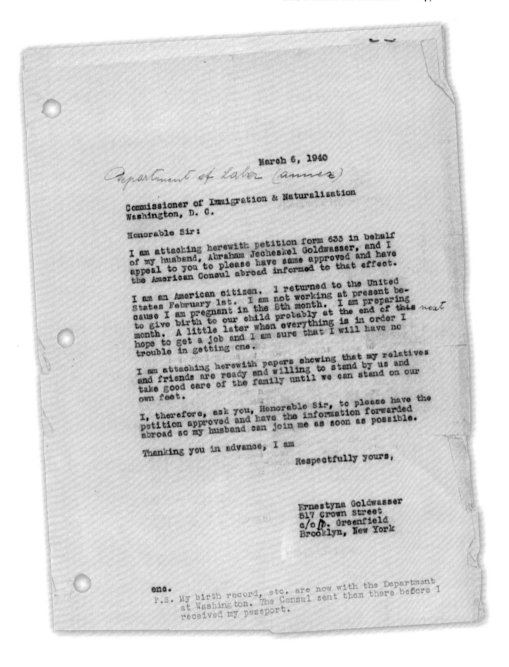

March 6, 1940

Department of Labor (annex)

Commissioner of Immigration & Naturalization
Washington, D. C.

Honorable Sir:

I am attaching herewith petition form 633 in behalf
of my husband, Abraham Jecheskel Goldwasser, and I
appeal to you to please have same approved and have
the American Consul abroad informed to that effect.

I am an American citizen. I returned to the United
States February 1st. I am not working at present because I am pregnant in the 8th month. I am preparing
to give birth to our child probably at the end of this *next*
month. A little later when everything is in order I
hope to get a job and I am sure that I will have no
trouble in getting one.

I am attaching herewith papers showing that my relatives
and friends are ready and willing to stand by us and
take good care of the family until we can stand on our
own feet.

I, therefore, ask you, Honorable Sir, to please have the
petition approved and have the information forwarded
abroad so my husband can join me as soon as possible.

Thanking you in advance, I am

Respectfully yours,

Ernestyna Goldwasser
517 Crown Street
c/o p. Greenfield
Brooklyn, New York

enc.
P.S. My birth record, etc. are now with the Department
at Washington. The Consul sent them there before I
received my passport.

My mother explains the fact of her unemployed status as being due
to her pregnancy, reflective of the mores of that era. She pledges to find
suitable employment as soon as her child (me) is born at the end of the
following month (another stretch since I was not actually due to be born

until May). Reading between the lines, one can tell she is striving to strengthen her case. The logic was that the US government ought to be interested in promoting full employment and, as a single mother, her ability to join the workforce is limited. With her husband at her side ("when everything is in order"), however, she would be financially able to hire a nanny and return to work.

MARCH 11, 1940
From the INS Dept. of Labor to My Mother

Receipt of the March 6 letter (above) and the accompanying petition and supporting affidavits was quickly acknowledged by the Department of Labor Immigration and Naturalization Service via a form postcard mailed on March 11, 1940 (see below).

The text of the postcard provides the following assurance: "Every effort will be made to avoid undue delay in considering and passing upon the petition." As we will later learn, these hollow words of subterfuge were intended to mask the US government's de facto policy of denial and delay when it came to granting visas to Jewish refugees.

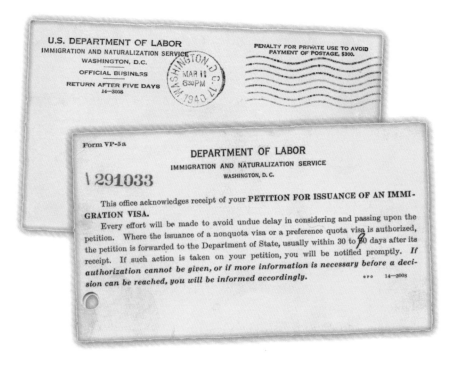

MARCH 18, 1940

From the Department of Labour, Immigration and Naturalization Service to Sigmund Hermann

Exactly one week after my mother received the postcard shown above containing the comforting message about "avoiding undue delay," my father's uncle, Sigmund Hermann, received a decidedly less promising response to the voluminous documents filed by his family in support of their petition.

Sigmund Hermann was curtly advised that the Immigration Service was not, in fact, the final government agency that would be able to grant the visa being requested for his nephew. No, the "alien" (my father) would now have to redirect his request to the US consulate responsible for granting US visas to citizens of Poland. Furthermore, Sigmund is told, none of the information already submitted to the Immigration Service, including the financial profiles of the prospective immigrant's US sponsors, could be passed on to the consulate because consular offices are "under the jurisdiction of the Department of State."

The Immigration Service returned all the affidavits along with this cover letter indicating their expectation that this notice – clearly an act of bureaucratic obfuscation – would close the books on my father's attempts to obtain a US visa. They had not, however, counted on my mother's obstinate determination.

Highlights from the form letter sent to Sigmund Hermann on March 18, 1940 (the actual letter is shown below):

- An alien...before proceeding to this country with the object of applying for...admission, is required to secure an appropriate visa from a United States consul.
- Any representations to be made in connection with the issuance of such a visa...should be addressed by interested persons directly to the United States consul to whom the alien has applied or will apply for the visa.
- The Department of Labor may not communicate with the consuls in connection with the issuance of visas to prospective applicants. Consular officers are under the jurisdiction of the Department of State, Washington, DC.

U. S. DEPARTMENT OF LABOR

IMMIGRATION AND NATURALIZATION SERVICE

WASHINGTON

ADDRESS REPLY TO COMMISSIONER OF
IMMIGRATION AND NATURALIZATION
AND REFER TO FILE NUMBER

VS Division

March 18, 1940

Mr. Sigmund Hermann,
    329 Kaighn Ave.,
        Camden, N. J.

An alien (with the exceptions referred to on pages 5 and 6 of the attached pamphlet), before proceeding to this country with the object of applying for either temporary or permanent admission, is required to secure an appropriate visa from a United States consul. Any representations to be made in connection with the issuance of such visa, such as the financial and moral standing of the prospective immigrant, or of his relatives or friends in the United States, should be addressed by interested persons directly to the United States consul to whom the alien has applied or will apply for the visa. The Department of Labor may not communicate with the consuls in connection with the issuance of visas to prospective applicants. Consular officers are under the jurisdiction of the Department of State, Washington, D. C.

Admissibility under the immigration laws is determined by officers of this Service only after an alien arrives at a port of the United States. Advance assurance of admission or readmission to this country cannot be given. It cannot be determined until actual arrival at a port of entry to this country whether a bond will be required by this Service for the admission of an alien. When a bond is required, interested persons may obtain the appropriate bond form and information relative to its preparation from the officer of this Service in charge at the port.

Aliens who have been lawfully admitted to the United States for permanent residence may obtain preference in the issuance of quota immigration visas for their wives and their unmarried children under 21 years of age. Brothers, sisters, stepchildren, uncles, aunts, nieces, nephews, cousins, and grandparents of citizen or alien residents of this country are not entitled to exemption or preference in relation to the quota restrictions.

Cordially yours,

Enclosures:
Affidavits of support.

C-3a.

U. S. GOVERNMENT PRINTING OFFICE   14—4009

MARCH 18, 1940
From My Grandmother to My Mother

While the Hermanns were coming face to face with the roadblocks erected by the US government (of which more will be said) to stanch Jewish immigration, my grandmother, Leah, was making progress in her efforts to rejoin her daughter in America. Since Leah, like both her daughters, was a bona fide US citizen, she was not required to go through an arduous process. She merely had to present proof of her US citizenship and she would be granted a treasured US passport and be free to "return" to the US – just as her daughter had previously done.

In this postcard, my grandmother, Leah, points out that she has informed the US consulate that she is waiting for a visa to be granted to my father (her son-in-law), because she plans to travel with him to America. This was part of the effort by my grandmother to urge the US authorities to allow entry to my father.

The reverse side of the postcard asks the recipients – my grandmother's brother-in-law and sister-in-law (Aron Grunfeld and his wife, at that time living in Romania) – to place the postcard into an envelope and forward it to my mother in care of Bernard Greenfield in New York. My grandmother's decision to use such a circuitous route through Romania to reach my mother by mail probably resulted from the fact that my grandmother had still received no mail from my mother, which, in turn, caused her to wonder whether mail from Krakow was being received in the US.

My dearest, dearest daughter,
    Still no mail from you. I saw a letter that Mrs. Bax received from her husband where he states that you are in America. I wrote to you, my dear child. I received a letter from the consulate that I can get a passport as soon as I get a ticket for the ship. So I answered the consul and I asked them to send me a telegram. I also told them that I am waiting for my son-in-law so that we may travel together.
    Stay healthy and may all your roads lead to happiness.
    Your mother

My dear brother-in-law and sister-in-law,
    Please put this postcard in an envelope and send it to my sweet
daughter in America. She has been there for two months already.
    The address is:
    B. Greenfield / 520 Crown Street / Brooklyn, New York
    Please do it immediately after you receive this postcard.
    Regards and many thanks.
        Leah Grunfeld

MARCH 27, 1940

From My Father to My Mother

Finally one of my mother's postcards from America reaches my father. He responds with a hastily drafted postcard of his own.

My dearest darling Erna,
    Thank you very much for your postcard. It made
me very happy. We are, thank God, healthy and I hope
to hear the same from you. We are waiting so long for
your letters and also I do not think that you receive letters frequently from us.

    . . .

    When do you think that we will see each other? I cannot wait.
It should be today!

                            Kisses a thousand times,
                                Chaskel

CHAPTER FIVE

Flight and Frustration

April–May 1940

APRIL 10, 1940

From Isadore Hermann to My Mother

The month of April 1940 was one that saw the plight of Europe's Jews, including my father, grow dramatically more desperate. On April 8, the three-day secret slaughter of twenty-six thousand Polish officers (many of them Jews) in the Katyn Forest by Soviet troops got underway. Atrocities across Poland abounded. Among them was an account dated April 23 of dozens of captive Jews at Stutthof, Poland, who were forced by local fascists to jump into open latrines. Most drowned or were beaten to death attempting to escape.

But it was also during this month that the extent of the widespread antisemitic attitudes harbored by the British Foreign Service were openly exposed. These sentiments, like those dominating the US State Department, served to strengthen Hitler's hand as he advanced his genocidal agenda. On April 27, British Foreign Service official R.T.E. Latham recorded in minutes of a meeting that fellow official H.F. Downie proclaimed the Jews to be "no less our enemies than the Germans" and asserted that Nazis and Jews were connected by "secret and evil bonds."*

The month ended with the major Jewish ghetto in Lodz, Poland, being

---

* Cited in Shlomo Aronson, *Hitler, the Allies, and the Jews* (Cambridge, UK: Cambridge University Press, 2004), 57.

sealed off, dooming its inhabitants to a slow death by disease and starvation.

It was against this backdrop of encroaching terror in Poland, and worldwide indifference, that my mother pressed on in her valiant attempt to free my father. On April 10 she received discouraging news from my father's cousin, Isadore Hermann. Isadore and his father Sigmund had submitted copious documentation of their financial solvency to the government and sworn out affidavits attesting to their willingness to support my father once he was granted entry to the US (see "The Hermann affidavits" in the February 28, 1940, entry above). These documents were submitted in late February along with a completed "Petition for the Issuance …" form (Form 633). The Hermanns received a form letter response from the government dated March 18 (see above).

In the following letter, Isadore informs my mother that the documents supporting his petition for an entry visa for my father have been returned to him. Instructions direct the applicant, my father, to contact the closest US consulate – now in Berlin.* Isadore, probably aware of the absurdity of such an instruction, suggests that my mother turn to HIAS (Hebrew Immigrant Aid Society) for help.

---

* The US embassy in Warsaw was closed shortly after the German invasion. On the night of September 5, 1939, Ambassador Anthony J. Drexel Biddle Jr., his family, and staff were evacuated by car and then train to Paris along with the Polish government-in-exile. After the fall of France, the embassy and exiles relocated to London, where they remained until after the war.

APRIL 11, 1940

From the Jewish Hospital of Brooklyn to the US Dept. of Labor

To substantiate the fact of her pregnancy, my mother requested that the Jewish Hospital of Brooklyn, where she was receiving prenatal care, send a supportive letter to the government. In it, the hospital's medical social worker attests that my mother is expected to give birth in the early part of May. She goes on to express her wish that this information be helpful to the department as it considers my mother's petition for an immigration visa for the baby's father.

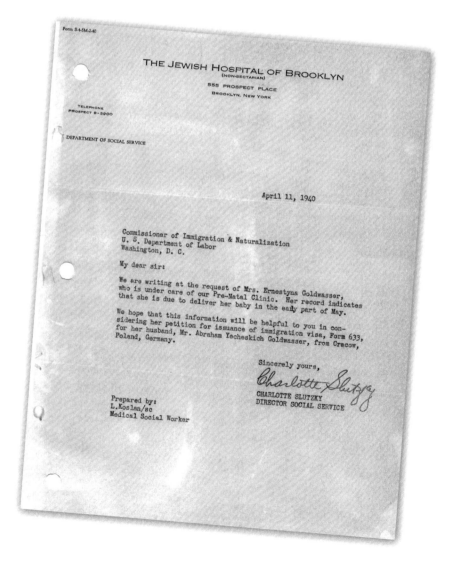

Form S-4-5M-2-40

THE JEWISH HOSPITAL OF BROOKLYN
(NON-SECTARIAN)
555 PROSPECT PLACE
BROOKLYN, NEW YORK

TELEPHONE
PROSPECT 9-3900

DEPARTMENT OF SOCIAL SERVICE

April 11, 1940

Commissioner of Immigration & Naturalization
U. S. Department of Labor
Washington, D. C.

My dear sir:

We are writing at the request of Mrs. Ernestyna Goldwasser, who is under care of our Pre-Natal Clinic. Her record indicates that she is due to deliver her baby in the early part of May.

We hope that this information will be helpful to you in considering her petition for issuance of immigration visa, Form 633, for her husband, Mr. Abraham Yecheskich Goldwasser, from Cracow, Poland, Germany.

Sincerely yours,

Charlotte Slutzky

CHARLOTTE SLUTZKY
DIRECTOR SOCIAL SERVICE

Prepared by:
L.Koslan/sc
Medical Social Worker

APRIL 16, 1940

From the INS Dept. of Labor to My Mother

It was more than a month before my mother received a response to the petition she had filed on March 6, 1940. In this form postcard, identified as Form VP-1, sent to my mother in care of her lawyer, Bennett Aron, she is advised that her petition for issuance of an immigration preference status (Form 633) for her husband has been approved. The text goes on to say that the approval has been forwarded to the US State Department for transmittal to the appropriate consular office.

This positive message does contain an ominous caveat, however. It explains that if the applicant is "your husband"(which he is), and if the marriage occurred on or after July 1, 1932 (which it did), then the granting of the preference status does not necessarily mean immediate issuance of the visa. It merely grants the application "a certain priority on the waiting list for quota visas." The note concludes with a reminder that it is necessary for the applicant to now apply outside the United States to an American consul in order to obtain such a visa.

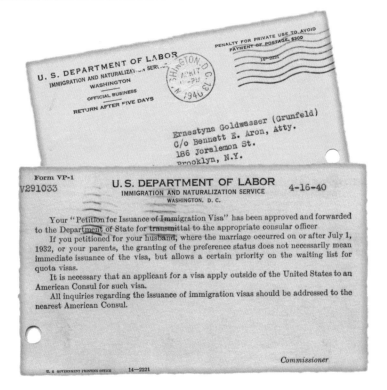

Thus, while the postcard of approval carried some apparently good news, it also reinforced the seemingly innocuous but actually deadly message that control of the issuance of the visa would be carried out by a consul located in Europe, which in turn was controlled by the US State Department.

Considering the timing of this message, one may easily presume that it is reflective of the new policies being implemented by the State Department and the Immigration and Naturalization Service. These new policies, designed to create a bureaucratic barrier to Jewish immigration into America, were being put into place during these early months of 1940 by the newly appointed assistant secretary of state, Breckinridge Long.

Postpone and Postpone and Postpone

One month before my mother arrived in the US and began her quest to free my father, a seemingly routine government appointment took place in Washington that would produce the devastating result of dooming her dream of reuniting with him.

Breckinridge Long was a close and wealthy friend of President Roosevelt and had been previously appointed by FDR to serve as ambassador to Italy. It was during his tenure there that Mussolini shocked the world by launching an unprovoked invasion of Ethiopia. When Roosevelt was being urged to impose an oil embargo against Italy as a means of protesting this aggression, it was Ambassador Long who attempted to convince FDR not to do so.

Called back from Italy when war broke out in September 1939, Long was placed by Roosevelt into the number two position in the State Department: assistant secretary of state. An isolationist, an antisemite – and, some (such as Eleanor Roosevelt) would argue, a closet fascist – Long used his high office to block any and all attempts to rescue persecuted Jews such as my father. He wielded his control of the diplomatic consular system as a weapon against what he saw as a potential Jewish onslaught.

Long's policies of intentional bureaucratic delay were being first fashioned during this period in early 1940. It would be several months before Long felt secure enough to record them in the form of the April 1940 memo

Assistant Secretary of State Breckinridge Long, who exercised his influence within the State Department to prevent the United States from becoming a place of refuge for European Jews, intentionally named Bermuda as the site for the famed 1943 sham refugee conference because of its inaccessibility. Long's xenophobia influenced practically every move he made during the war as he led the State Department action to deny visas to political and intellectual refugees. Photo: US National Archives.

recreated below, circulated within the State Department. And it would be several more years before such evidence of his perfidy would come to light.

While the format of the memo below is simulated, the content is a word-for-word instruction from Assistant Secretary of State Breckinridge Long in which he directs his bureau chiefs to advise all US consulates to place bogus obstacles in the way of refugees seeking to immigrate to the US. In carrying out Long's directive, the US consul in Berlin and State Department officials in Washington effectively sealed my father's fate.

CONFIDENTIAL MEMO

```
From: Breckenridge Long, Asst. Sec. of State
To: All executive bureau chiefs
Date: April 12, 1940
Subj.: Stopping the flow of immigrants


We can delay and effectively stop, for a
temporary period of indefinite length, the
number of immigrants into the United States.
We could do this by simply advising our
consuls to put every obstacle in the way and
to require additional evidence and to resort
to various administrative devices which
would postpone and postpone and
postpone the granting of the visas.
```

APRIL 17, 1940

From US Department of Labor to My Mother

Almost immediately after receiving Isadore Hermann's discouraging April 10 letter, my mother was contacted by the government with a highly unusual and somewhat terrifying list of demands. In the following letter, which begins with an explicit reference to "the visa petition filed by you in behalf of your husband," my mother is instructed to report, six days after the date of the letter – on the first day of Passover – to Ellis Island in New York Harbor. The standard form letter ignores the fact that my mother had previously explained her unemployed status (due to her pregnancy) and insists that she present detailed documentation of her financial condition (including her bank book and a sworn statement from her employer) as well as proof of her claim to be a US citizen. In a specially prepared footnote, the letter further demands that my mother bring along Jakob Grunfeld's naturalization certificate and her own birth certificate or other documents to establish her relationship to him.

Finally, she is instructed to enlist a US citizen as a witness – someone other than her relative and host, Bernard Greenfield – to attest to the proceedings. This exclusion of Uncle Bernard could have been made because he had previously been identified as my father's possible sponsor.

It is safe to assume that these bizarre instructions, directed to an observant Jewish woman whom they knew to be in her ninth month of pregnancy, were prompted not merely by the visa application that the INS had approved on April 16 (the previous day), but also by the government's desire to place insurmountable hurdles in my mother's path. Failure to appear would constitute grounds for the government to deny her petition and possibly even to deport her back to Europe.

The intent of this letter is clearly to intimidate. But once again, the bureaucrats had not counted on the stiff-necked determination of my mother. According to another handwritten document, there is strong evidence that my mother, with the assistance of her attorney, Bennett Aron, set out to comply with the outrageous demands set forth. Given that her appearance was slated to coincide with a major Jewish holy day, it is unclear whether or not my mother did, in fact, make an appearance at Ellis Island on that day. But I am confident that all the requested documentation was submitted, as requested, in one way or another.

U. S. DEPARTMENT OF LABOR
Immigration and Naturalization Service
Ellis Island, New York Harbor, NY

File No. 99491/299

April 17, 1940

Mrs. Ernestyna G. Goldwasser
517 Crown Street (c/o B.Greenfield)
Brooklyn, N. Y.

Dear Mrs. Goldwasser:

Reference is had to the visa petition filed
by you in behalf of your husband.   Re-entry Permit
You are requested to call at the ~~ixx~~/Division,
Ellis Island, New York Harbor, on Tuesday,
April 23, 1940,   at three p.m., and bring
with you evidence to substantiate the statements
made in your petition regarding your financial
condition. You should also bring your passbook
showing bank deposits. It is further suggested
that you obtain a statement, under oath, from
your employer, stating the length of employment,
and the amount of salary paid you. If you are
an employer, evidence should be obtained to show
your assets and liabilities.

If the beneficiary is in the United States (s)he
should accompany you to this office.
          Report to Room 240,
~~ftxx~Ellis~Island~and~ferrytransitisawe~~ the Barge Office, at South Ferry, New York City, at the above time,
and this letter will serve as your pass. Besides the
documents on the attached sheet, please bring with you
those noted below. *
          Respectfully,

          Byron Uhl

          BYRON H. UHL
          District Director
          New York District

CGMc

* Bring with you your father's naturalization certificate
and a certificate of your birth or some other document
that will show your relationship to the person through
whom you are claiming United States citizenship. In addition bring with you a witness--other than Bernard Greenfield
--who is qualified along the lines set forth in the attached
instruction sheet.

APRIL 18, 1940

From My Mother to Raymond H. Geist

Having learned from Isadore Hermann's April 10 letter and the INS's April 16 postcard that the US consul in Berlin would decide whether or not to grant a visa to my father, my mother immediately wrote an impassioned letter in German on April 18 to "Hon. Raymond H. Geist, American Consul, Berlin."

Geist was, until the end of 1939, actually serving as deputy consul in Berlin under Consul General George Messersmith. Both men had served in Berlin during the 1930s and issued frequent and largely ignored warnings to Washington about Hitler's intentions for the Jews. Geist was running the American embassy after the US withdrew its ambassador to the Third Reich, William E. Dodd, in the wake of Kristallnacht. Dodd had claimed that both Messersmith and Geist were partly Jewish and had for many years discounted their pleas for America to rescue German Jews. By the time my mother's letter reached the Berlin consulate, Geist had already been sent back to Washington. Another ray of hope extinguished.

The letter is depicted below and translated immediately thereafter.

My mother starts by referencing an enclosed letter of support from US congressman Andrew L. Somers (D-NY). While the letter from Somers itself has been lost, the fact that he responded to her at all indicates he was sympathetic to her plea. This assumption is further supported by the fact that Somers took to the airwaves after the sham Bermuda Conference in 1943 and decried it for what it was, saying that "the Jews have not only faced the unbelievable cruelty of the distorted minds bent upon annihilating them, but they have to face the betrayal of those whom they called 'friends.'"*

---

* Cited in Rafael Medoff, "'The Monuments Men' Shows How America Saved Paintings While Letting Jews Die," *Tablet*, January 29, 2014.

Ernetine Goldwasser
c/o reenfeld.

517 Crown Street
Brooklyn,N.Y.C.
4/18/1940.

Hon.Raymond H.Geist
American Consul
B e r l i n
Germany.

19/4 1940

Beiliegend uebersende ich Ihnen einen Brief des Congressmannes Andrew L. Somera,mit welchem Schreiben meine Angelegenheit empfohlen wird.

Ich bin amerikanische Buergerin und wohne unter obiger Adresse. F Mein Mann,Abraham Jecheskel Goldwasser befindet sich derzeit in Karkau Josefsgasse 9.

Ich moechte meinen Mann auf raschestem Weg hierher bringen und bitte Sie daher hoefl.alle noetigen Formulare die er auszufuellen und zu unterschreiben hat,an seine Adresse nach Krakau zu schicken. Weiters wollen Sie ihm bitte aufgeben,welche Dokumente er zur Erlangung des Visums benoetigt.

Inzwischen hoffe ich,dass Sie in den Besitz meiner Petition No 633 direkt aus Washington gelangt sind,damit mein Mann auf Preferenz Quota sein Visum bekommen kann.

Ich danke Ihnen im Vorhinein fuer Ihre Bemuehung und zeichne
hochachtungsvoll
Ernestine Goldwasser

F Jetzt befinde mich in der Schwangerschaft und erwarte bald ein Baby.

Ernetine Goldwasser
c/o reenfeld.

517 Crown Street
Brooklyn,N.Y.C.
4/18/1940.

Hon.Raymond H.Geist
American Consul
B e r l i n
Germany.

19/4 1940

I am enclosing a letter from Congressman Andrew L. Somers in which letter he describes what my situation is.

I am an American citizen and I live at the above address. My husband Abraham Jechezkel Goldwasser is now in Kraków at Josefsgasse 9.

I would like my husband to come here as quickly as possible and I beg you to send to him at his address in Kraków all of the forms that he needs to fill out and to sign. Please tell him what documents he needs in order to get a visa.

In the meantime I hope that you received my petition number 633 which came directly from Washington so that he may receive a visa under the preference quota.

Thank you in advance for all of your efforts on my behalf.

Sincerely.
Ernestine Goldwasser

I now find myself to be pregnant and I am expecting a baby shortly

From My Grandmother to My Mother

While all of these machinations by the US government were unfolding unbeknownst to my mother, my father and grandmother also remained totally in the dark about my mother and her efforts to free them from Germany's grasp. Not until April 22, 1940, more than three months after my mother left Krakow, did her mother and her husband acknowledge receiving a letter from her. In this letter, sent immediately to her daughter, my grandmother Leah presents news about her progress toward rejoining my mother in America. While she expresses the hope of arriving before my mother gives birth in May, she clearly does not appear confident that she will be there in time. She also repeats her strong desire to travel with my father, and extends hope to my mother that they will arrive in America together.

Most significant is Leah's comment that the US consulate she must deal with is no longer in Warsaw, but rather in Berlin. She asks for my mother's advice about whether she ought to travel to Berlin by herself to secure her American passport.

April 22, 1940, Krakow

My sweet Ernusha,

Your letter gave me a lot of happiness. I received it today and I am rushing to answer you. I want to give you some news regarding my departure. I want to leave here the fifth of May because I want to be there when you give birth. But I do not know if I can manage that because it is already too late and I prefer to travel with Chaskel. It would be much nicer and easier. You know the way I am and I would like to go with Chaskel.

You, my sweetheart, in the meantime, have an easy birth and with mazel. I am sure that everything will be okay because you deserve it. I have an easy heart and I hope that God will be good to us. Chaskel is very lonely, but I hope and I think that he will leave soon.....

I sent a letter to Genoa to find out about my passage on the ship. But first I have to go to the consul. The consul is now in Berlin and I do not know if I will have to go there. What do you think, should I go there? Stay well and happy and I wish you all the best. With God's help all will be fine.... And I hope to see you soon.

Mother

APRIL 22, 1940
From My Father to My Mother

My father adds the following words to the letter begun by my grandmother (above). His words are saturated with love and longing. He yearns to be at my mother's side to witness the birth of their "son" (how does he know the gender?). He reassures her that the family is faring well and he has managed to retain his job. Most Krakow Jews have not.

My father again points out that my grandmother wishes to wait until he is free to travel with her before leaving for America. Whereas before, he thought it best that she not do so and proceed alone, he now appears to be sympathetic to her position.

My father states that "We have everything that we need for the holidays." This refers to the matzah and other items required to observe the Passover holiday. The first Passover Seder in 1940 was to be conducted on the evening that this letter was written. Certainly the theme of liberation must have resonated deeply in the heart of my father, and in the hearts of my family members, as they pondered their collective future. For almost every one of them, it would be their last Passover Seder together.

My dearest darling in the whole world Ernusha,

Thank you so much for your wonderful letter, my dearest. You cannot imagine how happy we were and it was so wonderful to hear from you. I think that we will be together on my son's day of birth. God should help us as soon as possible.

...We are okay and we do not lack anything. I hope it doesn't get worse. I still work at Mr. Amand.

Your dear letter of March 29, we received today. This is the second letter that we received. God should help you to have an easy birth with mazel.

We have everything that we need for the holidays. We can get everything…

Mother is very lonely without you. She wants to be with you already, but she wants to wait for me. It may be better that way.

Regards and kisses a hundred times. See you as soon as possible. Regards to everyone. Thank you so much for your postcard.

Chaskel

MAY 1, 1940
From My Father to My Mother

Nine days after my father sent his April 22 letter, the family in Krakow received a packet of accumulated mail from my mother. Although I do not have copies of this correspondence, it is clear from my father's response below that one of the letters contained a key piece of information. By this time my mother had been made aware by the US Department of Immigration that her petition for a visa preference had been approved (see April 16, 1940, postcard above) but that my father must apply for a visa from a US consulate. In this May 1 letter, my father states that he wrote to the US consul (presumably in Berlin) right away. He goes on to express his confidence that the consulate will soon grant him the visa he has requested and that "with God's help, we will be together soon."

My dearest Ernusha,

I want you to know that this week I received three postcards and two letters from you. I wrote a letter to the consul right away on April 26.

I was very happy to receive all your letters. There will be even greater happiness when I receive the visa from the consul and from you a mazel tov.

With God's help the birth will be easy because you deserve the best. There is no other person in the world like you. My darling, I just want to be together with you. I miss you so very much, but with God's help, we will be together soon.

Chaskel

MAY 5, 1940
From My Father to My Mother

Correspondence is now flowing more smoothly between my parents. My father again mentions the fact that he sent a visa request to the US consul on April 26 and has yet to receive a reply. He explains that my grandmother (his mother-in-law) has received a letter from the Cook travel agency and is now waiting for him to receive his visa so they may travel together to America. While my father is still working, he does not earn much and the weekends are difficult for him (presumably due to boredom).

May 5, 1940

My dearest darling Ernunia,

I received your precious letter yesterday and I thank you very much for it. I am not complaining anymore. I receive letters every week now, sometimes even two or three times a week from you, my dearest. My wish is to be together with you and not have to write any more letters.

After receiving your letter of April 13, I wrote to the consul on April 26. I am waiting impatiently for an answer. I think that it will not take too long and we will see each other in happiness and with mazel. God should help us to be together soon. Amen.

Mother wants to travel together with me because she received a letter from the Cook travel agency on April 30. I think that soon I will be able to travel so the two of us will go together.

I am still working but don't earn much money. 35 zlotys a week is not much, but I am occupied. The worst is on Saturday and Sunday, but this will pass.

I am healthy and have everything I need. I only want to be together with you. You cannot imagine how I miss you. Stay healthy.

I kiss you many times.

Yours forever,
Chaskel

MAY 5, 1940
From My Grandmother to My Mother

In this postscript to my father's May 5 letter, my grandmother sends her congratulations to the new baby (me). Although these tidings were written a week before my birth, I had no doubt arrived by the time the letter was received by my mother.

My grandmother goes on to comment that they were able to quickly prepare the visa application for my father after receiving my mother's letter of April 13.

The family my grandmother inquires about in Camden is the Hermann family. The balance of the letter is confusing. She explains that the reason she has not yet received her US passport is because "…the consul went away." It is likely that she means the US consulate in Warsaw has been closed and that she must now await word from the Berlin consulate.

She concludes by informing my mother that she is having difficulty getting the ticket for the ship.

I want to send congratulations to the newborn baby. I want to wish you good luck. All the best and a lot of mazel for you and the whole family.

The letter to the consul went only 13 days after we received it and that is fast.

What is new with the family in Camden?

A letter came that the consul went away. That is why I did not get the pass so far.

We write to you every week, sometimes twice a week. We are waiting for an answer from the consul. I still do not have the visa. The ticket for the ship is hard to come by but I will let you know when I get it.

I send you warmest regards. We pray to God to be able to enjoy together.

Your mother

MAY 5, 1940

From My Great-Aunt Hedwig Hirsch to My Mother

In this letter to my mother, Aunt Hedwig (my grandmother's sister-in-law) alerts my mother to an emerging problem and enlists her assistance. It appears that Hedwig, as well as other family members, are urging my grandmother to leave for America as soon as she is able and not wait for my father. Hedwig asks my mother to "do something to help" – in other words to send a plea to persuade her own mother to get out while she can – even though it means abandoning my father! As this letter illustrates, the choice confronting my grandmother and mother was not an easy one.

> *May 5, 1940*
>
> *My dearest Erna,*
>
> *I take the opportunity to write to you. From what I hear, you are doing okay. I can say the same about your husband and mother. I am advising your mother to start traveling and not wait for Chaskel. But you know her; she does not want to travel without him. I know that you are waiting for him, but I think it has to be done this way. Can you do something to help? We pray to God that our wishes come true and all of you will be together. Do not aggravate yourself. You have to stay healthy.*
>
> *...*
>
> *Again, Erna, I wish you all the best and hearty regards.*
>
> *Aunt Hedwig*

Hedwig and Shimon
Hirsch, circa 1935

MAY 10, 1940

From A. M. Warren, Chief of the Visa Division, US Dept. of State, to Bennett Aron, My Mother's Attorney

Avra M. Warren was a career diplomat who held numerous ambassadorships during his lengthy career. In early 1940, Warren headed the Visa Division at the US State Department and was thereby in direct control of monitoring immigration quotas and the granting of alien visas. Much to my father's misfortune, Warren was a close associate of Breckinridge Long and shared Long's reputation of stringently enforcing methods of denial and delay to keep America from being overrun by Jewish refugees.

Holocaust survivor and former Berlin rabbi Max Nussbaum wrote the following of Warren:

> During those days after the outbreak of war in Europe, the American Vice Consul Warren was the greatest misfortune for the Jews in Berlin. Inherently, emigration at that time was still possible since the USA had not yet entered the war and the Germans still approved applications. However, Warren sabotaged the whole emigration procedure and he is responsible for the death of hundreds of Jews.*

It was the chief of the Visa Division, Warren, who sent the following letter to my mother's attorney in response to Aron's having personally called on him to inquire about the status of the visa application she had filed. As was the case with previous correspondence from the Department of Labor, this letter also begins on an optimistic note, but cruelly concludes with yet another impossible hurdle blocking my father's freedom.

The good news that the American embassy in Berlin was authorized by Warren's office on April 17 to grant a preference status to my father is demolished by the letter's concluding words: "The American Consul (in Berlin)…will, of course, be responsible for determining whether a preference quota immigration visa may properly be issued to the alien above mentioned."

In other words, the buck has been passed. The State Department's

---

* Yad Vashem file 3549470, June 30, 1958 (K.J. Ball-Kaduri – Collection of Testimonies and Reports of German Jewry).

authorization for the American embassy to grant preferential status to my father's visa application is (incredibly) not enough! The wealth and strength of the documentation provided by my mother and others is not enough. A determination must now be made by the American consul in Berlin before a visa may "properly" be issued.

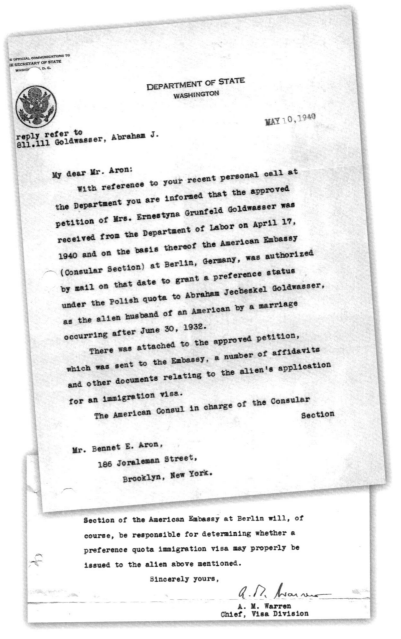

DEPARTMENT OF STATE
WASHINGTON

MAY 10, 1940

reply refer to
811.111 Goldwasser, Abraham J.

My dear Mr. Aron:

With reference to your recent personal call at the Department you are informed that the approved petition of Mrs. Ernestyna Grunfeld Goldwasser was received from the Department of Labor on April 17, 1940 and on the basis thereof the American Embassy (Consular Section) at Berlin, Germany, was authorized by mail on that date to grant a preference status under the Polish quota to Abraham Jecheskel Goldwasser, as the alien husband of an American by a marriage occurring after June 30, 1932.

There was attached to the approved petition, which was sent to the Embassy, a number of affidavits and other documents relating to the alien's application for an immigration visa.

The American Consul in charge of the Consular Section

Mr. Bennet E. Aron,
186 Joraleman Street,
Brooklyn, New York.

Section of the American Embassy at Berlin will, of course, be responsible for determining whether a preference quota immigration visa may properly be issued to the alien above mentioned.

Sincerely yours,

A. M. Warren
Chief, Visa Division

MAY 12, 1940

An American Baby Is Born

In May 1940, the German authorities announced that Krakow would become the first city in Poland to be made "*Judenrein*" (cleansed of Jews). The Jewish population of Krakow at the time the Germans entered the city was sixty-eight thousand, most of whom were to be either deported to rural areas or herded into the Krakow ghetto, which was completed in March 1941 in the Podgorze district.

Almost eight and a half months after the start of World War II, and more than four months after she had left Krakow, my mother – having successfully immigrated to America – was ready, indeed anxious, to give birth. On May 11, 1940, she arrived at Brooklyn Jewish Hospital, located just one and a half miles from where she had been staying with the Greenfield family. Both the hospital and the Greenfield home were situated in the Jewish quarter of Brooklyn that was then, as it is now, known as Crown Heights.

From what my mother shared with me about the delivery, I was apparently very reluctant to leave the warmth of her womb. She told me repeatedly, as I was growing up, that the delivery took more than twenty-four grueling hours. Despite the presence and good intentions of her cousins, without my father by her side, my mother felt painfully alone as she endured the lengthy labor. She was a stranger in a strange new land, separated by sea and circumstance from her beloved husband, mother, and sister, when I, at long last, emerged – appropriately enough on Mother's Day, May 12, 1940.

While still in the hospital, my mother was approached by one of the nurses, who offered to help her fill out the form needed for the issuance of my birth certificate. My mother again found herself alone when facing the question of what to name me. Cognizant of the Ashkenazi Jewish tradition of naming a newborn child after a deceased family member, she turned first to my Hebrew names. After some thought, she decided on Moshe Yaakov, naming me first for Moshe Goldwasser, her father-in-law (about whom I still know so little), and then for her own father, Jakob (Yaakov) Grunfeld, whose history has been discussed in an earlier chapter.

I never asked my mother why she picked this unusual ordering of my names. After all, she was closer by blood to Jakob, so his name should have come first. I always assumed that the reversed sequence was because she had a nephew (her sister Gusta's son) who was already named for their father, Jakob, while I would have been the first grandson of her father-in-law, Moshe. But I now feel there was another reason she selected her husband's father, rather than her own, to be my namesake. Having read and reread the numerous letters between my parents, it is now obvious to me that naming me Moshe Yaakov was a permanent way for my mother to demonstrate her undying love for my faraway father.

Next, my mother had to decide upon the English names. After all, I was to be a true American, so I definitely needed an American name. Although giving me Jack as a middle name was an obvious choice, my mother really had no clue about what my American first name, corresponding to Moshe, should be. The hospital nurse, apparently of Scottish or Irish descent, suggested Murray, which my mother accepted. Little did my mother or the nurse realize at the time how closely the two names, Moshe and Murray, are related to each other. The biblical Moses was named Moshe because he was drawn by Pharaoh's daughter from the waters of the Nile.* And Murray is Gaelic for a man of the sea. In either case, the name relates to surviving dangerous waters. The bearer of such a name, be he sailor, lawgiver, or the son of a Polish refugee, carries a special duty – after having been rescued from the waters of adversity – to make a difference on earth.

MAY 12, 1940
From My Father to My Mother

In this poignant letter, penned by my father in German-occupied Poland on the very day that I was entering the world in America, he empties his heart and expresses his deeply felt love for my mother.

He writes with disappointment that he has heard back from "the United States lines" and learned that the US consulate in Warsaw is no

---

* The verse in Exodus 2:10 says, *"ki min hamayim meshisihu"* (for I drew him out of the water).

longer issuing visas to Polish citizens. My father asks my mother to write to his cousins, the Hermanns, to urge them to move faster.

After expressing his longing and frustration at not being by her side to witness the birth of their first child, he closes by expressing his hope that the visa will be in Berlin shortly. My father had applied for a visa to the US consulate in Berlin on April 26 (as mentioned in his May 1 letter) and had somehow been given the assurance of receiving one within thirty days. Allowing time for the mails, he therefore at this point hopes that the visa will be in Berlin on June 10.

Dearest Ernusha,

I think and I hope that we deserve a mazel tov. God should help that it should happen as soon as possible and that we should be together soon. Amen.

Today we received a letter from the United States Lines and they say that the consulate still has not issued visas to Polish citizens. But he said that if I do get a letter from the consulate, I should let him know. Please, I would like you to write a letter to my cousins that they should move faster.

My darling, I know how you suffered and I hope that your birth was not too hard and that you and the baby are healthy. Please write exactly how it was. You probably know as much as I do as far as my departure is concerned; do what you can to help us to be together.

Darling, I miss you so much, you cannot imagine. It is ten days since I got a letter from you. How is our sweet little baby? Is it a boy or a girl? I do not care, the main thing is that it should be healthy and happy. My dearest one, I want only to be together with you as soon as possible. I am okay and healthy, but I miss you so much. It is already five months, but it seems like I haven't seen you for five years. Sweetheart, I have no strength without you. I cannot live without you. Please try so that we should be together. I know that you are doing whatever you can.

I think that the visa will be in Berlin on June 10. Stay healthy. I kiss you many times.

Yours,
Chaskel

MAY 12, 1940
From My Grandmother to My Mother

My grandmother, Leah, adds her words of congratulations on the birth
of her daughter's American-born baby (she also correctly anticipated my
gender). She goes on to confirm that the US consulate is no longer in
Warsaw and that she has contacted the consulate in Berlin to apply for her
passport. She explains that one must allow more time than before for the
application to reach Berlin. Presumably, my father applied for his visa at
the same time she did.

> *My dearest Ernusha,*
>
> *First of all, I want to wish you a mazel tov. From the bottom of my
> heart, I wish that the baby shall bring only happiness and nachas and
> that he should be a good baby and easy to manage.*
>
> *...*
>
> *I wrote to the consulate in Berlin, but have not received anything
> yet.*
>
> *How are you doing? Please write about everything exactly as it is. I
> am sad that I cannot be with you at this important time, but God will
> help us. It is possible that my letter to the consul came today because the
> consul is not in Warsaw anymore.*
>
> *Stay healthy and strong. Please write....*
>
> > *Many kisses,*
> > *Mother*

MAY 27, 1940
From My Father to My Mother

The weeks roll by and still no word from the US consulate regarding my
father's visa. Despite his suffering, he proclaims, he is determined to
survive. He informs my mother that he has received a certificate from
his employer, which apparently releases him from the need to obtain a
government form concerning his occupational status. Though he has not
heard from the consulate and he again urges my mother to write to Washington, my father remains fixated on the June 10 date on which he expects

to receive his US visa. He is counting the minutes. We know from other sources that on May 22, my father received a telegram from my mother advising him of my birth. He must see his wife again, he states, because "I am now both a father and a husband."

May 27, 1940

My dearest ones in the whole world,

On Friday I received two letters, from February 2 and April 2. Dearest, I would like to be with you before you get this letter. I miss you so much, you cannot even imagine. My dearest, how do you feel? Are you healthy? And the sweet little baby? Please write exactly about everything because I really want to know. Today I received a postcard from February 9. I would give all that I own to see you for a minute with my own eyes.

I received a certificate from Mr. Amand. I do not need my certificate of occupation right now. My dearest, I suffer so much but I am going to survive. I am waiting for June 10 and I am counting the moments till that time. Everything is the same as it was before. I am still healthy and I want to hear the same from you. I still work by Mr. Amand. I did not get any communication or letter from the consul and we do not know where the papers are. Maybe you can write to Washington to speed up the process. I have no time to lose. I have to see you with the baby because I am now both a father and a husband.

My dearest darling, I have to end this letter. I kiss you a thousand times. Send my regards to the whole family and regards from my whole family.

Chaskel

Actual first page of the May 12, 1940 letter from my father to my mother, written in Polish. Note the word "Mazeltov" at the end of the first line as my father somehow perceived that I had been born.

CHAPTER SIX

Closing the Golden Door

June–July 1940

JUNE 17, 1940
From My Father to My Mother

By mid-June, the dark cloud of German domination was rapidly spreading across Europe. The facility that was destined to become the most infamous Nazi death camp had been established in Oswiecim (Auschwitz), Poland. France had fallen and Paris was now occupied by German forces.

In the following letter my father again beseeches my mother to take his case to Washington, because all of his efforts to gain a travel visa to the US are proving fruitless. He goes on to suggest that perhaps if she wrote to the US consulate in Berlin, it might elicit a response. She of course has done exactly that, to no avail (see her April 18 letter above).

My grandmother, he reports, has received word from the consulate. This is probably due to her status as a US citizen. According to my father, she has been instructed to come to the consulate to claim her US passport. Contrary to my father's hope of accompanying her to Berlin, she is instructed to come alone.

The Josef mentioned in the letter is most likely my father's younger brother, Josef Goldwasser (born in 1912). Josef and his new wife Regina (whom he would wed a week after this letter was written) lived in Warsaw.

In this letter, my father expresses optimism that my grandmother and mother will soon be reunited in America.

My father closes with the sad but predictable news that he is no longer working because Mr. Amand has closed his store.

June 17, 1940

My dearest ones in the whole world,

It is almost two weeks since we received a letter from you. I hope and pray every day that a letter will come because it means so much to us. I really wonder how you are doing. Here everything is as it was before. I am healthy and I want to hear the same from you. Darling, I want to be with you so much. You cannot imagine how I long for you.

Could you please take care of something in Washington, because here we cannot do anything. I already wrote four letters to the consul and he has not answered. Maybe you can write to Berlin, maybe it would be better that way.

Mother received a letter from the consul that she has to go by herself to get her passport. I do not know how it will be. She wrote to Josef in Warsaw and if she gets something concrete maybe she will start traveling to you.

I think that we will see each other soon, with God's help.

That would be true happiness. I do not go to Mr. Amand anymore because he closed the store.

Stay healthy and I kiss you many times.

Forever,
Chaskel

JUNE 17, 1940
From My Grandmother to My Mother

My grandmother adds a message to my father's June 17 letter. In it, she confirms that she has received word about her passport from the US consul in Berlin. Oddly, she states that she "cannot go yet," without elaborating. It is clear that she is having second thoughts about joining my mother; she asks if it is possible to "take back the ticket for the ship because [she] cannot travel right now." What comes across is my grandmother's reluctance to leave Poland, likely due to her growing realization that her son-in-law, my father, will be unable to accompany her.

> My dearest darling Ernusha,
>
> It is already two weeks since we heard from you last. I finally received, after a lot of trouble, a letter from the consul telling me to come and pick up the passport. But I cannot go yet. How are you and the little son? What is his name?... But what can we do? Our dear God wants it that way and that is the way that it has to be.
>
> Does the little one let you sleep or does he cry at night? How do you manage alone with such a little baby? How do you go to buy something? Do you breast-feed him?... Please answer my questions because I am so anxious to know about everything.
>
> Maybe you can take back the ticket for the ship because I cannot travel right now... Your husband is no longer working.
>
> Everyone sends regards to you and your son.
>
> Stay healthy.
Mother

JUNE 24, 1940

From My Mother to A.M. Warren, Chief of the Visa Division, US Dept. of State

As requested in my father's June 17 letter, my mother again contacted the State Department. She had waited patiently for further word but received nothing for six long weeks. On June 24 she sent Visa Division Chief Avra M. Warren another letter in which she reminded him of his May 10 message. She pointed out that my father had written directly to the American consul in Berlin, Raymond Geist, on April 26. Just like my mother, who had written to Geist earlier (on April 18), my father had, at that point, received no reply from Berlin.*

---

* My mother eventually did receive a signed return receipt postcard from Berlin indicating that the US consulate had received her April 18, 1940, letter pleading for assistance (see above). Strangely, the return receipt was dated August 15, 1940. Why it took four months for my mother's letter to reach the US consulate in Berlin remains a mystery.

In an effort to appeal to Warren's emotions, my mother anxiously pleads that she is alone in America and has recently given birth to me. Finally, she begs for his help and concludes with "I should welcome hearing from you by return mail." She never did.

June 24th, 1940

Hon. A.M.Warren, Chief
Visa Division
Department of State
Washington, D.C.   Re: V.D. 811,111 Goldwasser,
                              Abraham J

Honored Sir:

Several weeks ago Mr. Bannet E. Aron of 186 Joralemon Street of this City made a personal call at your department in my behalf, and as a result you wrote to him under date of May 10th, 1940 that on the basis of the approved petition of myself, the American Embassy (consular section) at Berlin, Germany, was authorized to grant a preference status under the Polish quota to Abraham Jecheskel Goldwasser, my husband, as the alien husband of an American by a marriage occuring after June 30th, 1932.

On April 26th, 1940 my husband wrote to Hon. Raymone H. Geist, American Consul at Berlin, Germany, inquiring as to what documents he was to obtain in this matter. No reply was received by him to his inquiry.

I am alone here and have recently given birth to a child, so you can readily see the reason for my anxiety in trying to help my husband join me in this country.

If there is anything you can do to help me in this connection, I should welcome hearing from you by return mail.

Please accept my sincere appreciation for your co-operation.

Very truly yours,

Ernestyna Goldwasser
% Greenfield
517 Crown Street
Brooklyn, N.Y.

JUNE 25, 1940
From My Father to My Mother

In the following letter, my father reacts to the photo my mother has sent of his new son. This is the first time my father has seen my picture, and his pride shines through the heartbreak of his separation.

He again points out that the US consul has failed to respond to his inquiries and implores my mother to "write to him and ask him why he holds me up and does not let me go."

The letter contains a cryptic reference to a Mr. W.D., an American who has paid a visit to my father. My father admonishes my mother not to get in touch with him after he returns to the US, "because he is not a good man." The identity of W.D. and the reasons behind the ominous warning remain a mystery.

My father informs my mother that her sister, Gusta, is in Russia! He does not elaborate, and one may assume that Gusta was able to visit Russia and has returned, since my grandmother states in the same letter that "Gusta and her husband come here every day."

Evidently at this point, my father was able to travel as far as Warsaw where he reports that he attended his brother Josef's wedding, a match made by their sister Hanka. He reports that "everything is still okay" in Warsaw. What he doesn't know is that the German governor general over Poland, Hans Frank, has already started building the wall that will surround what is to become the notorious Warsaw ghetto. On October 16, Frank will order all Jews in Warsaw into the ghetto. Exactly one month later, the ghetto will be sealed off from the outside world, creating the world's largest prison camp.*

My father closes with kisses for me, addressing me by my Jewish name, Moshe Yaakov.

---

* The ghetto held approximately 400,000 Jews, or 30 percent of Warsaw's population, in a space equal to 2 percent of its area.

June 25, 1940

My dearest ones in the whole world,

Yesterday I received a photograph, and you cannot imagine how happy we were – wonderful boy! I am only sorry that I cannot be with you. But God will help and I think that soon we will be together.

I have not heard anything from the consul even though I wrote three letters to him, but he does not answer. I do not know what will happen. Maybe only you can write to him and ask him why he holds me up and does not let me go.

Your mother received a postcard from you before I received the letter. Please, at any time, go ahead and send a photograph of our sweet little son. He is so beautiful, the most beautiful in the world. Everybody loves him and they wonder how you learned to hold the baby so nicely. He is so little.

Ernusha, a man from America came to visit – his name is W.D.I am sure that you know who he is. Do not get in touch with him because he is not a good man.

Gusta is in Russia, and in Warsaw everything is still okay. I went this week to Josef because he got married. I am very glad about it. Hanka was the matchmaker.

Everyone sends regards. Stay healthy and happy. A lot of kisses especially for our little son Moshe Yaakov.

Chaskel

JUNE 25, 1940
From My Grandmother to My Mother

My grandmother again appends a postscript to my father's letter and articulates her reluctance to travel to America. She claims that the only route that is open is through Russia and Japan. This information may be the result of her other daughter Gusta's recent travels to Russia.

She points out that she must go to Berlin to claim her US passport before it's too late. Evidently, she accompanied my father to Warsaw to attend his brother Josef's recent wedding.

My sweet Ernusha,

Thank you for your letter and the photographs. It gives us so much happiness I cannot put it in words. I am glad that you are happy. He is a wonderful little boy. As far as my coming to you, unfortunately, I cannot go right now. The only road is through Russia and Japan. It is a roundabout way and the trip takes seven weeks and it costs a lot of money. I do not think that I will be able to do it. Maybe I will be able to go through Italy. I hope so. I am glad to hear that you have enough milk, but you have to take care of your breasts.

... My passport is at the consulate in Berlin. I have to go there to pick it up but I am afraid I will have to go soon because, if not, the passport will expire and I won't be able to get another one.

... Gusta and her husband come here every day and the children make a commotion. I went to Josef's wedding. Nothing new so far, everyone is okay and I hope that all is well by you.

Mother

JULY 8, 1940
From My Father to My Mother

Finally my father receives word from the US consul in Berlin, but the news is disheartening. He is instructed to come to Berlin, which for a Polish Jew in Krakow is simply impossible by this point. My father naively holds out hope that a "German" office, due to open in Krakow the following week, will be able to assist him. His naiveté is even more apparent when he implies that since she is in the US, my mother can somehow transform him into an American citizen. Evidently, in the letter to which he is responding, my mother made an error by noting their fourth anniversary as June 21 instead of August 20.

July 8, 1940

My dearest ones in the whole world,

Friday I received some papers from the consul, but I cannot use them, unfortunately. First of all, I cannot leave Krakow. Second of all, the roads are not open for me. I went to Cook and I will still write to Warsaw again to the same office that Mother wrote to for the ticket for the ship. The 15th of this month a German office is supposed to open up. Maybe there I can take care of something. Would it be possible to take care of things as an American because as an American, I would be able to leave sooner? God should help that soon we should be together.

...I hope that soon we will be together. Tomorrow it will be six months since you left us. It seems so long and I long for you so much. It is just hard to bear. I hope that we will be together for our fourth anniversary on August 20, not as you wrote June 21.

Please write how you feel and how you manage with the baby because I am very interested. I am happy that you have a baby, otherwise I do not know what you would do there all by yourself. But we will see each other soon with God's help.... I already know a little bit of English.

I greet you and kiss you a thousand times. Can I kiss our baby? I will kiss him when I come. In the meantime you do it for me.

Yours forever,
Chaskel

JULY 8, 1940
From My Grandmother to My Mother

My grandmother appends to my father's July 8 letter the following words. She explains that she has received a letter stating that she should come and pick up her American passport...in Warsaw! There are two possibilities. One, my grandmother was confused and meant to write Berlin, or two, some sort of US diplomatic presence still remained in Warsaw enabling her to go there instead of Berlin.

My sweet Ernusha,

...I am not sure what will be. Yesterday we received a letter from Warsaw that I should come in two or three weeks to pick up my passport.

How are you, my sweet child? Does the little one still drink from the bottle and who gives him a bath?... I would love for you to send us another photograph with your baby.... Stay well and I hope to see you.

Your mother

JULY 9, 1940
From My Mother to Avra M. Warren

It has now been two and a half weeks of silence since my mother implored State Department visa chief A.M. Warren for some word about the fate of my father. She dispatches the following brief reminder in the hopes of eliciting a response. She is soon to receive one (reproduced below), sent on the same day. The two pieces of correspondence cross in the mail.

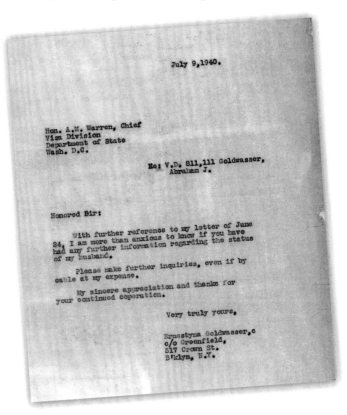

JULY 9, 1940

From Eliot B. Coulter to My Mother

On the same day that my mother wrote to Warren (above), the following letter was sent to her by the acting chief of the State Department's visa division, Eliot B. Coulter, to whom this case had been passed. Coulter would go on, some seventeen years later, to help rescue threatened Orthodox Jewish students from Egypt.

Coulter's response clearly exemplifies the tightening of visa controls implemented by Breckinridge Long and Avra M. Warren. Coulter explains that my father's application has been sent to the US embassy in Berlin. Coulter agrees to follow up with an inquiry and inform my mother when he receives word from Berlin.

Such bureaucratic obfuscation in the case of Jewish refugees from Europe fully complied with Long's directive of "postpone and postpone and postpone."

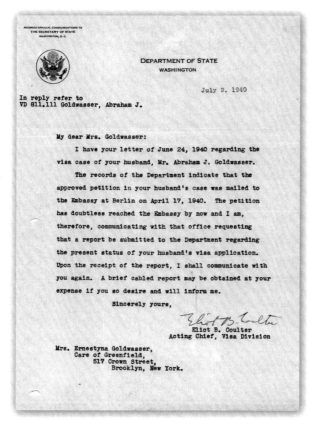

JULY 16, 1940
From My Father to My Mother

Another week passes during which my father has received more instructions from the US consulate in Berlin. But the documents have generated
more questions than answers. He reports visiting the "passport office" in
an attempt to gain information and being told to return on July 26. This
would indicate that there was a passport office of some kind still open in
Warsaw even though the US embassy had closed.

In an effort to sound an optimistic note, my father points to the fact
that at least he and my mother are able to stay in touch via correspondence,
unlike poor Chaluck (a family friend), who has disappeared. The Mrs.
Goldberg mentioned in the closing is our landlady at the home where my
mother and I were boarding.

July 16, 1940

My dearest, dearest ones,

*Your letters and photographs came here and made us very happy and
I thank you for them. Our little son looks beautiful, and you, darling, also.
My only wish is to be with you as soon as possible.*

*I received papers from the consulate, but the road on which I should
travel is not clear to me. I am waiting impatiently for the answer and
advice. I went today with Uncle Shimon to the passport office. They
told me to come next Friday (July 26). I pray to God that we should be
together soon.*

*As far as our little son, he is such a wonderful boy. You, my dar-
ling, look very nice and my heart prays that with God's help we will be
together and this will be the best.*

*We had a doctor that came to the house, but I feel okay. Mother was
here too and I feel better already. My darling, you have no idea how much
I want to be with you. I am waiting to hug and kiss my little one....*

*Even though we are not together, we are better off than Chaluck,
because we don't know what happened to him. We at least, thank God,
write to each other, and if God will help us we will be together soon. I
hope that nothing will stand in our way.... I long for you and only hope*

keeps me alive.... I just wish you happiness and I wish our son 120 years together with his parents.

I am ending my letter and kiss you and wish you all the best. Special regards to the family and to Mrs. Goldberg.

Yours,

Chaskel

JULY 18, 1940

From Eliot B. Coulter to My Mother

The following letter was sent by Coulter to my mother following his receipt of her July 9 reminder. In it she had agreed to cover any cable charges incurred by the State Department as they investigated the status of my father's visa application. Coulter again assures my mother that once he receives a reply, he will notify her.

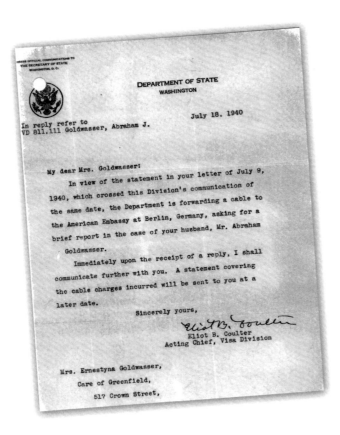

JULY 23, 1940

From My Grandmother to My Mother

Judging from this response (and a similar one from my father), my mother poured her heart out in a letter that arrived that day. In it, she evidently recounts her financial difficulties and shares the frustrations she is, by this point, encountering in her dealings with the US government. My grandmother informs my mother that she will soon travel to Berlin to obtain her US passport and that she has decided to immigrate to the US without my father. This suggests that she has given up on his chances of obtaining a visa any time soon.

My grandmother repeatedly scolds my mother for complaining about her situation when she should consider herself lucky for living in America. Perhaps to provide her daughter with some perspective, my grandmother points out that conditions in Krakow are deteriorating and that "you cannot buy anything for yourself."

> *My dearest Erna,*
>
> *We received your two letters. One is very, very sad and my heart was breaking. If you knew how people envy you that you are there, you would be happy. Don't worry that I cannot come yet, because I will come as soon as I can. I am going to the consul for the passport. I don't think I will wait for Chaskel. I was very upset reading your letter because it was so sad and because you have to go to work. Don't they pay you anymore? Don't they help you out with money? Please let me know. I am very anxious to know.*
>
> *People would be very happy to be in America and you complain. Please don't worry. With God's help everything will be okay and we will be together and you will be happy and healthy. As far as your little son, I am very happy that he is a good little boy and that he lets you sleep at night.*
>
> *Things are not so good here and Mala [Feiler, a neighbor] has no money. You cannot buy anything for yourself or the children. My dearest child, please write to me that you are happy and healthy with your baby.*

I kiss you a thousand times. Special regards to the whole family.
Please promise to be happy and not to be so sad.

Your mother

JULY 23, 1940

From My Aunt Gusta to My Mother

Gusta writes to her sister in desperation. She had hoped to send copies
of her old US passport with my grandmother when she travels to Berlin,
but discovered that they are in Washington and out of her reach. Evidently
my mother had previously written to Gusta and optimistically indicated
she would be able to bring her (and only her) to America. But this is not
so easy. Gusta is devastated at the thought of leaving behind her two children, as well as her husband, who does not want her to go. Nevertheless,
she states, "I will go. If I could have wings, I would fly."

Gusta writes:

*I wanted to send copies of the passport with Mother to Berlin because
there is no other way to do it. But the copies are lying in Washington.
Maybe you should write to Washington or to Berlin.*

*I was very happy to get your letter in which you write that you can
bring me over. I will go. If I could have wings, I would fly. If you decide
to take care of a little child, then I have some hope. My heart is breaking at the thought of leaving the little children and my husband. But
Shimeck does not let me go. In the letters I wrote to the consul, I asked if
I could go together with Mother. But in the meanwhile, I beg you to do
what you can.... This is so important.*

*Don't be upset and don't worry because you should be happy that
you are there and that you have your little boy with you.... We are with
Mother every day, but she is unhappy and worried about you.*

*I kiss you many times together with your sweet little son. I wish you
all the best and I know you will do all right. I love you.*

Regards from Yankush, Ruzunya and Shimeck.

Yours,

Gusta

JULY 31, 1940

From My Father to My Mother

As July ends, Jews, fueled by rampant rumors, are starting to scramble to get out of Krakow before ghettoization takes place. My father writes that his brother Yosek (Josef) and his new wife Regina, together with their parents and family, are going to be moved by the Germans to a village, Radomysl Wielki, located between Tarnow and Mielec. Coincidentally, as noted earlier, genealogical records indicate that my father's mother (Feige Pessel Honig) had been born in Radomysl, and that her parents lived there. Interestingly, my father indicates that he (referred to in code as "Abraham," his first name) and his mother may go there too.

With even more bad news, my father informs my mother that, not unexpectedly, he was unable to travel to the consulate in Berlin because "the roads are blocked." The reality of his imprisonment is beginning to emerge.

Finally, he asks if my mother has placed me into a "home." In those days, children from single-parent homes were typically institutionalized, as I soon would be. My father also hints at the eastward flight of Jews who were able to make it to Russia when he refers to "Alek and Ignac," apparently friends of his, who have disappeared.

> *My dearest sweetheart,*
>
> *I am so happy that you are not here and that you are in America. God should help us that I should soon be with you. Amen. Yosek and Regina are going to live in Radomysl Wielki with their parents and whole family. Abraham and Mother may go there also. I do not know yet, but I think so.*
>
> *Today I was supposed to go to the consulate for a medical examination, but the roads are blocked. I cannot go and I must stay here. Darling, do not worry, God will not leave us. I hope we will see each other soon.*
>
> *My sweetheart, how do you feel? How is our sweet, darling baby? Did you already put him in a home or are you still with him? He must be so sweet. I cannot wait to see you. I hope. I do not know what I would do if you were here. Alek and Ignac are deep in Russia. We have not heard from them in a long time.*

I am ending my letter, my dearest ones. Stay well and healthy. I kiss you many times.

Yours,
Chaskel

JULY 31, 1940
From Eliot B. Coulter to My Mother

Finally word arrives from the State Department that my father's visa application has been "provisionally approved" by the US embassy in Berlin. This seemingly good news is consumed by the ominous statement that my father is scheduled to make a "formal" application on this very day: July 31. While he does not say so explicitly, it is clear from the following sentence regarding "travel conditions" that this "formal" application must be carried out in person, in Berlin, before "final action" may take place. The mails, which were functioning effectively, will not be used to free my father.

In other words, as July draws to a close, my parents both realize that an insurmountable obstacle has been placed in their path. The very idea of a Polish Jew traveling freely from German-occupied Krakow to the German capital is ludicrous. "The roads are blocked," as my father puts it in his letter to my mother of the same date (see previous letter). Obviously, he was not in Berlin on July 31.

The letter closes with Coulter expressing due concern about the cablegram charges while expressing absolutely no concern about my father's impossible and desperate plight.

ADDRESS OFFICIAL COMMUNICATIONS TO
THE SECRETARY OF STATE
WASHINGTON, D. C.

DEPARTMENT OF STATE
WASHINGTON

In reply refer to
VD 811.111 Goldwasser, Abraham

JULY 31. 1940

My dear Mrs. Goldwasser:

Referring to my letter of July 18, 1940, a telegraphic report has now been received from the American Embassy at Berlin, Germany, regarding the visa case of your husband, Abraham Goldwasser.

It is stated in the Embassy's report that the evidence of support submitted in behalf of Abraham Goldwasser has been provisionally approved and that he is scheduled to make his formal application for a visa on July 31. It is added that the final action in his case will depend largely on travel conditions.

You will be advised at a later date of the cablegram charges incurred.

Sincerely yours,

For the Acting Secretary of State:

Eliot B. Coulter

Eliot B. Coulter
Acting Chief, Visa Division

Mrs. Ernestyna Goldwasser,
Care of Greenfield,
517 Crown Street,
Brooklyn, New York.

CHAPTER SEVEN

"*The Roads Are Closed*"

August–December 1940

AUGUST 7, 1940

From My Father to My Mother

My father reluctantly recognizes that "the roads are closed" in all directions and that his dream of reuniting with my mother and me in America is quickly fading. He is considering moving with his family to Radomysl, but indicates that for the time being he will remain in Krakow with my grandmother.

> My dearest ones,
>
> I received two letters from you . . . which made me very happy. As I wrote in my previous letter, we are probably going to Radomysl. My only other hope is that I will be able to stay with Mother in Krakow. I want you to know that I did everything in my power to be able to go to America. But the roads are closed. Maybe soon some roads will be open. If not, I will have to wait till after the war.
>
> I am happy that you, my darling, with the baby, are there. Please, darling, don't worry. I know that it is hard for you to give our little son to a home, but with God's help we will see each other soon. My mother and Hanka and my whole family are going to Radomysl. This is such a small town which the aunt from Camden can tell you about.
>
> . . .

My darling, I am ending my letter. stay well and healthy. I kiss you a thousand times.

Yours forever,
Chaskel

AUGUST 7, 1940
From My Grandmother to My Mother

My grandmother adds these words to my father's letter. She relays a newspaper report that travel to the US is available through Russia and Japan.

Surprisingly, my ever-resourceful grandmother expresses the desire to "bring you some money." Money that is undoubtedly going fast as the weeks drag by. My grandmother also states, "We are trying to stay in Krakow," reflecting the fact that Jews are being removed from the city.

Finally, my grandmother expresses her hope to be by my mother's side in five weeks, at which time she will be able to assist with my care and permit my mother to take me out of the "home" into which I had been placed.

My sweet Ernusha,

Today it says in the newspaper that one can travel through Russia and Japan. First of all, I have to have the ticket for the ship. You can imagine that I would be willing to go that way, but I don't know if I can manage to take money with me. I want to bring you some money, but who knows how long it will take till I will leave.

My sweet Ernusha, I envy you a thousand times that you are already there. We are trying to stay in Krakow, but we don't know what is going on.

Please write a long letter about yourself and how you are. Don't be upset that you have to give the baby to a home. I am sure it will not be long and God will help you to find a good job. I think that you can decide to put the baby in the home for five weeks. Gusta is completing her application papers to go to America.

stay happy and healthy together with your baby and your husband. Don't worry about anything and don't lose your health over it. Be happy.

I love you,
Mother

AUGUST 13, 1940

From My Father to My Mother

In this somewhat disjointed letter, my father's words are reflective of the turmoil that is engulfing the Jewish community of Krakow. He alludes to the fact that he should have been at the US consulate in Berlin on July 30 (actually July 31). Of course he failed to appear because he had no passport or viable travel arrangements to America. He expresses his inability to document his vocational skills. He closes with a picture of whole families being dislocated as the German occupiers prepare to imprison and eliminate the Jewish population of Krakow, and with a prayer that "Abraham" (himself, referred to in third person) should not have to change his address.

My dearest sweet ones in the whole world,

Yesterday our son was three months old and I received a beautiful letter from you that made me very happy. I received some forms from the consulate to fill out for an affidavit. I should have been at the consulate on July 30 to go to the doctor for an examination. Under one condition, that I have a plan of how I will travel. But I did not receive my passport yet. They tell me to wait. I pray to God that it shouldn't be long and difficult.

I long for you. You have no idea how much I long to be with you. I do not know my new address yet. I will find out any day now. Regarding my profession, I cannot get any papers. I only have what I had when I took my exam. I am very happy that we have a beautiful little boy. Now Mother is writing to Warsaw; maybe this will help with the trip. But you be happy that you are there.

Everybody comes here to ask me to ask you to help them. Hanka and the children are here because they are going to Radomysl. God should help that Abraham should not have to change his address.

Stay healthy and happy. I kiss you a thousand times.

Forever,

Chaskel

AUGUST 20, 1940

From My Father to My Mother

It is the eve of my parents' fourth anniversary. My father writes that the
path to America through Spain and Portugal is blocked, and it is necessary
to head east and travel through Russia. With the exception of his brother
Yanek, who went to the town of Walbrun, my father's entire family has
been forced out of Krakow to the small town of Radomysl.

Seemingly trivial items ("Abraham does not have a quilt cover anymore") have been magnified in importance with the impending winter
amid escalating deprivations.

He closes with a request for assistance in locating his own birth certificate and for a copy of my birth certificate – documents he needs to carry
on his quest for a visa to the United States. Despite the despondent tone
of his previous letter, my father is not yet prepared to give up.

My dearest, dearest sweetest in the whole world,

*I received your letter from August 5 today. As I wrote to you, I can-
not leave now, not because I do not want to, but because we cannot. We
cannot go through Portugal, only through Russia. Besides, they are only
letting American citizens go, and I will have to wait a little longer. Maybe
God will help and soon it will be over. My dear, my whole family, my
mother, my aunt, and all of them left for Radomysl Wielki. Maybe I
will go there soon. My brother Yanek left for the town of Walbrun to be
with his girlfriend. I hope that he will get married soon. God should
give them happiness.*

*Tomorrow will be a big holiday. It is our fourth anniversary. God
should help us that we should be together soon.*

*Abraham does not have a quilt cover anymore. You should be happy
that you are there. Especially our little Murray Jack. We have to suffer
a little bit, but God will help us and it will be good because our faith is
such.*

Please write to Warsaw.

*Yosek and Regina are very happy, as we are. But we are not together
now. I think that it won't take too much longer. My dearest, I have so
much to write to you. But when it comes to writing, I forget.*

Please write me to tell me who has my birth certificate because the consul told me that I need two birth certificates and our marriage certificate. I finally got our wedding certificate after trying very hard. Also, can you please send our sweet son's birth certificate? Maybe it will help that I have a son who is an American citizen.

I am healthy and feel well. I want to hear the same from you and our son, my dearest.

I kiss you a thousand times.

Yours forever,
Chaskel

AUGUST 20, 1940
From My Mother's Cousin, Leibek Ziller, to My Mother

In this message, appended to my father's letter, my mother's cousin Leibek responds to her words of greeting. Although his words are clearly restricted ("I could write a lot, but I cannot"), he nevertheless describes the state of exodus the Jewish community is being forced to undergo ("Most people are leaving Krakow").

My dear cousin,

Thank you for writing a few words to me and thank you for remembering me. God bless you. As Chaskel previously has told you, his family went to Radomyśl Wielki, and it is possible that I will go there soon too. Most people are leaving Krakow.

Please do not worry, we are all well and healthy. We are very happy that your son is progressing well with his growth. God will help that he will be the beginning of happiness for the whole family. I could write a lot, but I cannot. The weather is awful. I am running to do some work.

Hearty, hearty regards and a kiss for your son.
Leibek

AUGUST 20, 1940
From My Grandmother to My Mother

My grandmother adds another postscript that is partially reproduced below. In it, she expresses the state of confusion, turmoil, and desperation facing the increasingly entrapped Jews of Krakow. Rumors of new escape paths abound, "but Chaskel cannot leave yet because they will not let him."

> *My sweet Ernusha,*
>
> *Your letter gave us much happiness. But you don't tell us how to travel. Can you ask someone there if we could go from Berlin to America? I would leave this minute. But Chaskel cannot leave yet because they will not let him. They say that within nineteen days, people can go through Japan.*
>
> *People get food packages from New York. I do not want this from you because I know you have enough work. I do not know what to do with my trip....*

(The remainder of this letter is missing.)

AUGUST 28, 1940
From My Grandmother to My Mother

Intent on making Krakow the most *"Judenrein"* (cleansed of Jews) city in Poland, the Germans initiated the relocation of Jews in earnest on August 1. Most of Krakow's seventy thousand Jews would be forced to leave the city, leaving behind only those capable of hard labor and their families. Many were sent to Warsaw, although some, such as my father's family, wound up in smaller provincial communities like Radomysl Wielki. In this letter, my grandmother informs my mother that my father's family has now moved to Radomysl.

In the Podgorze district of Krakow, construction of tall concrete walls, designed to encase the Jewish ghetto, would begin soon. By the following March, Krakow's remaining fifteen thousand Jews would be forced to move into a space formerly occupied by three thousand souls. In an ominous foreshadowing, the walls were designed to resemble tomb-stones.

In her note, my grandmother is still unsure of her course and again asks my mother to advise her.

My sweet, dearest Ernusha,

Your letter gave us a lot of happiness, and it is very good that we get a letter from you every week. Gusta is very happy that you are taking care of her information to leave Poland.

...I do not know which way to go so please write to me.... By us, everything is fine and your husband's whole family is in Radomysl.

Stay healthy and happy with your sweet son. I kiss you thousands of times. I hope that we will see one another soon.

Regards and kisses from the whole family.

Yours,
Mother

AUGUST 28, 1940
From Thos. Cook & Son to My Mother

In this letter to my mother from the Cook travel agency, written on the same day as the previous letter from my grandmother, the agent quotes travel costs associated with bringing my grandmother from Berlin to the US via Japan. So although my grandmother is, at this point, uncertain about her ability to immigrate to America, my mother is proceeding on track by making such inquiries.

The agent explains that he is uncertain whether my mother is inquiring only about my grandmother or about my father as well. Clearly my mother is still holding out hope that somehow my father can also make it to Berlin to receive his visa and accompany my grandmother to the US. This possibility diminishes with each passing day.

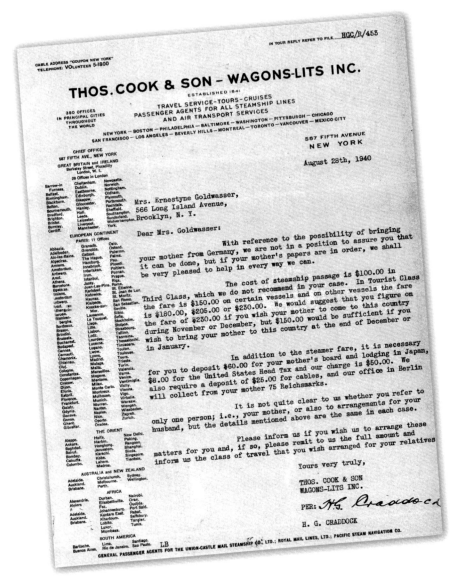

AUGUST 30, 1940

From My Father to My Mother

As August draws to a close, my father confirms the fact that his entire family has now relocated to Radomysl. He remains uncertain, however, as to whether he should join them there. He believes he should remain in Krakow because he feels responsible for the welfare of his mother-in-law, who will soon be off to Berlin and then America. It is likely that he is holding out hope that he will be able to join her on this voyage.

My dearest, darling, sweet Ernusha,

I received your very precious letter. It gives me so much warmth that I feel as though I am together with you.... [Our friends] are very upset because their husbands were sent to the depths of Russia. It is very bad over there.

My darling, we have to thank God a thousand times that we are at least able to write to one another and that we are healthy. I think that we will be able to stand it and that God will help us. Amen.

My whole family and my mother are healthy and they live in Rado-mysl. I do not know yet if I will change my address since dear Mother is here with me.

Stay healthy and happy. I kiss you many thousands of times.

Yours forever,
Chaskel

AUGUST 30, 1940
From My Grandmother to My Mother

In this letter of the same day, my grandmother finally confirms that she is prepared to fly to Berlin, even if she remains reluctant to travel by air. She has also overcome her resistance to confronting the fact that she will be leaving my father behind. My grandmother promises to go to the consulate when she gets to Berlin to plead my father's case, "because when you write to them, they do not answer."

The letter also references the fact that by this point I had been placed into an orphanage in order to allow my mother to return to work. Not surprisingly, my mother is not happy about this situation and is offered some palliative words of consolation by her own mother.

My dearest darling Ernusha,

Your letter gave us life. I cannot tell you how sweet the letters are and what they mean to us. I just pray to God that you will be healthy and happy with every step that you take.

Regarding my trip, if you can pay for my trip I will take a plane even though I do not want to take a plane. I will go to Berlin, to the consulate, because when you write to them, they do not answer.

Do not be upset that you put the baby into a home. Be happy that you can have him with you in America. God willing you will be together again. Be happy and healthy.

I kiss you thousands of times together with your sweet, darling son.

Yours,
Mother

SEPTEMBER 10, 1940

From My Father to My Mother

In this letter my father reveals his intention of remaining in Krakow and not joining his family in Radomysl. He also affirms his willingness to travel to the US consulate in Berlin despite the hazards.

My dearest darling Ernusha and my sweetheart Murray Jack,

I want to let you know that I have not received mail from you in two weeks, but I am sure that this week I will get something.

Darling, I am so lonely for you. I cannot tell you how much. I can't stand it anymore. God should help us that it should not take so long anymore.

[My] Mother and Aunt and the whole family are healthy in Radomysl. It may be that Yosek and I will stay in Krakow. I do not know for sure, but [your] Mother is with me and this may help. I wrote to the consulate and I am waiting for an answer. These days it is not very safe to travel, but I would go anyway.

I do not do anything. I just sit in the store. When Yosek comes, maybe I will be able to make some money.

Stay healthy and happy with our sweet, darling son and do not worry if you are putting him in a home. With God's help, we will be together soon so you will be able to take care of him. I feel healthy and do not lack anything but you and my son.

Why don't you write if you go to restaurants like you promised you would when you got a job. Tell me what kind of job you have and how much money you earn. I really want to know. I kiss you a thousand times.

Yours forever,
Chaskel

SEPTEMBER 10, 1940
From My Grandmother to My Mother

In the following somewhat lengthy postscript, my grandmother admits that "things are getting worse and worse." It looks as though my aunt Gusta and her family will soon be forced out of Krakow to a small town in the provinces.

Poignantly, my grandmother ponders, "I do not know why the consulate does not answer any letters." She does not suspect the real reason is that, like consulates throughout Europe, they have been instructed by the top officials to postpone and impede any and all channels of Jewish immigration into the USA.

Although we have not received any letters from you, we hope that tomorrow or the day after, we will receive one. Here everything is the same but things are getting worse and worse. Gusta rented an apartment in the town of Niepolomice but she is still here and we do not know what will be.

Dearest Ernusha, yesterday we got a message that Americans can go for free to America. Please find out. This would be wonderful if it were the truth. I do not know why the consulate does not answer any letters. We wait months and months and receive nothing.

Did you put the little sweetheart in a home? If you did, let it be with mazel. Do not worry about it because thousands of people are envious of you. We hope that as soon as possible we will see each other and that will be good.

Gusta wrote and telephoned to the consulate but they do not want to answer. She would like to have the papers in her hands already.

We miss you with every step that we take because if you would be here, I would be on my way and with you already. Do you still live in the same apartment? What do you plan to do? Always remember that you should not worry. You have nothing to worry about because everything is minor and it does not pay to be upset. Be happy and healthy. I miss you and want to be with you already. I send regards to Bernard and family and to Leon and family.

Yours,
Mother

SEPTEMBER 18, 1940
From My Father to My Mother

In this letter, my father again explains that his whole family has been relocated to Radomysl, but that he has decided to remain behind in Krakow with his mother-in-law. He points out that my grandmother strongly wishes to leave, but since Italy has now entered the war and because crossing Russia is difficult for a single woman, she has been unable to do so. He urges my mother to "take care of things" in America, thereby enabling him to immigrate as well and accompany my grandmother on her long journey.

Dearest darling Ernusha and Murray Jack,

I received your wonderful letter on Monday. It was such a beautiful letter you cannot imagine. It seemed to me that I was speaking to you in person. I would like to be with you as soon as possible and really talk in person because I have no friends anymore. God will help us and I hope that it does not take much longer. I beg God that you should at least be together with Mother and that our son should not be in a home.

My mother, aunt and the whole family are in Radomysl.... Regarding your mother, it is not that she did not want to go – she couldn't go. Because by that time Italy was already at war and to go through Russia is very difficult for her, but she wants to go very much. If you could take care of things as far as I am concerned then we could go together.

Unfortunately, I know that it is hard and that I will have to wait a little longer. I have to be patient and God will help us. Please do not worry. Everything will be all right.

How are you, darling? How is your health and how is the health of our little son? He must be a gentleman already, our little one. I would like to see him so very much. In the meantime, I am not changing my address.

Stay well and healthy.

Yours forever,
Chaskel

SEPTEMBER 27, 1940
From My Father to My Mother

In response to a telegram sent with some urgency by my mother, my father writes that my grandmother will soon go to the "passport office" in Krakow and obtain permission to travel to Berlin within a week. A Mr. Klugerman is mentioned as someone who will assist her. Based on previous correspondence, it appears that Klugerman is someone who, for a fee, assists people wishing to travel. It is not clear whether Klugerman is offering to accompany my grandmother to Berlin or not.

My father recognizes that his position will become more dire once my grandmother leaves Krakow, but he puts on an optimistic outlook. He again posits the vain hope that perhaps "something will come for me from the consulate" after my grandmother leaves.

It is the eve of the Jewish new year (Rosh Hashanah) and my father expresses the hope that things will be better in the coming year. He closes with the disturbing rumor that my aunt Gusta picked up at the shipping office: US citizens born in Europe now lose their citizenship if they are still living outside the US after they reach the age of eighteen. The rumor is false but it nevertheless strikes fear into the hearts of my aunt Gusta and my grandmother.

My dearest darling Ernusha,

We received your telegram last Friday as far as Mother is concerned. Mother and Mr. Klugerman are going to the passport office to get a piece of paper that will allow her to go to Berlin. He could also take care of it for me so that I can accompany Mother but he wants to take care of it himself. But you know the way he is. I do not know if even he will be able to go. I am not going to aggravate myself with it. Because if it is meant to be, I will go as soon as possible. With God's help, next week when Mother leaves, maybe something will come from the consulate. My darling, I am so upset with all this, but what can I do? Now, New Years is coming, so maybe it will be better.

I have not received a letter from you in two weeks, but I am sure I will get one any day.... Please, darling, do not worry that I am not going to Mr. Amand anymore, because they are in Bochnia already.... I just want to see you as soon as possible. I am tired of all this longing for you. Maybe God will hear us and finally we will be able to see one another. It is already nine months since you left. I feel well. I am not lacking anything, only you, and it will be my biggest happiness when we will be together.

Gusta went to a shipping company and they told her that a child of an American citizen who is born in Europe loses his citizenship when he is 18. This is what they told her. I wonder if it is true. If it is true, Gusta would be very upset because she would not be able to leave.

Stay well and healthy. I wish you a happy and healthy New Year. My mother and my whole family wish you a happy and healthy New Year.

I kiss you a thousand kisses.

Yours forever,
Chaskel

SEPTEMBER 27, 1940
From My Grandmother to My Mother

In this addendum to my father's letter, my grandmother pinpoints her departure from Krakow. She will have everything ready by "one day after Rosh Hashanah," that being Saturday, October 5. She plans to depart for Berlin on Sunday, October 6, without Klugerman or any other escort. There is no doubt that this moment was fraught with anxiety over leaving my father behind – as well as saying good-bye to her lifelong home and her culture.

My sweet, darling Ernusha,

Finally will come the time when we will be able to see one another. I am leaving when I have everything ready, one day after Rosh Hashanah, Sunday to Berlin and from there further. Klugerman will not accompany me. I do not know if he will be able to.

Please write how you are. I have been waiting the whole week for a letter from you and we have not received anything from you. I do not know what to ask you because I will see you soon in person. I am already anxious about traveling. I cannot help it, but the payment will be that I will see you and God should help that it will be as soon as possible and God should help that you will be together with Chaskel soon because he already misses you and the baby so terribly.

…I just wish for you health and happiness and all the best. Stay happy and healthy together with your sweet, darling son, and I wish you a happy and healthy New Year and whatever you wish should come true. I will be seeing you.

Mother

OCTOBER 6, 1940
From My Grandmother to My Mother

In this simulated telegram sent from Berlin, my grandmother notifies my mother that she arrived safely and that she is awaiting word whether she will be able to board a ship on either October 23 or 30.

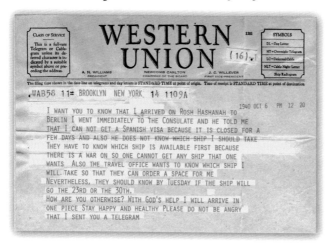

OCTOBER 11, 1940

From My Father to My Mother

In this letter my father informs my mother that my grandmother has left Krakow and is presumably en route to America. He is unaware that my mother has already been informed via the October 6 telegram. Evidently my grandmother left a few days ahead of schedule on October 1. She presumably spent Rosh Hashanah (and Yom Kippur as well) in Berlin.

My father expresses his unsuppressed envy at the sight of his mother-in-law fulfilling the most devoutly desired dream of his life. He attempts to remain cheerful and characteristically optimistic, ending his explanation that Jewish children are no longer allowed to attend school with the hollow words "...but maybe they will someday."

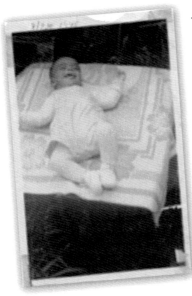

My dearest darling in the whole world,

Today is Erev Yom Kippur and I received your sweet letter and photographs with our beautiful, lovely boy. Everyone thinks he is beautiful and he looks six or seven months old. I cannot wait to hold him in my arms as well as you, my dearest little mommy. I would give everything to be able to see you in person. I am not complaining. Thank God I am not lacking anything but you. I think it will not take long and soon we will see each other, Amen.

Dearest Ernusha, Mother left on October 1 to Berlin and then on to America. How I would have loved to be with her or in her place. I envy her because I want to be with you so much. Darling, God should help us that with the New Year we should get our wishes and that we should be together soon.

...My darling sweetheart and sweet son, my own son, Murray Jack, I want so much to be with you. Gusta, Shimeck and the children come every day to see me. The children are wonderful and they love to hear your letters. They do not go to school anymore because they cannot, but maybe they will someday.

Darling, do not worry about me. I have everything that I need. Now I will start writing airmail. I thought that I was not able to, but I will try. Stay happy and healthy. I kiss you a thousand times.

Yours forever,
Chaskel

OCTOBER 15, 1940
From My Grandmother to My Mother

My mother learns, via this letter, that my grandmother's troubles are not over now that she has reached Berlin. She finds herself alone and stranded there. She had initially planned on being in Berlin only a few days, but has already been there for two weeks, staying at the home of a cousin. The cause of the delay is the intransigence or intentional incompetence of the US consulate. They claim to have lost my grandmother's ship ticket for passage to the US from Spain on November 28. The visa needed to enter Spain has also not arrived.

My grandmother is in a state of confusion and despair as she weighs whether she should return to Krakow or make her way to Spain to meet the ship. She implores my mother to send a telegram to the travel office, which is no longer Thomas Cook but American Express.

As the days drag on, my grandmother valiantly attempts to learn about the status of my father's visa to the US. She meets with more frustration and obfuscation. The consulate tells her that they are very busy and have no time to deal with this matter. "You understand what is going on," she ominously tells my mother.

It's the same story. American citizen or not. Visa or no visa. The US diplomatic corps in Europe was determined to block all avenues of entry for the endangered Jews of Europe.

Finally, my grandmother dispenses with the niceties and tells my mother exactly what her situation is: "…it is a matter of life and death."

My sweet, darling Ernusha,
I feel so completely alone. I was at the consulate in Berlin yesterday and they cannot find the ship ticket. They sent a telegram to Lisbon and

they also do not have it. So, it is not in the consulate or anywhere. I am
sitting here in Berlin and every day is like a year to me. Everything is
going very slowly and I do not know what to do. Should I try to go back
to Krakow or should I wait in Berlin until November 28? If you send a
telegram inquiring where the ticket is, I will travel November 28. If not,
I cannot sit here all year because there is also a question if I will get a
visa to go to Spain.

...I am also asking you to send a telegram to the consulate and to
the German mail office inquiring about my ship ticket and where I can
pick it up. I hope that they will answer.

I still get regular letters from Krakow. Yesterday, I received a package
of kosher meat. Everything is all right at home with Chaskel. He wants
to leave already, but I do not know how to do it. Whenever I ask the consulate about him they tell me that they have no time and that they have
too much work. You understand what is going on.

How are you? How is the sweetheart little baby and how are Uncle
Leon and his wife? Please write, because it is a matter of life and death.
I pray to God to see you as soon as possible. If I receive the fifty dollars
I will have too much to bring with me so I will have to have a special
certificate saying that I can do it.

I am giving you the address of the traveling office:
American Express Company / Berlin / Unter den Linden Street 73

Stay well and a thousand kisses to your little boy.
Mother

OCTOBER 16, 1940
From My Father to My Mother

This letter reveals that my grandmother had also written to my father from
Berlin. With him she was more direct and did not sweeten the situation
with the consulate. "They said that for no money in the world will I get
a visa." Despite this crushing news, my father does not focus on his own
misery but instead commiserates with my mother who is clearly despondent over having to place her baby into a "home."

My dearest darling Ernusha and Murray Jack,

Yesterday I received your wonderful letter and it gave me so much happiness. We have to be together, but who knows when? We have to hope, but I think it will take a long time.

I received a letter from your mother that the consul did not want to talk to her about my case. They said that for no money in the world will I get a visa. Not now, anyway, so in the meantime, I have to stay here still.

...Darling, I can imagine how you felt when you had to give the baby to the home. Darling, you have it better than me – at least you can see him whenever you want. But I also hope to see him soon. I know that you do not sleep at night thinking about how you can help.

Stay healthy and happy. I send you and our little son thousands of kisses.

Yours forever,
Chaskel

OCTOBER 23, 1940
From My Grandmother in Berlin to My Mother

This letter, advising that my grandmother will likely leave Berlin in the next few days, recounts her hectic activities in Berlin as she prepares to secure her passage to America. She mentions that she has run out of money and appeals to my mother for more to help her defray the many fees she is facing.

My grandmother carried with her pictures of my father, including the photo shown at the end of chapter 3.

My sweet, darling child,

Your telegram came on time and I will probably leave here on the 24th or the 25th. I received the passport with mazel and tomorrow I will receive the visa to Portugal and Spain. I have to take care of everything myself and I run around the whole day. The $120 is not enough, I need another $50. I sent a telegram to you but I have received no answer yet. I thank God that my travels have already progressed this far.

I do not feel like staying here much longer. Today I had to go to the police station to register myself. It took two and a half hours. That is how I have to run around all day. But I will be happy to board the ship already and be on my way. Please write if possible airmail. This is my third letter to you.

Stay healthy and well. I hope my legs hold out. Regards from all. I am staying here with some cousins of Aunt Hedwig and I am enclosing my new address. I have received seven photos from Chaskel. I hope to give them to you when I see you with mazel. Kiss the little one many times.

Your mother,

Leah

NOVEMBER 2, 1940

From My Father to My Mother

Conditions are clearly deteriorating in Krakow, a fact that peers through the cheerful tone adopted by my father in this letter. By now, Jews are being rounded up in the nearby provinces and being relocated in Krakow. My father alludes to the extremely cramped living conditions that result.

The "Uncle Pinya" to whom he refers is Uncle Pinya Rosehandler, married to my grandmother Leah's sister Manya. (In my parents' wedding picture, shown in the preface, Manya is sitting next to my father, holding on to Gusta's son Yankush.) The family of six who were also living with them, whose identity is unknown, were additional occupants (perhaps moved to the apartment by the Germans), so twelve people were sharing their apartment.

His mention that "some American governor proposed that whoever has a visa or has possibilities to leave can do so through a little island" could possibly be a reference to former Indiana governor Paul V. McNutt, who was appointed to serve as the high governor of the Philippines by FDR in 1937. McNutt, for humanitarian reasons, somehow convinced the State Department to permit the entry of twelve hundred European Jews into the islands every year during the war. This, at a time when far fewer Jews were being granted entry to the United States itself.

According to the Holocaust Encyclopedia published online by the United States Holocaust Memorial Museum, the State Department in 1940 greatly restricted Jewish immigration by ordering US consuls to delay visa approvals on national security grounds. After the United States entered the war in December 1941, the trickle of immigration virtually dried up, just as the Nazi regime began systematically to murder the Jews of Europe.

My father's references to Jews fleeing to Russia are ominous. While wholesale deportations have not yet begun, many Jews were being forcibly sent for "resettlement in the East."

My dearest darlings whom I miss so much, Ernusha and Murray Jack,

You cannot imagine the happiness in our house when we received your sweet letter and photograph. I am happy that you look very well and that our dear Murray Jack does too. I would like to hear his voice and see him already because I miss you so terribly much you have no idea.

I sent to you with Mother a dress and a robe. I would like to have a letter [from the American consul] that would allow me to be together with you. In the meantime, I will stay in Krakow. Gusta also thinks that she will stay in Krakow. I am in the store with Yosek, and thank God I earn money for my keep but I miss you.

Ernusha, my dearest. I am happy that you and the little sweet baby, Moshe Yaakov, are there. I suffer a lot but I live with the hope that with God's help we will see each other soon. My darling, I get letters and packages from my mother and my family with all different articles. They send you hearty regards and kisses.

Darling, they say that in one of the newspapers it said that some American governor proposed that whoever has a visa or has possibilities to leave can do so through a little island. I am not sure of the name. Please do me a favor and find out if this is true.

A lot of people are in Russia and someone sent a package to some people, but they did not receive it. So you can see, darling, how things are with us. I feel good that we can write to each other.

Uncle Pinya also lives with me. He was in Warsaw and came back to

Krakow. He sleeps in our apartment with me in the kitchen. As you know, a whole family of six people is with us. Pinya and I are in the kitchen and Gusta and her husband and children are all in the same room.

Stay together and happy. God should help us that we will be together soon.

Yours forever who always thinks of you and kisses you thousands of times,

Chaskel

NOVEMBER 2, 1940

From My Aunt Gusta to My Mother

In these words, appended to my father's letter, my aunt Gusta informs my mother that she has been advised to travel to Vienna to apply for a US passport. This instruction seems contrary to that received by my father and grandmother, which directed them to the US consulate in Berlin, not Vienna. It is possible that either the consul or my aunt made an error.

My aunt is caught in a tragic dilemma and clearly is anguishing over what she should do. Should she abandon her children and husband to join her mother and sister in America, or should she abide by her strong desire "to be together with my husband in Krakow"? She appeals for advice to my mother, who also, I am sure, shared her turmoil over this decision.

Dearest Ernusha,

You know about everything already. I received a letter from the consul that I should go to Vienna to make the application for a passport. Mr. Neustater says that I cannot take my children because they are not ten years old yet. But God should help me that maybe I will be able to do so. The main thing is that I want to be together with my husband in Krakow. What do you think about it and what do you think I should do? I am walking around very nervous and upset and I do not care about anything anymore.

How are you, my dearest? How is your sweet baby and how is your job?

I want to know so much about you but I can't. I would like to already receive the news that dear Mother is with you. I think that any day now she will be there.

Kisses,

Gusta

NOVEMBER 15, 1940

From the National Refugee Service to My Mother

Prodded by word of her mother's distress in Berlin, my mother swung into action. Among those she contacted was the National Refugee Service, a largely ineffectual agency created in 1939 and headed by FDR appointee J.P. Chamberlain. The agency was created in the wake of the notorious 1938 Evian Conference, where the US was represented by another FDR crony, Myron Taylor. It was the nearly unanimous position of the conference attendees that their nations could not accept any Jewish refugees that convinced Hitler to pursue the "Final Solution" – the policy of Jewish genocide.

In this response letter, my mother is advised that her mother is "probably" no longer in Berlin and en route to Lisbon. Should she discover that, in fact, her mother remains stuck in Berlin, my mother is asked to let the NRS know and they will pass the buck to the Hilfsverein der deutschen Juden (Aid Association of German Jews). The Hilfsverein's activities were restricted in 1939 by the Reich to assisting Jews emigrating from Germany. Once the Nazi policy of forced emigration changed to extermination in 1941, the Hilfsverein was disbanded.

CABLES: NACOMREF, New York
TELEPHONE: BRyant 9-2102

NATIONAL REFUGEE SERVICE, INC.

AN ORGANIZATION DESIGNED TO CARRY ON THE ACTIVITIES OF THE NATIONAL
COORDINATING COMMITTEE FOR REFUGEES AND CERTAIN OF ITS AFFILIATES

165 WEST 46TH STREET
NEW YORK CITY

November 15th, 1940

Mrs. Ernestine Goldwasser
566 Coney Island Avenue
Brooklyn, New York

IN REPLY PLEASE REFER TO:
GRUENFELD, Lea
Case #A 13207

Dear Mrs. Goldwasser:

We have your recent postal card and can well understand your anxiety over your mother's difficulties.

However, we have not sent a cable because your mother, by this time, has undoubtedly left Berlin. As you will recall, she was supposed to remain there only four weeks. Our cable to Berlin was dated October 7th, 1940. By this time she undoubtedly is on her way to Lisbon and we hope that matter will move smoothly from this point on.

If you have information to the effect that your mother cannot leave Berlin, however, please notify us immediately and we will communicate with the Hilfsverein.

We assure you of our interest.

Sincerely yours,

Augusta Mayerson
Augusta Mayerson
Acting Director
Migration Department

HKohn:sk

NOVEMBER 29, 1940
Passenger Manifest from the S.S. Exeter

While my grandmother apparently left Berlin and arrived in Lisbon at the end of October, it was not until November 29 that she sailed from Lisbon, along with eighty-nine other passengers, aboard the S.S. *Exeter*. She arrived in the Port of New York on December 9, 1940. Note that the manifest incorrectly lists her gender (circled) but correctly identifies her, and several others, as US citizens by marriage.

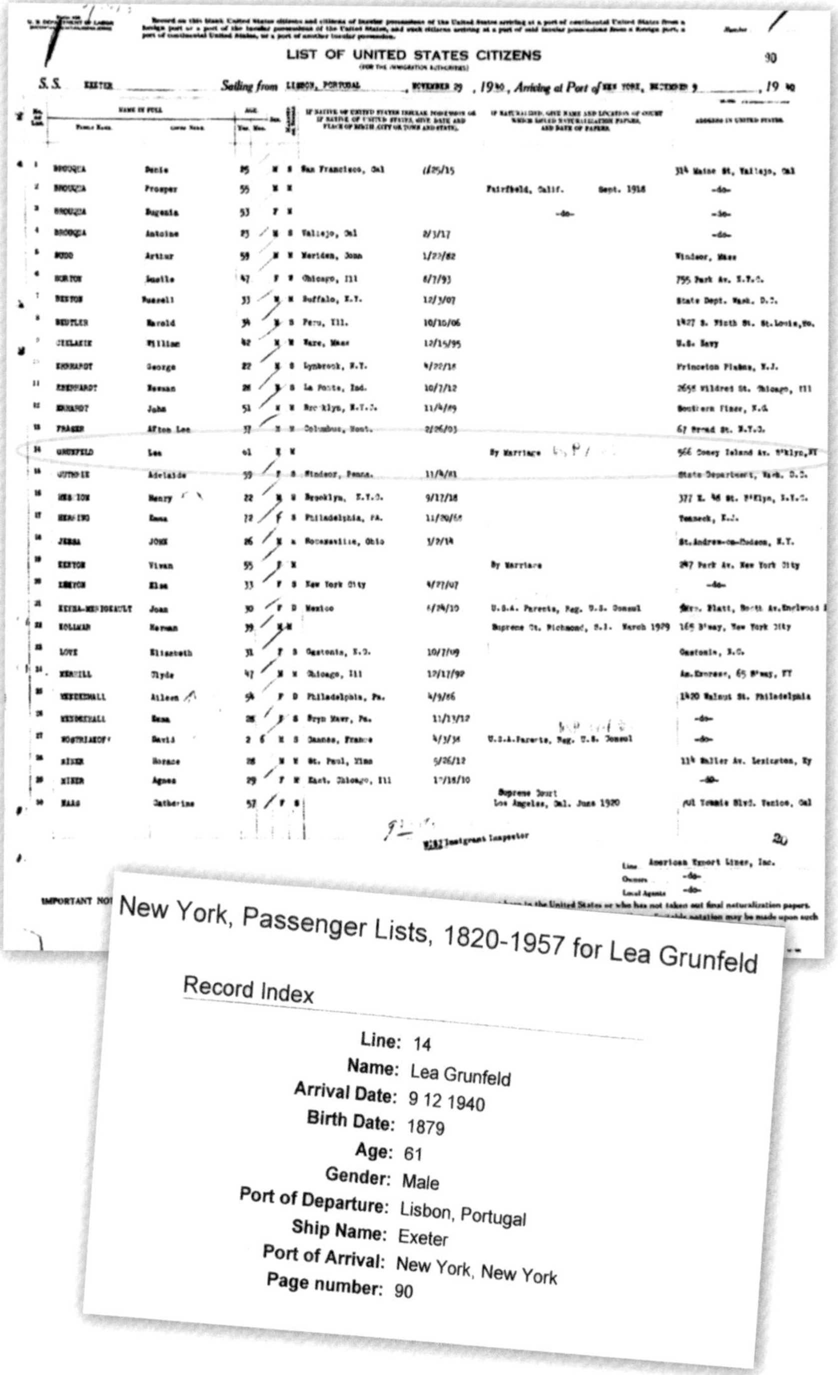

LIST OF UNITED STATES CITIZENS

(FOR THE IMMIGRATION AUTHORITIES)

S.S. EXETER Sailing from LISBON, PORTUGAL, NOVEMBER 29, 1940, Arriving at Port of NEW YORK, DECEMBER 9, 1940

90

No. on List	Family Name	Given Name	Age	Sex	Married or Single	If native of United States, give date and place of birth		If naturalized, give name and location of court which issued naturalization papers, and date of papers	Address in United States
1	BROUQUA	Denis	25	M	S	San Francisco, Cal	1/25/15		314 Maine St, Vallejo, Cal
2	BROUQUA	Prosper	55	M	M			Fairfield, Calif. Sept. 1918	-do-
3	BROUQUA	Eugenia	53	F	M			-do-	-do-
4	BROUQUA	Antoine	23	M	S	Vallejo, Cal	2/3/17		-do-
5	BUDD	Arthur	59	M	M	Meriden, Conn	1/22/82		Windsor, Mass
6	BURTON	Lucille	47	F	M	Chicago, Ill	6/7/93		755 Park Av. N.Y.C.
7	BESTON	Russell	33	M	M	Buffalo, N.Y.	12/3/07		State Dept. Wash. D.C.
8	BEUTLER	Harold	34	M	S	Peru, Ill.	10/10/06		1427 S. Ninth St. St. Louis, Mo.
9	CIELAKIE	William	42	M	M	Ware, Mass	12/15/95		U.S. Navy
10	EHRHARDT	George	22	M	S	Lynbrook, N.Y.	4/22/18		Princeton Plains, N.J.
11	EBERHARDT	Herman	28	M	S	La Porte, Ind.	10/7/12		2655 Mildred St. Chicago, Ill
12	EHRHARDT	John	51	M	M	Brooklyn, N.Y.C.	11/4/89		Southern Pines, N.C.
13	FRASER	Afton Lee	37	M	M	Columbus, Mont.	2/26/03		67 Broad St. N.Y.C.
14	GRUNFELD	Lea	61	M	M			By Marriage	566 Coney Island Av. B'klyn, NY
15	GUTHRIE	Adelaide	59	F	S	Windsor, Penna.	11/4/81		State Department, Wash. D.C.
16	HEARSON	Henry	22	M	S	Brooklyn, N.Y.C.	9/17/18		377 E. 46 St. B'klyn, N.Y.C.
17	HEARING	Emma	72	F	S	Philadelphia, PA.	11/20/68		Teaneck, N.J.
18	JERSA	JOHN	26	M	S	Roseville, Ohio	3/2/14		St. Andrew-on-Hudson, N.Y.
19	KENYON	Vivan	55	F	M			By Marriage	247 Park Av. New York City
20	KENYON	Elsa	33	F	S	New York City	4/27/07		-do-
21	KEENA-MENTONNAULT	Joan	30	F	D	Mexico	6/24/10	U.S.A. Parents, Reg. U.S. Consul	Mrs. Platt, North Av. Englewood
22	KOLLMAN	Herman	39	M	M			Supreme Ct. Richmond, S.I. March 1929	165 B'way, New York City
23	LOVE	Elizabeth	31	F	S	Gastonia, N.C.	10/7/09		Gastonia, N.C.
24	MERRILL	Clyde	47	M	M	Chicago, Ill	12/17/92		Am. Express, 65 B'way, NY
25	MENDENHALL	Aileen	54	F	D	Philadelphia, Pa.	4/9/86		1420 Walnut St. Philadelphia
26	MENDENHALL	Emma	28	F	S	Bryn Mawr, Pa.	11/13/12		-do-
27	MOSTRIAKOFF	David	2 6	M	S	Cannes, France	4/3/38	U.S.A. Parents, Reg. U.S. Consul	-do-
28	MINER	Horace	28	M	M	St. Paul, Minn	5/26/12		11 Waller Av. Lexington, Ky
29	MINER	Agnes	29	F	M	East. Chicago, Ill	12/18/10		-do-
30	MAAS	Catherine	57	F	S			Supreme Court Los Angeles, Cal. June 1920	401 Venice Blvd. Venice, Cal

U.S. Immigrant Inspector

20

Line: American Export Lines, Inc.
Owners: -do-
Local Agents: -do-

IMPORTANT NOT…

New York, Passenger Lists, 1820-1957 for Lea Grunfeld

Record Index

Line: 14
Name: Lea Grunfeld
Arrival Date: 9 12 1940
Birth Date: 1879
Age: 61
Gender: Male
Port of Departure: Lisbon, Portugal
Ship Name: Exeter
Port of Arrival: New York, New York
Page number: 90

DECEMBER 10, 1940

From My Father to My Mother

As winter descends on Krakow, my father tries to relay cheerful news of weddings and other *simchas* (family celebrations). He writes cryptically about visiting a Mr. Koppner. Prudence demands that he not say more, but it is evident that this represents another attempt on the part of my father to get out of Poland.

Giza, referred to at the end of the letter, was the daughter of the sister of my cousin Mala Sperling's mother.* Mala was named in memory of Giza's mother.

My dearest darling in the whole world,

Today I had a big holiday. I received a telegram and your sweet letter with a photograph of our little boy. My darling, I long to be with you already. Amen. As soon as possible.

Thank God I do not lack anything but if I could, I would pin wings on myself and fly to you. Darling, please write to Mother's address, the letters somehow get there quicker …

Darling, I long for you so much. I cannot wait to be together with you. Whatever I do here, I think of you, and God should help that we be together forever. I think that I have suffered enough for my sins. …

Darling, my whole family is in Radomysl and they are happy and they feel okay, but we have to have strength to be able to take everything that is coming to us. Today I am going to go to Mr. Koppner to take care of things. I cannot say any more because I cannot. Giza is the only one I can talk to. She would do anything for you also. I kiss you and send you hearty regards a thousand times and kiss you.

Yours,
Chaskel

---

* It was Mala who translated all of the Polish letters included in this book.

Please send kisses for our sweet darling son a thousand times, and please tell him that his daddy sends him the kisses and that he will come to see him soon. Special regards from my whole family.

DECEMBER 10, 1940

From My Aunt Gusta to My Mother

Gusta, apparently learning from a telegram sent by my grandmother that she had arrived safely in New York on December 9, adds these words to my father's December 10 letter.

Gusta discusses receiving a call from the consul, telling her to go to Vienna (or Berlin) for her passport. She did so, but her application was denied. Unlike my mother, who acted immediately and presented voluminous proof of her US citizenship, Gusta had delayed until the situation was desperate, and showed only her marriage to Shimeck, a Polish citizen. The consulate correctly told Gusta that this was not sufficient. Gusta asks my mother for help in proving that she is an American citizen. She then refers to several family members who now work at home, including my father, who wishes to join his family in Radomysl; her husband who refuses to give her money to even take passport photos; and to her (and my mother's) cousin Gusta Hoffnung, the mother of Mala Sperling.

My aunt Gusta also refers mysteriously to "the woman who was supposed to travel with Mother [and] paid one hundred zlotys," – presumably a reference to herself and to her dashed hopes to come to the United States with my grandmother. It is not known what Gusta paid for, but, whatever the case, her efforts and her payment were to no avail.

My dearest ones,

I can imagine your happiness when Mother came and how you greeted one another. Mother must be very tired from that long trip, but everything was worth it. I cannot even tell you what I would give to be with you.

Now I will tell you the story with my papers. The consul called me and said to go to either Vienna or Berlin to take care of my passport. Unfortunately, the first time I tried I could not get it because the magistrate says that I have no right since my husband is a Polish citizen.... I would like to have some kind of papers proving that I am an American citizen.

...I forgot to tell you, my dear husband does not want to give me money to have photographs made to send to the consulate. I strongly believe that this is one reason that I cannot get out of this terrible situation. Chaskel works a little bit at home, but he wants to go to his mother and family. I do not know how this will work out.

Please write if there is any hope that Chaskel can go to you soon. The woman who was supposed to travel with Mother paid one hundred zlotys.

I kiss you many times. The children are behaving very well. Chaskel took the telegram that you sent and went to Gusta Hoffnung because everyone is very happy with news from you. I do not know if we will be able to send this letter airmail. I could talk to you forever and ever.

I kiss you many times.

Gusta

DECEMBER 27, 1940

From My Father to My Mother

As 1940 draws to a close, both my parents, separated for nearly a year by oceans and circumstance, look ahead to the new year with trepidation and a grain of optimism. In this letter, my father explains that he has contacted a member of the Judenrat (a council the Jews were forced by the occupying Germans to establish, in order to run the ghetto and eventually to organize the deportations) to assist him in leaving the country.

He again mentions the mysterious Mr. Koppner in what appears to be some sort of code. Are potatoes a code name for dollars, or perhaps zlotys? The identity of Yehudah, to whom my father says he gave potatoes, is also unknown.

My father closes by expressing his grief that he is not by my mother's side earning a living so that she would not need to work and therefore leave me in an orphanage.

My dearest ones in the whole world,

It has been three weeks since I have received a letter from you. But every day I hope that one will come. I want you not to worry about me. I am okay. Leon Auerbach [Giza's father] is a macher [influential person] on the Judenrat, so he is trying to help me leave. God should help him. You, my darling, should prepare the ticket for the ship. I pray to God that it shouldn't take too long because I have to have strength to be able to take it. I feel okay and healthy and make enough money for my keep. I want to hear the same from you.

From my dear Mother and whole family I get letters, and they are okay.... My dear Ernusha is the smartest one from us all. It is almost a year since you left, but I hope that soon we will see each other....

Now, dear Mother, the way you wrote to me, I gave Yehudah 250 kilograms of potatoes because they do not have anymore. I have some left so I gave [my] Mother another 70 kilograms of my potatoes and I hope that they will have enough for a while. How is everything there? I go to Mr. Koppner and he is upset that nobody writes to him....

What is new? How is our dear, sweet son? Is he home? How is dear Mother? And you, are you earning more money already? I cannot tell you how much I would like to be together with you so that I could work and you could take care of the house and baby. Stay healthy and happy. Thousands of kisses to all of you.

Yours forever,
Chaskel

CHAPTER EIGHT

"Here Everything Has Changed"

January–June 1941

From Gusta Stern, a Cousin, to My Grandmother

It is a new year in a new world for my grandmother, Leah. The following letter is included because it reveals that my grandmother was, at that time, residing with my mother and me as boarders at the Goldberg home in Brooklyn. The letter speaks of the deprivations being suffered by my grandmother's cousin (formerly a very wealthy woman) in Berlin.

> *Mrs. E. Goldwasser*
> *c/o Goldberg*
> *556 Coney Island Avenue*
> *Brooklyn, New York*
>
> *My dearest cousin Laicha [Leah Grunfeld],*
> *   I read your telegram and I am very happy that you, thank God, arrived in New York okay. I also found out how much you had to go through. My children informed me too late about your departure and I could not make it to the train station.*
> *   How are you doing, my cousin? Together with your dear daughter and grandson you should be strong and well.*

Did you already get used to the new world? How is your health? Please write to me everything.

...You know my situation, dear Laicha. Besides the fact that I became a widow, I lost my store and I have to struggle in my old age even to take care of my old brother who is under constant doctor's care and cannot take care of himself.

...I feel terrible to have to ask for clothing for my children. My brother also has nothing and cannot do anything for me. I managed to get some clothing for him.

Regards and kisses,
Gusta Stern

JANUARY 18, 1941

From My Father to My Mother

In this letter, my father says that he is still in Krakow, but does not know for how much longer. He asks my mother to find out how a Mr. Belfore was able to obtain a passport for his wife. My father asks whether my mother could do the same for him (overlooking the legal differences between alien husbands and wives concerning citizenship) and asks whether he can go through Havana or somewhere else. He also mentions visiting the Lachters, cousins of my mother (and Leon Lachter) who remained in Krakow.

My dearest ones whom I miss so much,

It is six weeks since I received your last letter. I am still in Krakow, but I do not know for how much longer. So please, I beg of you to write to my mother in Radomysl.

I would like to be with you already. Mrs. Belfore is supposed to receive a passport soon, she does not know what kind yet, so please I beg of you to go to Mr. Belfore and ask him how he took care of it. Could you, my darling, do the same for me? Maybe I can go through Havana or somewhere else.

You cannot imagine how much I want to be with you already. I have everything that I need – only you are missing. God should help us that it should not take so long because I do not know if I have enough strength to take it much longer.

. . .

How is our sweet little baby? He must be a big man already because he is eight and a half months old. How is dear Mother? I can imagine the happiness that you have together. At least the two of you are together and I hope to be with you soon.

Three times a week I go to Mr. and Mrs. Lachter. . . . Please write to me and tell me everything that is happening.

Stay healthy and happy and remember that I think about you always.

Yours,
Chaskel

FEBRUARY 14, 1941
From My Father to My Mother

My father here discusses the mail situation and how he and my mother should continue to communicate with each other. Oddly, at several points, he refers to himself in the third person, first as Abraham and then as Murray's father and as "your husband." He mentions the "presents" he received from my mother and from his uncle. These are presumably cash or negotiable valuables and it is these that may account for the third-person usage. The identity of Natan, to whom he suggests packages be sent along with his brother Josef, is unknown, as are the identities of Mrs. Malaker and others mentioned in the letter.

My father at this point, several weeks before the opening of the Krakow ghetto in Podgorze, which had been a very poor part of the city, realizes that his ability to remain at his current address is tenuous and advises his wife to address all future correspondence to his mother in Radomysl.

My dearest darling ones whom I miss so much,

I received your letter this week and the first letter from Mother. It is not my fault that you do not get letters from me. I cannot send them airmail so I try to send them through Berlin. Maybe that way you will get them sooner. I write again now even though I did not get an answer from you. I will write and write and write because at least you will have letters from me. I write every week, anytime I can.

The wool you sent to Abraham you should not have sent because he is warm and he has everything he needs. Darling, you would do better if you would send it to Josef or Natan because they are in Russia and it is very cold. I really worry about it because Murray's father does not need anything. He still has the present from his wife and half from his uncle. He does not need anything, but only counts the days till he can travel to see you.

You cannot imagine how happy it makes me that you have a good job. It should be with mazel and your husband should also have a job with you, Amen.

I still live in Krakow together with Gusta and the whole family. God should help us that I should be with you for your birthday. Leibek still lives with his wife in the same apartment. Every week I receive a letter from my dear mother and the whole family. They are okay.

My dearest, I received the letter from December 30 but I found out from Mr. Zelberger what a difficult time of traveling dear Mother had. I would be willing to go through it gladly myself only to be with you. Mrs. Malaker and her children are leaving. I do not know where they are going, but she is trying to get out of here.

I very often go to the Goldcorns' and I sit there days on end. [My brother] Yanek and his wife live in Walbrun, and every week, he and his wife come to Krakow. She is a very enterprising woman and she knows how to make money. Shimeck does not earn too much money. The children do mischief and they are disobedient except when I yell at them, and then they listen.

If you write to me, write to me at my mother's house because I do not know how much longer I will be allowed to stay here.

Stay healthy and happy. I send thousands of kisses to you all.

Yours forever,
Chaskel

P.S. The most important thing I want to ask you about is our sweet little *boy. Is he with you? I hope that God will help and that he will be with you soon. Our Murray Jack is already nine months old. I am so sorry that I cannot give him a kiss, but please give him thousands of kisses and hugs from me and tell him it is from his daddy.*

FEBRUARY 28, 1941

From My Father to My Mother

My father now informs my mother that soon he will be moving in with his own mother and his whole family. He writes that he has enough money to live and that with money one can get everything. He refers to Aunt Dvora, who was the wife of my father's great uncle Mozes Pinkus Goldwasser, and to Mala Feiler, a neighbor at 9 Josefa. She was a widow with three children. (See my mother's July 1973 letter listing victims reproduced at the end of chapter 11.)

He then says, "I sold everything of mine except for a few suits that I can sell later on." He writes that "yesterday Mrs. Belfore left. Please try to be in touch with her and she will tell you everything." Presumably this means she will explain how she was able to obtain a visa and also, without constraints of the postal censors, she will be able to draw my mother a true picture of current conditions in Krakow.

My dearest ones whom I miss so much,

Even though I have not received any letters from you, I write anyway and it is not my fault if you do not get any news from me. I have been here the last few days but soon I will go to my mother and my whole family. Thank God I am not lacking anything except, of course, you, and I would like so much to be together. I hope that we will see each other soon. Do not worry about me because I have enough money to live. I do not lack any food. With money, one can get everything.

…I sold everything of mine except for a few suits that I can sell later on. Did my family from Mr. Stern come to see you? Mrs. Stern is very anxious to know what is going on. Aunt Dvora and my whole family are in Radomysl and they are content there. They had to leave where they were staying before.

*Shimeck earns a little money, but I do not know for how much lon-
ger. Gusta still has some money. Mala Feiler asked me to ask you to go
to her brother so that he can send her something because she is very
poor. Yesterday, Mrs. Belfore left. Please try to be in touch with her and
she will tell you everything. I want to remind you of my address in
Radomyśl Wielki.*

*Stay healthy and happy. I have never forgotten about you and I love
you forever. Please write to me about how much you earn and if you earn
enough for your keep. Does dear Mother earn any money? Is our sweet son
standing and walking already? Please send me a photograph.*

Yours,
Chaskel

MARCH 17, 1941
From My Father to My Mother

By the spring of 1941, the SS had expelled more than fifty-five thousand
Jews from Krakow. Only about fifteen thousand remained. On March 3
the Krakow ghetto was formally opened – not in the Jewish district of
Kazimierz, but in Podgorze, south of the city. The Jews of Krakow were
ordered to report to the ghetto by March 20. Non-Jews forced to give up
their homes in Podgorze were compensated with the much finer homes
formerly occupied by Jews. Meanwhile, by March 21, all of Krakow's fifteen thousand Jews were stuffed into a barbed-wire and brick-walled area
formerly inhabited by three thousand souls. The ghetto consisted of 320
buildings containing 3,167 units. Initially one apartment was issued to
every four Jewish families. Many, however, were rendered homeless and
forced to live on the street.

The initial purpose of the ghetto was to centrally house the city's
Jewish population in order to facilitate their use as slave laborers in the
local factories – including the German Enamelware Factory owned by
Oskar Schindler. But with the onset of Operation Reinhard the following
year, the ghetto became a staging area for deportations and mass murder.
Despite heroic resistance efforts, in little more than two years nearly all of
the ghetto's residents will have been slaughtered.

In the following letter, my father describes the dispersal of our family in the wake of the establishment of the ghetto – which he conspicuously does not mention. He gives my mother his new address in Radomysl. He then describes bitter family quarrels with Gusta and her husband.

Without elaboration, he states: "Here everything has changed and it is not like it used to be." He informs my mother that her sister Gusta is suffering greatly and will soon be going to Niepolomice, a town about fifteen miles east of Krakow.

For the time being, it appears, my father and family are to be spared the deprivations of the Krakow ghetto. He speaks of his little nephews and nieces with affection, invoking the lyrics of the well-known Yiddish lullaby "Rozhinkes mit Mandlen" when he compares them to raisins and almonds.

We also learn that my father is no longer working. His words, for the first time, betray that he is confronting his own mortality when he writes: "I would like to be able to live till we will be together."

My dearest ones in the whole world,

Last week I received your letters. Thank you for them. I do not understand why you do not get any letters from me. I write every week. My address now is: E.P. Goldwasser, by Teichman, Radomysl Wielki. You have no idea how much I miss you, our dear son and Mother. I want nothing more but to be with you. You have no idea, but thank God at least I am with my family now. I am not working now.

My dear darling, you do not know what I went through, and I feel so sorry for Gusta and the children. They really suffer. At least Shimeck gives them money for food. I did not speak to him at all which was good. But twice I really argued with him. Can you imagine, Uncle Pinya went to Warsaw and when he returned I told him to come live with me. Shimeck got angry and did not speak to me for a whole week. I do not know where to turn. I feel very lonely and I do not like to be shunned. Uncle and I slept in the kitchen and I gave my room to Shimeck and Gusta and they still were not happy. We split the rent and electric and this was not good either.

I am happy at least for you the situation is better. Here everything has changed and it is not like it used to be. I would like to be able to live till we will be together. This is my only dream because I need you terribly.

...

Thank God that I do not need anything. I just need to be with you. My aunts and their children are like almonds and raisins. They are cute children. When I hold them in my arms I think when will I be able to hold my own son. Every day I learn your language.

Yanek, Mr. and Mrs. Kaufman, Josef, Regina and Zesha come to see me and so do Lola Feinster and the children.

Gusta and her children are going to Niepolomice and Leibek is going to go to Dabrowa to Zofsha and her family. Nothing else is new and I cannot write anymore.

Stay happy and healthy. Thousands of kisses. I love you forever.

Chaskel

APRIL 1, 1941

From My Mother to the New York City Housing Authority

In this letter, my mother appeals to the Housing Authority for lodging in one of the city's projects. She explains that she and my grandmother are boarding with the Goldberg family, where she is unable to live with her infant son, and is forced to put me up at the Brooklyn Infants' Home.

In pleading her case, my mother cleverly invokes the spirit of Teddy Roosevelt by closing with the words "I know I shall get a square deal."

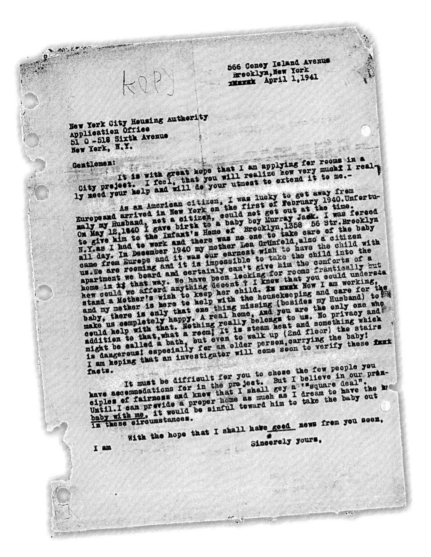

566 Coney Island Avenue
Brooklyn, New York
~~March~~ April 1, 1941

kopy

New York City Housing Authority
Application Office
51 0 -518 Sixth Avenue
New York, N.Y.

Gentlemen:

It is with great hope that I am applying for rooms in a City project. I feel, that you will realize how very much I really need your help and will do your utmost to extend it to me.-

As an American citizen, I was lucky to get away from Europe and arrived in New York on the first of February 1940. Unfortunaly my Husband, not a citizen, could not get out at the time. On May 12,1940 I gave birth to a baby boy Murray Jack. I was forced to give him to the Infant's Home of Brooklyn,1358 56 Str.Brooklyn N.Y. as I had to work and there was no one to take care of the baby all day. In December 1940 my mother Lea Grünfeld,also a citizen came from Europe and it was our earnest wish to have the child with us.We are rooming and it is impossible to take the child into the apartment we board and certainly can't give him the comforts of a home in it that way. We have been looking for rooms frantically but hew could we afford anything decent ? I knew that you could understand a Mother's wish to keep her child. Now I am working, and my mother is here to help with the housekeeping and care for the baby, there is only that one thing missing (besides my Husband) to make us completely happy. A real home, and you are the only one who could help with that. Nothing really belongs to us. No privacy and in addition to that, what a room! It is steam heat and something which might be called a bath, but even to walk up (2nd floor) the stairs is dangerous! especially for an older person,carrying the baby! I am hoping that an investigator will come soon to verify these facts.

It must be difficult for you to chose the few people you have accommodations for in the project. But I believe in our principles of fairness and knew that I shall get a "square deal". Until I can provide a proper home as much as I dream to have the baby with me, it would be sinful toward him to take the baby out in these circumstances.

With the hope that I shall have good news from you soon,

I am   Sincerely yours,

APRIL 4, 1941
From My Father to My Mother

In this letter, my father informs my mother that he has once again written to the American consul to inform them that he has changed his address. But he does not even bother expressing the now futile hope that he will hear back from them.

He also expresses the fear that he may not survive to see my mother again when he writes: "I would like to live until the moment that we are together."

He urges my mother to write to him frequently and also to write to a Mr. Gold, apparently an American relative of a family the Grunfelds knew in Poland, who were – like so many Polish Jews – in desperate need of assistance. My great-aunt Hedwig's April 28, 1941, letter to this Mr. Gold is below.

My father goes on to explain that he is living together with his entire extended family and somehow they are all okay. He wishes my mother a healthy Passover and he expresses the hope that he will be with us both in time to celebrate my first birthday on May 12.

My dearest ones in the world,

I received your letter from March 31st and it gave me a lot of happiness. I like to receive letters from you. They make my life easier.

I wrote to the American consul when I came to Radomysl so that they can know that I changed my address. Dear Gusta, Shimeck and the children are in Niepolomice.... We also received the present for Leba and Regina.

Now, my dearest ones, I want to let you know that we are all fine and that I feel well. But I miss you terribly and I would like to live until the moment that we are together. This is my only wish. I am very happy to hear that our son gives you a lot of happiness and I pray that I live to the day that I am together with both of you. Please write a lot and also write to Mr. Gold.

My dearest Ernusha, I hope that I can write to you that I am ready to go, but not yet. Please also write to me at M. Pheiffman, for Goldwasser, Radomysl Wielki, this is my new address. I live together with the whole family and thank God this is good. My dear mother, aunts, uncles, sisters-in-law, brothers-in-law, and children are okay. Lola Feinster and the whole family are okay.

I send you hearty kisses and regards from the whole family and also best wishes for a healthy Passover. I hope that I will be with you for our son's first birthday. I love you and miss you.

Chaskel

APRIL 11, 1941

From My Father to My Mother

The following letter, written by my father on Erev Pesach (the day before Passover) is a particularly poignant and emotional one. In it, he begs my mother not to cry so much because she needs to be a healthy mother. His depiction of celebrating the Passover Seder while staring at a photo of his beloved and distant wife is truly heartbreaking.

He explains that he has written again to the consul, but they have not answered yet. While the words speak of patience, they are dripping with frustration. He again mentions my upcoming first birthday and expresses the hope that I will grow up to be "a good man."

> *My dearest darlings in the whole world,*
>
> *I received your letter from March 9. Today is Erev Pesach and you gave me a lot of happiness. Please, darling, do not cry so much. You have to be a healthy mother and wife. At the Seder I will ask God for all the best and I will put a picture of you in front of my eyes and I will imagine that we are together.*
>
> *I wrote again to the consul; they have not answered yet. You wait for it and I wait for it. I have all the photographs and everything is in order. I just have to wait for the answer.*
>
> *I no longer go to Kepshen and Mrs. Cohen. Gusta writes to me often and she also wrote to you. My son's birthday is coming up and I want to wish him a lot of mazel and happiness and that he should grow up to be a good man. I hope that soon I will be together with you. I wish my son good health as well.*
>
> *. . .*
>
> *I go to my friends to make the days seem shorter. I have much correspondence because I write to the whole family and this also keeps me busy so the day goes by faster.*
>
> *Everything here is the same. I wish to be together with you. Dear Mother writes to me that you cry a lot. Please don't, because you will get sick and this won't be good. I hope that dear God will hear and help us.*

Nothing else is new. My dearest Erna, I send you, our son and Mother greetings and kisses.

Yours,
Chaskel

APRIL 28, 1941

From My Great-Aunt Hedwig to Mr. Gold in America

In this amazing letter, which was found together with the letters from my father to my mother, my great-aunt Hedwig (who was married to my grandmother Leah Grunfeld's brother Shimon) addresses a Mr. Gold, living in New York, whose sister, Mrs. Eichen, is suffering greatly in Rado-mysl. Hedwig advises Mr. Gold that her sister-in-law (my grandmother) will deliver this letter to him and inform him about conditions back in Poland. Hedwig admonishes Mr. Gold for failing to write to his sister or inquire about her welfare. Hedwig explains how dire circumstances have forced everyone to overcome their pride and embarrassment at asking for assistance from others. "Please believe me that the help is needed," she pleads. "I cannot describe to you what is going on here."

Mr. Gold,

I hope you remember me and I am taking advantage of this situation. I am here now with the Eichen family and I decided to write to you. My sister-in-law, Mrs. Grunfeld, will come to see you and she will tell you all about us. Her brother does not know why you do not write and why you are not interested in what is happening here. The situation here is very difficult and is very bad. Please believe me that you should be very happy that you are where you are because it is really bad here.

The Eichen family is living under one roof with five other families. They cannot do anything about it because there is a war going on, but we have to live even though it is very hard. If you are able, it is your duty to write and find out and even to help. It is very sad that we have to ask people to do things for us, but this is the only way that we will survive. Life is very dear and if you have no other way then you ask people and you are not ashamed. I could tell you a lot of things, but please believe

me that the help is needed. I cannot describe to you what is going on
here. Please, I beg of you, do not let the people down and write to them.
I wish you all the best and greetings.

Hedwig Hirsch

MAY 12, 1941
From My Father to My Mother

In this letter my father notes that today is the first birthday of the son he
has never met. He extends his best wishes that they will soon be together.

Although my father makes the oft-repeated claim that he lacks for nothing except his wife and son, he no longer advises my mother to refrain from
sending packages. In fact, he twice requests that she send them (if she can),
indicating that conditions continue to deteriorate.

To my dear ones whom I love,

It has already been three weeks since I received anything from you
but I write every week because I know that you like to receive letters from
me.... It would be better if you would write to me because we all read
all your letters.... Thank God we are okay. If you want to send packages
we would be very happy because we could use the things that you send.

...

Darling, our sweet son has a birthday today and I know what type of
party you will make for him. He should be happy and healthy and I hope
that soon he will see his father and I know that this is your wish too.

Now I will tell you a little bit about the people around here. Regina,
Yosek's wife, is about five months pregnant. I hope that God will help her
and it will be okay. I already received four packages, but if you cannot
send me more then you should not.

I am, thank God, healthy and I want to hear the same from you. The
only thing that I'm missing is being with you.

...

My mother and family are okay and they send you hearty regards.
I am always thinking about you.

Chaskel

MAY 30, 1941

From My Father to My Mother

It has now been six years since my parents first met – the last year and one half of which they have been forced to live far apart. My father mentions that he has forwarded one of my mother's packages on to her sister, Gusta.

Despite his anguish, he signals a positive tone when he advises my mother that soon she will be able to bring me home from the orphanage. Finally, he again complains about rowdy children; this time it's the neighbors. Conspicuous in its absence is any mention of the consulate or his visa application. It appears that hope is beginning to flicker out.

Yesterday I received your sweet letter and I am very happy to read it. First of all, I am happy to hear that you got a raise.... Oh, another thing, Gusta is angry at me because I do not write to you about her. She said that I completely forgot that she exists. So please tell her that I did not forget and that I sent her a package because she needs it more than I. I do not lack anything except for you.

I am very happy that you write so much about our sweet son. He looks so beautiful. God should help you that you should be able to take him home soon and that his daddy should be able to give him a kiss because he misses him so much. It is already six years since we first met, and God should help that we should be together as soon as possible.

...Gusta writes that her husband earns very little money.... Please, I beg of you, send me another picture of Murray Jack because I have no patience to wait anymore. I hope that he is not sick or anything.

I will finish my writing for today. There is so much commotion going on next door from me. I cannot stand it. The children run back and forth.

I kiss and greet you thousands of times.

Yours forever,
Chaskel

JUNE 15, 1941

From My Father to My Mother

As the days drag by and conditions become more desperate, my father clearly is focused on happier days of the past. He notes the upcoming anniversaries of his engagement and wedding to my mother as he expresses hope that "things will not get worse." In something of an about-face, he now advises my mother that she should send more "packages," which represent a lifeline for him and other family members. Times are very bad and the whole family is asking for packages. Finally, he speaks of how quickly his nieces (his sister Chana's daughters) are growing up and despairs that he is not witness to his own son's childhood development.

> My dearest ones in the whole world,
>
> I received your letter, and it gave me so much happiness that I cried, and I pray to God that we should be together soon. My dearest darling Ernunah, our sweet son is so wonderful. God should help that I should see him with my own eyes very soon. On July 3rd it will have been six years since we became engaged and August 20th it will have been five years since we got married. We have certainly gone through a lot. I just hope that everything will be all right.
>
> ...
>
> Thank you very much for the congratulations for my birthday [June 17]. I hope that our wishes will come true and that we will say happy birthday to each other in person someday soon.
>
> ...I am writing you the truth. I hope things will not get worse than they are now. I have milk, butter and sugar; the only thing that I am missing is you....
>
> When it is nice here, we go for walks. I miss you with every step that I take. I hope that I can leave here soon. I am so upset that I am unable to see my own child. I hope when you get this letter at least you will see him for me. I live with the thought of seeing and being with you. Rechela and Bronka [Chaskel's nieces] are already young ladies and they play around. They remember their Aunt Erna.

I received all the packages that you sent. If you can, please send some more. In the last letter, I wrote that you should not, but times are very bad and I hope that everything will turn out okay....

The whole family asked me if I can send some packages. They are no longer in Krakow.

I greet you and kiss you many thousands of times and I always think of you.

Chaskel

JUNE 30, 1941

From My Father to My Mother

The year is half over and my parents are not one bit closer to reuniting than they were a year earlier. In this letter, my father responds to my mother's recently received June 4 letter in which she evidently expresses her concerns about my father's welfare. He seeks to calm her fears but soon turns to sharing his inconsolable frustration over the inequity of his situation. "I, who dreamt to have a child, and now I have to sit and wait...."

He goes on to say, somewhat cryptically, that he received the coffee and the tea but that my mother "will not be able to send us anymore." He does not explain why. My father closes this highly emotional letter by again invoking one of his frequent tropes: "I want to live to reach the time that we will be together."

To my dearest ones whom I miss so much,

I was very happy to receive your letter from June 4. I do not know why you are so upset and why you worry about us so much. We are okay, please believe me. I also want to hear the same from you. I cannot live without you. I miss you so much. All day and night I think about you and that is how my life goes without you. I, who dreamt to have a child, and now I have to sit here so long and wait. I hope that God will help us and that we will be together soon.

I am with my mother and whole family. I have everything that I need. All I'm missing is you. I hope to live until the moment that I will be with you. I received coffee and tea, my darling, but you will not be able to send us any more.... I am very happy that our sweet son is already grown up. He is such a good-looking boy, too. I think he looks like you, and I cannot wait to see him in person.

You write to me that I am nervous. No, I am not. I remember when he was born....

Every day I go for a walk in the meadow. I am not hungry; we have enough to eat. Rechela and Bronka always ask about Aunt Erna. They remember you and point you out in the photographs. Thank God that our darling son is okay and that he does not get sick. God should help us.

...

Dear Mother is okay, but her stomach hurts. I want to live to reach the time that we will be together.... You can tell Leon that he should not be upset about his family. They are okay but his sister cries all the time....

No more for now. Regards and kisses. I love you forever.

Yours,
Chaskel

CHAPTER NINE

Living on Hope

July 1941–April 1942

JULY 23, 1941
From My Father to My Mother

In this response to a letter received from my mother, it appears that she
has managed to bring me home from the orphanage. My father, now living
with his family, claims not to be in need. Amazingly, he states he is even
able to assist others. He includes an update for Leon Lachter from his sister Ewa Lipshitz, saying that she and her family "cry a lot."

> To my dearest Erna whom I miss so much,
>
> I received your letter from June 8 yesterday and I was so happy with
> it that I read it over and over....
>
> My darling, I am so happy that you will be together with our sweet
> son and that he looks so beautiful and that he walks already. I am happy
> that you will take our son home. At least the two of you will be together.
> I would like to hold and hug him.
>
> ... Darling, if you could only send some photographs I would be the
> happiest person in the world. I also pray to God that I should be together
> with you soon. I may send something to Gusta....
>
> Our whole family is together, which is very good.... God should
> help that everything will be over soon. I am happy that I do not need
> anything from anyone. It also makes me happy that you do not need
> anything either. I try to even help some people....

Ewa Lipshitz and her family are okay, but they cry a lot. Tell Leon
that he should not worry about it because we are all together. Gusta
reads all of your letters.

Dearest Mother, thank you for the few words that you wrote to me. I
am happy to hear that you are healthy and I am happy that you are not
sorry that you are there. I wish that I were there also.

Nothing new. I send you regards and kiss you a thousand times. Spe-
cial regards from my whole family.

Chaskel

AUGUST 13, 1941

From My Aunt Gusta to My Mother

My aunt Gusta and her family are at this point living in Niepolomice, about
fifteen miles east of Krakow. This places them, like my father's family, outside the grip of the Krakow ghetto. In this letter to her sister, Gusta twice
mentions that she has a good appetite (a sign of good health) and that
she is trading her son's suits for food. He no longer needs them since he is
becoming a real "peasant boy," from living in the countryside.

Gusta offers a glimpse of the desperation she faces: "…I do not care
about anything." For the first time we learn that my mother has included
cash in the packages she has been sending to my father. Cash he generously
passes on to his sister-in-law.

My dearest ones,

You complain that I do not write too often, but that is because I am
unable to afford the postage. Do not worry about us. The main thing is
that Chaskel should be with you.

…I have a good appetite and we eat a lot of peasant bread and
butter. Thank God that we are not lacking that yet. I have exchanged
Yankush's cotton suits for many things. The main thing is that every-
thing should end.

We hope to hear good news from you. The children are okay and they
are growing nicely. They have a lot of freedom and fresh air. Ruzunya
misses you terribly, especially her bubbie [Yiddish for grandmother], and

she often cries. I cannot help her. Yankush has become a real peasant boy and he has even started to talk like a peasant. Shimeck earns very little money, but he hopes that everything will be okay.

…I do not look bad and I have a good appetite, but I do not take care of myself because I do not care about anything. I miss you so much that I cannot even talk about it. I am happy when the children are away so that I can cry.

Is Mother better? The baby looks beautiful and God should help that his parents should be together in happiness and health.

…Shimeck is also healthy, but he complains that he has nothing to do.

Do you have nice furniture? What does dear Mother do during the day? Chaskel sent me kasha [buckwheat] and money from the package that he received from you.

Nothing else is new. I kiss you a thousand times and I beg Mother not to worry because I want to see her happy and healthy. Bye-bye to my dearest ones. Regards from the children and Shimeck.

Gusta

AUGUST 17, 1941
From My Father to My Mother

We learn of several new developments in this letter from my father. My mother – presumably as a result of her April 1 letter to the New York Housing Authority – has found a new apartment, and my grandmother has found employment, not a trivial accomplishment given her age and language skills. My father notes their soon-approaching fifth anniversary and bemoans the fact that nearly two of those years have been spent apart from each other.

My dearest Ernusha,

I received your sweet letter yesterday. Thank you very much for the photographs; I can hardly believe how beautiful our son is. He is really something to look at. You are right, I feel like screaming from happiness. Congratulations on your new apartment. I wish you a lot of happiness

My mother with me at age fourteen months on July 14, 1941

and I hope that we will all be together as soon as possible. You are doing a good thing that you are staying at home with the baby in the meantime. I also want to congratulate dear Mother on her new job. I hope that it will not be too difficult for her....

Thank God I have everything that I need; the only thing I don't have is fruit and vegetables. Really, it is only you that I am missing with every step that I take.

My dearest ones, you know that on August 20 it will be five years since we have been married, and I hope that finally we will be together.... It is very hot here now so we go to the forest sometimes.

...My dearest Ernusha, I miss you so terribly much. I cannot wait until the moment that we are together again. It has already been nineteen months since you left me. Stay healthy and happy. I kiss you countless times.

Yours,
Chaskel

OCTOBER 13, 1941
From My Father to My Mother

As my father pens this impassioned letter, little does he realize that on this day the German authorities have begun deporting Jews from central Europe to the ghettos of Poland as Operation Reinhard gets underway. It will succeed in murdering nearly two million innocent people.

As summer turns to fall, my father's anguish over his prolonged separation bleeds through his words. At the same time he jokes that being forced to sell all his possessions may have a benefit: "He will have less luggage" when he arrives to the US. My father again mentions the need for money and explains that he, along with everyone else, is living on hope alone.

As they struggle to resist the imposed dehumanization, conditions inside the filthy, overcrowded Jewish communities become life-threatening as disease, starvation, and inadequate clothing and shelter begin to ravage the Jews trapped inside.

My dearest ones in the whole world,

I received a letter from you after a few weeks. Your letter was sweet and I thank you very much. The letter was dated September 18. My dearest Ernusha, I want to tell you how much I miss you, how much I love you and how much I pray to be together with you, our sweet son and Mother.... My dearest, I dream about you every day. I dream that we are together at last and I have a feeling that we will be.

I am very happy that you sent photographs of our sweet son. I wrote you that we received the three packages of cocoa and sugar. If you can, please send some more. Abraham does not earn anything; he is selling everything that he has.

Maybe he will have less luggage that way. But he looks okay.... I get letters from Gusta every week. She writes so so, but she has what she needs. Leon also writes. Cousin Hela went to the doctor and he gave her some medicine and she feels a little better. Here, thank God, you can get everything as long as you have money.

My dearest Ernusha, I long so much to see you. I have no strength anymore and I only live thanks to hope. I am healthy and I feel well, only I miss you....

Stay healthy and I kiss you thousands of times.

Yours forever,
Chaskel

DECEMBER 20, 1941
From My Father to My Mother

As another year draws to a close, my father speaks of collecting candles for the Hanukkah menorah. He also writes of a mysterious Mr. Jehovah. Is this a real person or a code name, perhaps for God?

Denied access to any news, the Jews of Radomysl are unaware of the Japanese attack at Pearl Harbor and America's subsequent entry into the war. There is also no doubt that my father was unaware that the attack postponed by one month a high-level meeting of fifteen Nazi leaders (seven of whom held doctorate degrees) in the Berlin suburb of Wannsee. The conference would consolidate and implement the Reich's genocidal "Final Solution" by extending Operation Reinhard beyond Poland to all areas under German occupation. The conference formally marked Europe's eleven million Jews – including my family – for extermination.

Attendees at the Wannsee Conference, January 20, 1942

My dearest darling ones in the whole world,

It has already been seven weeks since I received a letter from you, but I hope that everything is okay with you. . . .

My dearest Ernunah, I miss you so terribly much and I would like to live until the moment that I can be together with you and I pray and hope that we will be together as soon as possible.

. . . If you have money then you can buy everything.

It has already been two years since we separated and I clearly remember the day that we said good-bye. You looked so beautiful and I see you every day that way. My dearest Ernunah, I would like to see you and our sweet son with my own eyes. He must be beautiful. I would like to hold him in my arms, hug him and kiss him all over.

How is dear Mother? Is she healthy?

I do not know why but I have not received any letter from Mr. Jeho-
vah. I do not think anything will come of it.... But do not worry, my
darling, God will not leave us.... I live with Yosek and Regina and they
have a beautiful daughter. She looks a little bit like our son.

I am going to light some candles for Chanukah and we managed to
get some fat, like we used to. I am going to the Feinster and the Reitgers
families. I have a lot of people who invite me, but the only thing that I
wish is to be with you.

I send you thousands of kisses.

Yours,
Chaskel

FEBRUARY 6, 1942
From My Father to My Mother

By this date, the nearby Lodz ghetto has been liquidated. The Wannsee
Conference has come and gone, putting into motion the "Final Solution"
for Europe's Jews. It establishes "extermination" camps throughout occupied Poland including Auschwitz-Birkenau, Treblinka, Sobibor, Belzec,
and Majdanek. These killing centers engage in round-the-clock mass murder on a scale never before seen in human history.

Obviously unaware of the atrocities and carnage surrounding him, my
father carries on everyday mundane correspondence in which he states,
"everything is the same as it was." In truth, unbeknownst to my father and
the other Jews of eastern Europe, nothing was the same. Using many forms
of falsehood and concealment, the Germans kept the Jews totally in the
dark about the looming Holocaust.

My dearest darling ones that I miss so much,

It has been such a long time since I received a letter from you, but
I hope and pray that everything is okay with you. My dearest Ernusha,
you cannot imagine how much I miss you, our dear son and Mother.
How are you all? I am okay, I am not missing anything except you. I
get letters from Gusta every week. She writes that she is well. Ruzunya,

Yankush, and Shimeck are also well.… By us, thank God, everything is the same as it was.

My dearest Ernunah, I miss you and I do not stop thinking about you for a single moment. I just long to be together with you. My mother and my whole family are okay. I just want to be with you, that is all that I want. That is my only wish.

I finally received a letter from Mr. Checkov. It was not a nice letter and I did not write back.

There is no more news. I kiss you thousands of times.

Yours,
Chaskel

FEBRUARY 21, 1942
From My Father to My Mother

As the war drags on, mail service becomes spotty, cutting off my father's heart-line to my mother. Nevertheless, he continues to write about the mundane and the monumental. At the midpoint, the handwriting of the letter changes from that of my father to that of his brother, Yosek. Yosek, with whose family my father has been living, explains that he was forced to rewrite my father's words because "otherwise it would have cost too much to send." It is possible that Yosek's handwriting is more compact, or that he deleted parts of the letter, thus using less paper and hence less postage.

My dearest darling ones whom I love so much,
It is already four months that I have not received a letter from you. But I hope that everything is okay with you.… My dearest Ernunah, you should know how much I miss you. It is already five and a half years since we got married. I would like to live until the moment that I can be together with you again.

I get letters from Gusta every week and I send all kinds of packages. I also get letters from Leibek. I am really okay and I have a good apartment. I still live with Yosek and Regina; they have a nice little girl and a very warm apartment.

(Chaskel goes on, but it is now in Yosek's handwriting.)

Thank God I have everything that I need and it is only you that I am missing. Maybe you can do what Sylvia is doing. She writes to her husband and he asks her about me.... I miss you and I yearn to be with you.

My dearest Ernunah, how are you? Are you healthy? How is our dearest son? Does he miss his father? Also, how is dear Mother? Does she still have pains from her legs? Does she have lots of problems from her little grandchild?

I kiss you thousands of times and I love you very much and I do not stop thinking about you.

Chaskel

From My Father to My Mother

As the first Polish Jews are unloaded at the Majdanek death camp in Lublin – under the direction of Operation Reinhard – my father pens the following letter to my mother. It will be the last letter she is to receive from him. He has not heard from her for six months. He tells of his new baby niece who "brings sunshine into the house," and who reminds him so much of the son he has never seen.

In just a few weeks the Sobibor extermination camp, in eastern Poland, will begin conducting industrial scale mass murder – first using carbon monoxide and then Zyklon B (hydrogen cyanide) gas. More than 250,000 men, women, and children will be murdered there over the next eighteen months.

April 27, 1942

My dearest darling ones that I miss so very much,

I send you regards from [Leon's brother] Yosek Lachter and I am sure that I will get something from you soon. My dearest darling Ernusha, you cannot imagine how much I miss you and how much I would like to be with you. I have everything that I need but you.

Regina and Yosek thank you very much for your congratulations on the birth of their daughter. She is a cute little girl. She is beautiful like our Murray Jack. She looks a little like our Murray Jack too. She really brings sunshine to the house – that is what a child does.

You, my darling, must be very happy to bring Murray Jack home. When I look at the photographs I feel as though I will be home soon also. Soon it will be his birthday, he will be two years old. So kiss him a lot from me. Kiss him every day one hundred times and I am sure that I will see him soon.

You will probably get a letter from Gusta very soon....

Everything is okay and everyone is well. Nothing else is new.

I kiss you a thousand times.

Yours,

Chaskel

This picture, brought to the US by my grandmother as promised in her October 23, 1940, letter (in chapter 7) is the last picture that I have of my father. His worsening condition is evident when this picture is compared to earlier pictures of my father.

CHAPTER TEN

Records of My Father's Journey

After opening the April 27, 1942, letter from my father, my mother never received another from him. While her efforts at learning of his whereabouts and his eventual fate over the following years remain mostly undocumented, there is little question that she continued her struggle long after losing contact with him. Despite facing an unending set of roadblocks that impeded her efforts to bring her husband to America – intentionally put in place by the US State Department's "closed door" policy toward Jewish immigration – I do not believe that she really gave up hope of finding him. As of October 15, 1945, five months after the war in Europe had ended, my mother was still addressing letters directly to my father. She did not learn of my father's ultimate fate until nearly a year later (see chapter 11).

The details of my father's journey are, for the most part, shrouded in the fog of war. Yet thanks to the scrupulous efforts of Yad Vashem, records assembled by the US Third Army, and other sources, I have been able to piece together a chronology, based on witness testimony, camp records, and historic data that, at this juncture, represents the most plausible accounting of my father's fate – up to a point. A point after which documented evidence is no longer available.

In this chapter I chronicle my father's path as far as verifiable and documented sources are able to take me. In the following chapter I will describe my mother's valiant efforts to obtain information about what became of my father, her sister, and their other relatives.

As you will read, both the documented and anecdotal evidence is sometimes contradictory and often confusing. I have, out of necessity, been required to accept the veracity of certain sources over others. While I cannot claim that the following narrative is a definitive recounting of my father's experiences, I do believe that it represents the most accurate account possible given the information available today. Copies of the most significant documents are included at the conclusion of this chapter.

As noted above, in March 1941, my father escaped being herded into the recently constructed Krakow ghetto by relocating to Radomysl Wielki, where he lived with his family. Fifteen months later, on June 30, 1942, an order was issued for all other Jews living in the surrounding countryside to relocate to Radomysl. Some twelve hundred men, women, and children from the region were soon absorbed by the town's Jewish households – where they nervously awaited their fate.

As in all similar towns throughout German-occupied Poland, the Jewish community of Radomysl had been ordered to form a Judenrat, a committee of community leaders forced by the Germans to facilitate the mechanics of its program of genocide. On July 2, the Judenrat received an order to provide a listing to the SS of all Jews aged sixty and older residing in Radomysl. Apparently the members of the Judenrat expressed some misgivings and the order was changed the following day. The list was now to contain the names of ALL Jews living in Radomysl...including the names of my father, his mother, his siblings, their spouses, and other family members, all of whom had previously moved to Radomysl.

On July 7, approximately five hundred Jewish men of the town, mostly those holding valued trade skills, were issued certification documents signed by the Gestapo. My father, an experienced furrier and machinist, was no doubt among them. This certification would prove extremely valuable in the days that lay ahead.

The Judenrat members quickly realized that the list they were being asked to provide was intended to serve as a deportation order and, out of desperation, they valiantly attempted to negotiate. The SS responded that if a certain sum could be raised by July 15 and turned over to them, the deportation order would be canceled. Amazingly, the money was raised in full and on time from an already impoverished Jewish population. It was turned over to the SS, but the deportation order was, in fact, not rescinded. The offer was a vicious lie intended to extract the last drop of wealth from the trapped Jews of Radomysl.

On July 15, according to plan, the Germans blocked all roads to and from the town. On the 17th, they summoned all Jews to appear in the central market square, where they performed an *Auswahl* or selection. The elderly and the infirm were segregated to one side of the square. Any person objecting to being separated from a loved one was shot openly on the spot. Dozens of children, including, in all likelihood, three of my father's nieces (my cousins) were murdered in plain sight.

The groups of elderly and infirm were marched to the nearby cemetery, where open pits had been prepared. They were shot at the edge of the pits and their bodies kicked into the mass grave. The remaining Jews, including my father, his brother Josef, and his brother-in-law Shmuel Kohane, were herded onto horse-drawn carts and taken to nearby Debica, a centralized concentration point for the entire region. There they waited under armed guard in an open field for two days.

On July 19 an *aktzia* took place at Debica. Those Jews not holding the special Gestapo-issued *protekzia* documents were savagely murdered by bludgeoning and gunfire. The *aktzia* was eagerly carried out by local Poles enlisted by the SS. Had my mother not acted bravely and managed to immigrate to the US in January 1940, this would have been the time and place where she, her mother, and her two-year old son (if he had not already been killed two days earlier) would also have been savagely murdered. But for my mother's courage and the grace of God, the murdered two-year-old boy would have been me.

The survivors of this bloodbath – the men who held the labor certifications, including my father, his brother, and his brother-in-law – were then packed onto waiting trains and deported to various destinations in the German camp systems.

On July 21, 1942, my father, along with hundreds of other Jewish men from Debica, including Josef and Shmuel, arrived at the notorious labor camp in the town of Mielec, about seventy miles from Krakow in southeastern Poland. Mielec was one of the first towns in occupied Poland to be made completely *Judenrein* by the SS. The nearby camp housed roughly eighteen hundred Polish and Austrian prisoners. My father, along with about 250 men, was assigned to work in the Ernst Heinkel Flugzeugwerke factory (previously known as the Polish National Aircraft Company), where, as a machinist, he was required to fabricate aircraft parts for the Luftwaffe.

As my father adjusted to life inside the Mielec labor camp, Jews in neighboring parts of Poland were being swallowed up by the Nazi killing machine. On August 27, 1942, the Jewish community of Niepolomice, where my mother's sister Gusta and her family had fled from Krakow, was liquidated. While it is not known if they were murdered during the *aktzia* in the town or deported to a death camp (my mother's cousin Leibek Ziller told Yad Vashem that Gusta and her family were murdered in Belzec), no member of that family was heard from again.

My aunt Gusta Hirschprung and her children Ruzunya and Yankush, who are presumed to have perished or been deported on August 27, 1942

One day in September 1942, a prisoner named Henek Sperling arrived in the Mielec labor camp. (Henek is now the husband of my cousin Mala.) He had been assigned to work at the Heinkel aircraft factory. There he encountered my father along with my uncles Josef and Shmuel. The four men worked together at the plant for the better part of the ensuing two years.

The following passages contain speculative assumptions about my father's experience while interned at the forced labor camp (later a concentration camp) at Mielec. They are drawn from various survivor testimonies including those collected in the book *Mielec, Poland: The Shtetl That Became a Nazi Concentration Camp* by Rochelle G. Saidel (Jerusalem: Gefen Publishing House, 2012). While my father was unable to record a testimony of his time at Mielec, I feel it safe to assume that his story closely paralleled the experiences of those who were able to do so.

In the fall of 1943 the Mielec camp was placed under the direction of SS Kommandant Hering. At about this point in time, the status of the camp was officially changed from a labor to a concentration camp. The fence around the camp was fully electrified. One touch meant certain death. My father, like all prisoners, was forced to endure the *Appells* or torturously lengthy roll calls that were held at 5 A.M. each day. A Polish Nazi collaborator, Rudolf Zimmermann, would routinely stride along the rows of prisoners each morning, looking each man in the eye. One blink could result in the prisoner being selected, taken away, and never seen again. Somehow my father managed to endure and survive these daily death rituals.

As the winter of 1943–44 dragged on, conditions became increasingly more extreme in Mielec. In February 1944, the camp was placed under the control of the obese and sadistic Oberscharfuehrer Josef Schwammberger, who replaced Kommandant Hering. My father, along with all of the camp's other prisoners, was forced to watch a public punishment of a young Jewish girl who was falsely accused of lying to Schwammberger. She was given twenty-five lashes on her naked body as Schwammberger and his wife stood by laughing.*

In March 1944, after having worked in the same street clothes he had been wearing when he was deported to Mielec nearly two years earlier, my father was issued a striped uniform bearing a yellow star. He was also tattooed on his right wrist by another prisoner with the letters KL, which stood for *Konzentrationslager* (concentration camp).

By late July, Soviet forces had advanced westward to within fifty miles of Mielec. On July 28, prior to the camp's liquidation set to take place in

---

* Josef Schwammberger escaped in 1948 to Argentina, where he lived openly until 1987. Thanks to the efforts of the Simon Wiesenthal Center, he was tracked down and eventually extradited to Germany. Schwammberger was convicted in 1992 in Stuttgart and sentenced to life imprisonment in Mannheim. He died in 2004 at age ninety-two.

August, my father and thousands of other prisoners were transferred to various labor and death camps. My father, his brother Josef, his brother-in-law Shmuel, and Henek Sperling were sent to Wieliczka, the site of a well-known salt mine.

On August 4, after spending but a few days in Wieliczka, my father, Josef, Shmuel, and Henek, along with a contingent of other prisoners, were transferred inside locked cattle cars to Flossenberg concentration camp in Germany. Once there, my father received the prisoner number 14788. His profession was there recorded as "mechanic." Flossenberg was the main camp of a broad system composed of nearly one hundred forced labor sub-camps. In addition to Jews, the camps interned political prisoners, German criminals, homosexuals, and Jehovah's Witnesses. The father of Ukraine's future president Viktor Yushchenko was also interned there. By this time, more than four thousand inmates were imprisoned in the main camp at Flossenberg.

On August 9, my father was transferred from Flossenberg to one of its largest sub-camps, Leitmeritz (also known as Arbeitslager Leitmeritz), about forty miles from Prague and near Terezin, in what is today the Czech Republic. More than eighteen thousand prisoners would pass through Leitmeritz during 1944 and 1945. As many as 4,500 inmates would perish in less than a year due to the Germans' ruthless exploitation of slave labor and the inhuman living conditions.

It was the Germans' plan to employ Leitmeritz laborers to construct an aircraft factory inside a nearby mountain that would provide camouflage and protection from Allied air raids. The man-made caves were also intended to house an underground munitions factory and two synthetic rubber plants code-named Richard I and Richard II. My father was likely put to work excavating the mountain, where he was forced to work under Czech engineers who handled the explosive charges. Polish Jewish prisoners were assigned to load the fallen debris and rocks onto carts and then remove them from the excavation site. It was hazardous and strenuous physical labor, which, coupled with the meager food rations, spelled death for many prisoners. In addition to starvation and exhaustion, many perished due to the frequent cave-ins and even more due to rampant outbreaks of typhus.

One of my father's co-prisoners, Meyer Megdal, gave the following account of daily life (and death) in Leitmeritz:

> As we were marched daily to work, surrounded by SS guards, we passed POW barracks. We noticed that the garbage cans in front of their kitchen contained potato peels. Our SS guards forewarned us not to touch those cans – that anyone caught helping himself to the potato peels would receive a lashing. This could not stop the starving inmates from doing it. We would hide the potato peels inside our shirts until we returned to our barracks.
>
> Each barrack contained a small iron stove with a pipe extending from the stove upward through the roof to the outside, permitting the smoke to escape. Upon return from work to our barrack, those of us who managed to get some potato peels would line up in front of the stove and [each would] wait for his turn to bake the peels on its hot top before devouring them....
>
> We did not always succeed in helping ourselves to the potato peels unnoticed. I remember the day when one of the SS guards caught me grabbing a few potato peels from a garbage can. He made me put them back in the garbage can and wrote down my ID number. The next morning during the *appel* my number was called and, before departing for work, I received 15 lashes from one of the SS guards.*

According to recovered German transport lists, on October 3, 1944, my father's brother Josef was transferred from Flossenberg/Leitmeritz to Bergen-Belsen. He was never heard from again. Shmuel was transported to Dachau, then to Natzweiler-Struthof (the only Nazi concentration camp on French soil), and then to Leonberg in the upper Seestrasse, where he perished on December 25, 1944, while working under catastrophic conditions as a forced slave laborer for the Messerschmitt AG aircraft company.

On October 13, something unusual happened. My father's name appeared on a transport list of prisoners being moved from Flossenberg/

---

* Meyer Megdal, *My Holocaust Testimony*, copyright © 1994 by Meyer Megdal; second edition © 2000 by Meyer Megdal, http://www.megdal.com/Meyer/Testimony.html. Used by permission.

Record card obtained from Yad Vashem documenting the date and place of Shmuel Kohane's death, as reported in July 1955

Leitmeritz to Mauthausen concentration camp, but it does not look as though he was actually on board the transport. Examining the transport manifest, one spies a small handwritten question mark to the left of my father's name. To the right of his date of birth there is a dash and a zero, instead of a check mark as is the case with almost all of the other names on the page (other than those that have a line running through them; see list below). These handwritten markings appear to indicate that my father was scheduled to be on this transport, but was not checked off as ever having boarded. Extensive searches in the voluminous documents recovered from Mauthausen have been unable to turn up a Mauthausen prisoner card issued to my father. His name is not listed in any Mauthausen memorial book, database, or genealogy record that either Yad Vashem or I have been able to locate.

Hence, I am left with the conclusion that, in all likelihood, my father was scheduled to travel on, but never actually boarded, the transport to Mauthausen on October 13, 1944. I suspect that this may be due to the fact that he was too ill, or perhaps too contagious, to travel.

At this point the trail of concentration camp records grows cold. Whatever actually happened to my father after October 13, 1944, can only be a matter of speculation. because there is no extant official documentation beyond this point. Nevertheless, my mother picked up the trail in early

1945. Initially trying to contact my father directly (not knowing if he was alive or dead) and later through inquiries to various agencies, letters from survivors, and eventually through the efforts of a *beit din* (Jewish court), she was able to obtain some indications about what became of her beloved husband. Her quest for the truth is chronicled in the following chapter.

Concentration Camp Records Concerning My Father

This card, created in 1951 by the US Third Army, contains information gained from the original German listing page shown on the next page. They both document that my father, Chaskel Goldwasser, Prisoner No. 14788, a Polish Jew, born June 17, 1908, arrived at the Flossenberg camp on August 4, 1944, from the Krakow/Plaszow area, which encompassed Mielec.

{Next page} Prisoner ledger page documenting the entry of my father (Chaskel Goldwasser) and his brother (Josef Goldwasser) into Flossenberg concentration camp on August 4, 1944. Once there, my father received the prisoner number 14788 while Josef was assigned number 14790. This page documents the transport of my uncle, Josef, to Bergen-Belsen on October 3, 1944.

14771	J. Pole	Goldmann Jankel	20.4.96	4.8.44 v. Plaszow	7
2	"	Goldmann Mortka	15.12.18	"	Berg-Belsen 15.45
3	J. Pole	Goldmann Markus	10.12.19	"	13.10.1944 Dachau
4	"	Goldmann Salomon	19.6.16	✝ 22.3.45	
5	J. Pole	Goldmuns Juder	9.10.05	"	9
6	"	Goldner Firvel	5.10.12	"	Berg-Belsen 10.44 Bolzen
7	J. Pole	Goldner Jankiel	1.4.22	"	14.10.44 Dachau
8	"	Goldner Pinkas	29.3.06	"	
9	"	Goldreich Chaim	12.1.28	"	11
14780	"	Goldreich Scil	20.4.28	"	11
1	J. Pole	Goldschein Joel	21.2.24	"	13.10.44 Dachau
2	J. Pole	Goldschmied Jakob	12.4.25	"	13.10.44 Dachau
3	J. Pole	Goldschein Adam	12.4.23	"	13.10.44 Dachau
4	J. Pole	Goldstein David	25.5.24	"	13.10.44 Dachau
5	J. Pole	Goldstein Jakob	1.10.05	"	13.10.44 Dachau
6	J. Pole	Goldstein Jakob	7.9.10	"	13.10.44 Dachau
7	"	Goldstein Josef	25.2.95	✝ 27.9.1944	
8	"	Goldwasser Chaskel	17.6.01	4.8.44 v. Plaszow	
9	J. Pole	Goldwasser Pinkus	2.1.23	"	13.10.44 Dachau Beigh
14790	"	Goldwasser Josef	26.3.4.	"	5.10.44 Bozen
1	J. Pole	Solowiczyk Leyba	16.5.16	"	13.10.44 Dachau
2	J. Pole	Golsauer Mortka	2.10.04	"	13.10.44 Dachau
3	J. Pole	Golter Berec	20.3.24	"	13.10.44 Dachau
4	J. Pole	Gorielow Benjamin	1.12.05	"	13.10.44 Dachau
5	J. Pole	Gottlieb Willi	23.1.19	"	13.10.44 Dachau
6	J. Pole	Gootnich Majer	27.3.17	"	14.8.44 Flossenbürg
7	"	Golsdanker Chaim	27.7.10	"	9.8.44 Leitmeritz
8	J. Pole	Gosdanker Bendes	28.6.06	"	13.10.44 Dachau
9	J. Pole	Gosdanker Michel	22.2.09	"	13.10.44 Dachau
14800	"	Gottmann Osriach	14.8.21	"	

Vor- und Zuname Goldwasser CHaskel   P.J.Haft-Nr. 14788
Beruf: SCHlosser   geboren am: 17.6.08   in: Krakau
Anschrifts-Ort   Straße Nr.
Eingel. am 24.8.44   Uhr von   K.L.Kra.– Entl. am   /   Uhr nach

Bei Einlieferung abgegeben   Koffer   Aktentasche   Paket
___ Hut/Mütze   ___ Paar Schuhe/Stiefel   ___ Kragenknöpfe   ___ Feuerzeug   ___ Wehrpaß
___ Mantel   ___ Paar Strümpfe   ___ Halstuch   ___ Tabak   Pfeife   ___ Fremdenpaß
___ Rock   Bade   ___ Paar Gamaschen Zub   ___ Taschentuch   ___ Zigarren/Zigaretten ___ Arbeitsbuch
___ Weste/Kletterweste ___ Kragen   ___ Paar Handschuhe Zub ___ Zig. Blättchen ___ Invalidenkarte
___ Hose   ___ Vorhemd   ___ Brieftasche mit ___ Ziertuch
___ Pullover   ___ Binder/Fliege   ___ Papiere   ___ Messer   Schere   /
___ Oberhemden   ___ Paar Armelhalter   ___ Sporthemd/Hosen ___ Bleistift/Drehblei
___ Unterhemden   ___ Paar Sockenhalter   ___ Abzeichen   ___ Geldbörse
___ Unterhosen   ___ Paar Mansch.-Knöpfe ___ Schlüssel a. Ring ___ Kamm   Wertsachen: ja—nein

        Abgabe bestätigt: Effektenverwalter

     Goldwasser   Grünla

My father's personal effects registration card at Flossenberg. This ruse was intended to convince prisoners that there was some hope of their eventual release when their personal items would be returned. My father, having been transported from a slave labor camp, had no personal items whatsoever.

Date	14.11.49/ LL	Flossenb.No. 14788 Pole Jude.
Name	GOLDWASSER, Chaskel	File GCC 5/IC/2
BD	17.6.08 BP	Nat Polish Jew.
Next of Kin		
Source of Information	Uberstell. v.AL Leitmeritz nach Mauth.	
Last kn. Lokation	(Juden)	Datel. 13.10.44
CC/Prison	Flossenb/Leit- Arr. meritz	lib.
Transf. on	13.10.44 to Mauthausen	
Died on	in	
Cause of death		
Buried on	in	
Grave		D. C. No.
Remarks	Lfd.No. 145	

This index card, prepared by the US Third Army in 1949, indicates that my father was scheduled to be transported from Flossenberg to Mauthausen on October 13, 1944. It is now believed that he never boarded that transport.

In this critical, circled detail of the original transport listing of prisoners being moved to Mauthausen from Flossenberg on October 13, 1944, my father's name is listed at line 145. Yet note the question mark to the left of his prisoner number. Also note the dash, rather than a checkmark, next to his date of birth on the right. Finally note the zero next to the far right column. It is presumed that this manifest document was used at the time of departure to check off prisoners as they boarded. The fact that my father's name was not checked off in the column on the right,, along with the absence of any record of my father's presence in Mauthausen, together indicate that he never boarded this train and was never interned at Mauthausen.

				- 324 -				
Goldwais,	Grischa	49085	,		lo.12.09	13. 2.45	lo. 3.45	Bu
Goldwasser,	Beuajon	26521	PJ		1. 9.00	lo. 9.44	.lo. 1.43	T
Goldwasser,	Blanka	64334	PJ		2o. 2.21	8. 3.45	,	
Goldwasser,	Blima	52877	PJ		1. 6.18	15. 9.44	.6. 2.45	Ra
Goldwasser,	Chaskel	14788	PJ		17. 6.08	4. 8.44	,	
Goldwasser,	Josef	1479o	PJ		26. 3.1o	4. 8.44	.3.1o.44	BB
Goldwasser,	Rosa	54635	J		12. 4.2o	9.1o.44		
Goldwasser,	Tinkero	14789	PJ		2. 1.23	4. 8.44	13.1o.44	Da
Goldweiss,	Wolf	46521	PJ		5. 5.11	6. 2.45	,	
Goldyn,	Josef	4o 58	P		4. 3.12	12.1o.43	13. 8.44	T
Goldyriew.	Iwan	2662	Rp	,	12.12.21	7.12.43	,	

This detail from a list of Flossenberg inmates, prepared by the US Third Army from actual handwritten German transcripts similar to the one shown on page 162, corroborates the fact that my father was not transferred to Mauthausen. The second from the right column lists the date of each prisoner's transfer, and the last column lists an abbreviation of the camp to which the prisoner was sent. Both columns remain blank in my father's case. Compare it to the following listing, which names my father's brother Josef, who arrived on the same date as my father, but was transferred on October 3 1944, to BB (Bergen-Belsen).

22/1/1993

Dear Murray;

I am sending to you the information you requested to the best of my knowledge and as much as I remember in a very short version.

I arrived in Mielec (a K.Z. camp in Poland) from Nei Sandz (Nowy Sacz) ghetto in the beginning of September 1942. We worked there in an airplane factory "Henkel No. 111". There I remember seeing your father Haskel Goldwasser. I remember him always beeing in the company of two other men, another Mr. Goldwasser and Mr. Kahane.

Sometime in July or August of 1944 as the Russian front was advancing from the east, the camp Mielec was liquidated and we were transported in locked box cars to another camp in Wieliczka Poland to work in underground previously existing salt mines that were changed into airplane factories where we were forced to manufacture parts for airplanes.

After approximatly three weeks to a month we were again put into locked box cars and sent to Flossenburg, Germany. There we were seperated into different groups and sent to different camps.

I was sent to Chechoslovakia to the K.Z. camp Leitmeritz (Zytomiezyce) There we had to build underground tunnels which were to be used as war industries.

Part of our people were left in Flossenburg, Germany and I have no knowledge of what happened to them.

From Leitmeritz, as the Russian front kept advancing closer, we were again transported in box cars to the camp Mauthausen in Austria. That was sometime in October 1944.

We stayed there for about a week and then again transported in box cars to K.Z. camp Guzen Il in Austria. Every day we were taken in box cars to work to underground tunnels to a place called St. George. We worked there at Messerschmidt airplanes No. 109. The distance from camp to work was approximatly 10 to 15 miles.

Finaly we were liberated by the American army on May 5th 1945. From there I and some other fellow prisoners walked to the city of Linz, Austria.

When we arrived from Austria to America to your house on 822 Emerson Ave. in Elizabeth, I recognized a man from a photo on the wall as beeing with me in camp Mielec and Mala told me that it was your father Haskel Goldwasser. That is all I remember pertaining to your father.

Warm regards to Linda, your children and grandchildren and the whole family.
If you have any questions do not hesitate to ask me.

Love and best wishes
Henry and Mala.

This 1993 letter from my cousin Mala Sperling's husband, Henry (Henek), to me confirms the journey of my father, his brother, his brother-in-law, and Henry from Mielec to Wieliczka to Flossenberg and to Leitmeritz.

CHAPTER ELEVEN

The Search for Abraham Goldwasser

As the world emerged from the conflagration of World War II, the American public began to gain glimpses – slowly at first and then with accelerating frequency – of what had actually transpired in the Nazi death camps. Mostly via horrific newsreel footage of emaciated naked bodies being bulldozed into pits and stacked like cordwood under the disgusted gaze of General Eisenhower, the depravity of Hitler's "Final Solution" played out across movie screens and into the consciousness of many Americans.

My mother's efforts at locating my father, from whom she had not heard since mid-1942, began during the closing days of the war in Europe. She understood fully that a great many Jews had perished, but that some had survived. Armed with this knowledge and her boundless optimism, she began to piece together the facts surrounding my father's fate. At that time my mother knew nothing of the records discussed in the previous chapter.

By late February 1945, an Allied victory in Europe was all but assured. The Red Army had liberated Auschwitz, and US troops would soon do the same at Buchenwald. My mother, believing that with such Allied advances, mail service might have been restored, sent an impassioned postcard dated February 27, 1945, to her long-lost husband.

The postcard was addressed to my father in care of the Teichman family in Radomysl, the last address given to her by my father. It did not reach Radomysl until months after the war had ended, on August 24, 1945, at which time it was forwarded to Mielec. It was ultimately returned to my mother in Brooklyn as undeliverable.

The text of the postcard is shown translated to English below. Note my signature (MURRAY) in the lower right corner of the original postcard.

My dearest Chaskel,

It's been so long since we had any news from you and from my dear family, and we are worried. I found out today that the mail will again be delivered, so I am writing to you at the last address I knew.

I am praying very hard to God that you personally will be able to receive this writing.

We are waiting for news from everyone with terrible longing.

We are healthy, our darling son is very sweet and he always talks about his darling father. Please write to us as soon as you can about you and the family.

I kiss you, Erna. Kisses from Murray and mother.

AUGUST 15, 1945

Postcard from Moses Grunbaum to My Mother

On February 27, 1945, my mother also wrote to her sister Gusta at her last known address in Niepolomice. She received a response dated August 15, 1945, from the Jewish Committee of Niepolomice, informing her that Gusta and her family had all been deported in 1942 and were presumed dead. My mother also was informed that her cousin Markus Goldwasser and his entire family had all been killed.* The original is shown in Polish below the English translation.

---

* This, in fact, was not true. At least three of Markus Goldwasser's children survived and later lived in Israel.

OCTOBER 15, 1945

Final Letters from My Mother to My Father and Her Sister

With the war finally ended, Jews around the world embarked on the task of reassembling their lives and their families. By October 1945, mail service had been restored in Europe and so my mother here attempts to contact my father by sending this tragic note to him in care of "Concentration Camp in Germany." In my mother's case, as with most Americans, the enormity of the Holocaust had not yet sunk in. The very idea that innocent noncombatants like her husband and her sister had been senselessly murdered was still very difficult for her to accept at this point.

Not yet ready to face the finality of her sister's death, despite the message from Moses Grunbaum, my mother sent a similarly addressed letter to Gusta. Both letters were returned.

10/15/1945

My dearest Chaskel,

Even though I am trying so hard, I still don't have any news from you and have no idea where you are.

I know you were in Mielec in 1942 at the Flugzeugwerke [airplane factory], and then what?

I pray so hard to God that you should receive this letter.

Where is the rest of the family? My sister Gusta Hirschprung?

We are awaiting news from you with great longing.

Mother and I are healthy and our son is sweet and wonderful. He talks about you.

Please write very soon, we will do whatever we can to help you.

Your wife Erna, Mother and Murray

The letters sent by my mother to my father and to her sister bearing the generic address "c/o Concentration Camp in Germany" were returned. Both envelopes were stamped "MILITARY CENSORSHIP." But the letters themselves were unmarked. A pencil-written note on the returned envelope to Gusta read: "Not UNRRA."

The United Nations Relief and Rehabilitation Administration was a

Envelope of my mother's October 15, 1945, letter to my father. Both this letter and a similar one addressed to her sister were returned due to insufficient address.

largely US-sponsored postwar agency established to deal with Europe's war-stricken refugees. By the time my mother's letter reached Europe, the concentration camps had been converted to UNRRA-managed refugee camps. My mother now turned from attempting to contact her relatives directly to approaching and seeking out help from volunteer and governmental agencies.

On November 20, 1945, my mother wrote to the Joint Distribution Committee's Paris office (see below). The Joint Distribution Committee (JDC or "the Joint"), on whose board I have served for several years, is a worldwide Jewish relief agency that celebrated its one hundredth anniversary in 2014. The massive task of rescuing and resettling hundreds of thousands of Jewish DPs (displaced persons) fell squarely on the shoulders of the Joint in the aftermath of the Holocaust. If any agency would be able to assist in locating her husband, it would be the Joint.

My mother's November 20 letter noted that she had not received any correspondence from her husband for three years. My mother pointed out that she had recently received correspondence from a cousin, sent from Krakow on September 26. In the cousin's letter, he informed my mother that he had just returned to Krakow from a German concentration camp and that my father had been in Dachau in 1944. I have been unable to identify this cousin of my mother's or to find his September 26 letter. The Krakow genealogical records identify two sons of Markus Goldwasser as among my mother's male cousins.* It may well have been one of these men who provided the information (about my father being in Dachau) to my mother. In any event, based on this newly received "sighting," my mother asked the Joint to try to locate her husband.

---

* My maternal great-grandmother, Gittel Goldwasser, married Wigdor Hirsch in an unregistered ceremony; some of her children therefore carried the surname Goldwasser, while others were known as Hirsch. Markus was a brother of my grandmother Leah Grunfeld. On her wedding certificate my grandmother's maiden surname was recorded as Goldwasser.

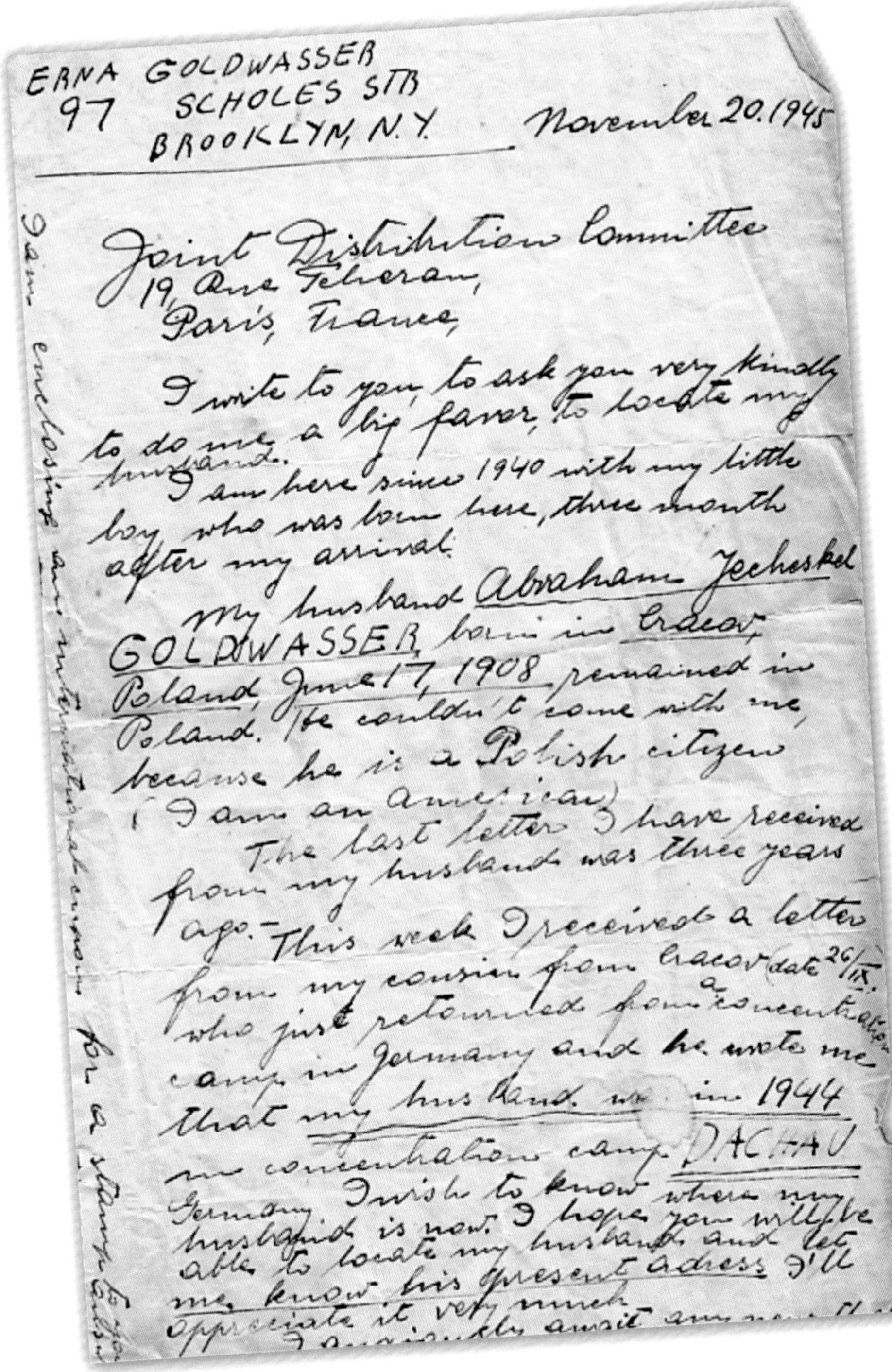

ERNA GOLDWASSER
97 SCHOLES STB
BROOKLYN, N.Y.   November 20. 1945

Joint Distribution Committee
19 Ave Teheran,
Paris, France,

I write to you, to ask you very kindly
to do me a big favor, to locate my
husband. I am here since 1940 with my little
boy who was born here, three month
after my arrival.
My husband Abraham Zechaskel
GOLDWASSER, born in Cracov,
Poland, June 17, 1908, remained in
Poland. He couldn't come with me,
because he is a Polish citizen
(I am an american)
The last letter I have received
from my husband was three years
ago. This week I received a letter
from my cousin from Cracov date 26/IX.
who just returned from concentrations
camp in Germany and he wrote me
that my husband was in 1944
in concentration camp DACHAU
Germany. I wish to know where my
husband is now. I hope you will be
able to locate my husband and let
me know his present adress. I'll
appreciate it very much
I anxiously await answer. ...

I am enclosing an international answer for a stamp ...

In November 1945, my mother received this stark and tersely worded postcard in response to her inquiry made nine months earlier. It is from an official of the town of Mielec, in which he coldly states that there is no information about the whereabouts of any of her family members and that they are all "most likely" dead. The original is displayed below the English translation version.

```
POST CARD                              [stamp: POCZTA POLSKA 1]

Honored Lady,

I am letting you know that of the
family Goldwasser, no one is in Mielec
and most likely, not alive.

Regards.
H. Stieler (?)
```

HIAS, the Hebrew Sheltering and Immigrant Aid Society, was founded in the US during the late nineteenth century to assist in the settlement of newly arrived Jewish immigrants from Russia and the Pale of Settlement. By the 1940s HIAS was operating around the world in providing aid to displaced Jews.

On January 8, 1946, my mother completed this HIAS form designed for American relatives to communicate with Jewish refugees in Europe. Apparently based on the information she had received from her cousin in his September 26, 1945, letter, my mother gave my father's address as "Concentration Camp Dachau," noting that he "was there in 1944." But the handwritten note at the top of the form, presumably written after it was received by HIAS, reads, "Are not in Dachau."

On February 16, 1946, my mother again wrote to the JDC Paris office (see below). She provided them with an update based on a recently-received letter from a friend of my father's in Poland. The friend had written that he was interned together with my father in several concentration camps in Poland and then in a camp in Germany. The friend advised that in November 1944 my father was transferred from Augsburg in Bavaria to Dachau among a transport of sick prisoners. My mother again asked the JDC to see if they could locate her husband based on this newly unearthed information.

Not having heard back from HIAS, on February 17, 1946, my mother again wrote a letter using a HIAS form. The letter was written in Polish this time and addressed to my father in Dachau, Germany, where she believed he was last seen alive. In this letter, my mother identifies Henryk Metzendorf as the source of her information that my father was transferred in November 1944 from Augsburg to Dachau.

The English translated version and the original of this letter are both included below.

According to German concentration camp records, Henryk Metzendorf was in Mielec, Flossenberg, and Leitmeritz at the same times as my father. He was transferred to Augsburg (a sub-camp of Dachau) on October 25, 1944, and then transferred to the Natzweiler and Leonberg camps in December 1944.

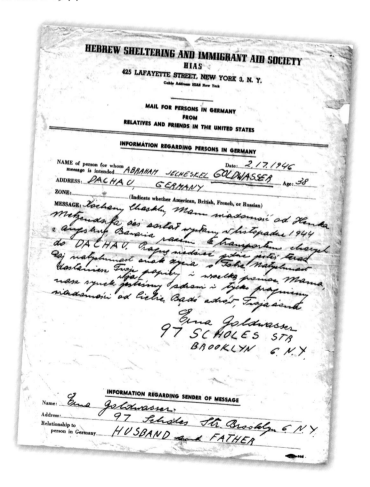

February 17, 1946

Dearest Chaskel,

*I received some news from Henryk Metzendorf that you were trans-
ported in November 1944 from Augsburg, Bavaria, with a transport of
sick people to Dachau.*

*I long to know where you are now. Please send me an immediate sign
of life and you will right away get your papers and any help you need.*

*Mother, our sweet son and I are healthy. We only long to hear from
you. Stay well, your wife,*

Erna Goldwasser, 97 SCHOLES STR, BROOKLYN 6, N.Y.

On March 16, 1946, my mother was advised that the JDC had received
her February 16 letter of inquiry. They informed her that JDC representatives in Germany had been contacted about the case. They asked my
mother to forward my father's last known address.

On March 22, 1946, my mother responded (see below). She informed
the JDC that our family's long-standing address had been 9 Josefa Street
in Krakow. She explained that prior to the establishment of the Krakow ghetto, in 1941, my father and his family (including his mother) were forced to relocate to Radomysl Wielki, near Mielec. She retraced his path as she understood it at that time, explaining that he was taken, along with his brother Josef and brother-in-law Shmuel Kohane, to Mielec, where the men worked for several years in an aircraft factory before being sent to various concentration camps throughout Germany.

My mother stated that Josef died of typhus at some point prior to April 1944. This information is contradicted by the German passenger manifests that listed Josef as having been transported into Flossenberg on August 4, 1944, and out of Flossenberg to Bergen-Belsen on October 3, 1944 (see previous chapter). She placed my father in Augsburg in Bavaria and believed he was part of a transport of sick prisoners taken to Dachau in November 1944. This is information she had gathered from Henryk Metzendorf's letter.

My mother wrote that she "knows for sure" that my father is not in Krakow, in Radomysl, or in Mielec. She closed by imploring the JDC to search and help her locate him.

Weeks of waiting culminated in further disappointment. On May 16, 1946, a telegram arrived from her attorney Ben Aron. It was addressed to my mother and stated:

> Records checked at War and State Departments as well UNRRA fail to disclose any information concerning parties. Investigation here ended.

On July 9, 1946, the Jewish Information Office at Dachau advised my mother, in German, that *"Abraham Jecheskel Goldwasser bei uns nicht registriert ist und auch nicht war"* (Abraham Jecheskel Goldwasser is not registered with us and never was).

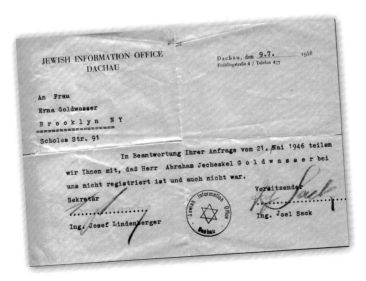

At the time my father was presumed to have been transported to Dachau, it was unlikely that the Germans were recording the names of all of the sick prisoners being evacuated from eastern camps. Although neither my mother nor I were able to obtain official confirmation of the fact that my father was transported to Dachau, other evidence (including Henryk Metzendorf's September 26 letter mentioned in my mother's correspondence, as well as the letter from my mother's unnamed male cousin) suggests that Dachau was a stop along his journey. In addition, and apparently unbeknownst to my mother, in December 1945, Pola Goldwasser, the daughter of Markus Goldwasser, submitted a report to the Stockholm office of the World Jewish Congress, in which she said that my father was in Dachau in 1944.

Despite these reports of my father's presence in Dachau, Yad Vashem conducted its own research and concluded, as was stated in the letter from the Dachau Jewish Information Office, that he was never there.

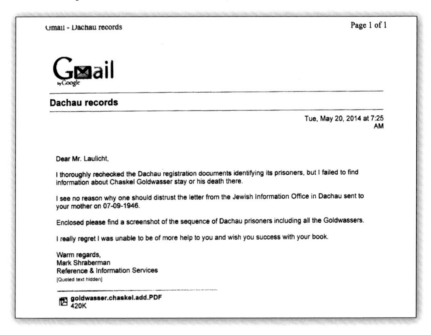

In this e-mail correspondence dated May 20, 2014, from Mark Shraberman, Director of Reference and Information Services at Yad Vashem in Jerusalem, with whom I had spoken numerous times, Mr. Shraberman recounts that he was unable to find any information about my father among the Dachau archives. The e-mail was accompanied by a screenshot listing all the prisoners at Dachau named Goldwasser. My father, Chaskel, is not among them.

More bad news for my mother's efforts to learn my father's fate followed on the heels of the letter from the Jewish Information Office in Dachau. On July 18, 1946, my mother heard back from the JDC once again. They still had no information about my father:

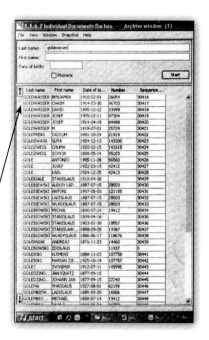

> ...to date we have had no report from our German offices with reference to your husband. We are still keeping open our files, and should we have any definite information we will communicate with you immediately.

My father's name, Chaskel Goldwasser, should have appeared here if there were a record of his being interned at Dachau.

The following day, July 19, 1946, brought another reply, and although it provided no information about my father's fate, it did contain a name that would figure largely in the days and years ahead.

In its letter to Bennett Aron, the US State Department responded to the attorney's June 12 inquiry in behalf of two of his clients who were searching for missing spouses. One, of course, was my mother. The other was the husband of one "Chana Scheindla Laulich" (shown as Scheindel Chana Laulicht in the Krakow genealogical records) who had been taken from Krakow to an unknown fate. She was being sought by her husband, Philip Laulicht, who, like my mother, had managed to immigrate to America.

The letter afforded precious little hope. It explained that the State Department was, at that time, examining the records of numerous German concentration camps. Once that review had been completed, and the data collated, it would be turned over to the respective governments of the nations that were affected. Mr. Aron was advised to contact the Polish government – either directly or via its acting consul general in New York – to learn the fate of the two missing people he was seeking.

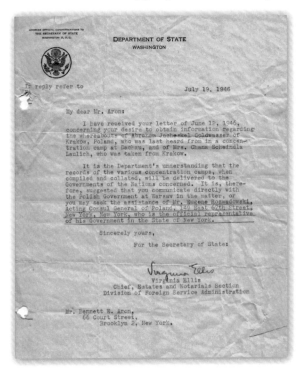

Mr. Aron's other client, Philip Laulicht, who had likewise been advised that his wife had perished, was introduced to my mother by their mutual friends Sol and Ann Gutfreund in 1945 or 1946. During the summer of 1946, Philip Laulicht and my mother decided to marry.

But as both my mother and Philip Laulicht were observant Jews, there was a serious question that had to be resolved before any wedding could take place: Was my mother an *agunah*? The state of *igun* (being an *agunah*, meaning literally "chained" or "anchored") is the Talmudic description of the status of a wife who is unable to remarry because her husband has disappeared or is unwilling to grant her a *get* (a legal bill of divorcement). According to Jewish law, a woman may not be married to more than one man simultaneously; any previous marriage must be definitively terminated before she is free to marry again. In the case of a missing husband, there is some concern lest he reappear, in which case the woman would turn out to be married to two men at once. A missing spouse must therefore be declared dead by a *beit din* (a Jewish court) – assuming there is plausible evidence to support this conclusion – before the surviving spouse may be permitted to remarry.

Sol and Ann Gutfreund, good friends who introduced my mother to my second father, Philip Laulicht, in 1946

As did many observant Jews who found themselves in similar straits in those days, the couple contacted the major Orthodox rabbinic authority, the Agudas Harabonim, also known as the Union of Orthodox Rabbis of the United States and Canada, located in New York. They presented whatever information they had collected about the likely fates of their respective spouses and awaited a reply. It was soon forthcoming.

In the case of my mother's inquiry, the members of the New York *beit din* had gone to the length of contacting their counterparts in Poland, the Chief Rabbinate of Krakow, to investigate this matter. After hearing back, they formulated the following determination and forwarded it to my mother in August 1946:

At a sitting of the *beit din* that took place in the office of the Agudas Harabonim on Thursday, the 11th day of Av (August 8, 1946), in which Rabbis H. Bick, M. Falik, and Y. Chamudos participated, they adjudicated the matter of the *agunah* Mrs. Esther Chaya Goldwasser.

And after receiving testimony from the Chief Rabbinate of Krakow, that witnesses came and testified that they saw that her husband Avraham Yechezkel ben Moshe Goldwasser had died and afterwards he was burned, relying upon this and in combination with additional letters attesting to this, the *beit din* decided to permit her to marry. If the civil government agrees based on its laws that she may remarry, then there exists no barrier, from a halachic point of view, to her marrying someone else according to the laws of Moses and of Israel.

This certificate is given by us to her as a sign and as proof.

Sealed by me on this date.

Signed:

Rabbi Mordechai Schustman,

Recording Secretary in *agunah* matters

For the Agudas Harabonim

אגודת הרבנים דארצות הברית וקנדה
THE UNION OF ORTHODOX RABBIS
OF THE UNITED STATES AND CANADA
132 NASSAU STREET
(SUITE 1221)
NEW YORK 7, N. Y.

RECTOR 2 - 2376
2377

ב"ה

בישיבת בית דין שחיתה בלשכת אגודת הרבנים ביום ה י"א מנ"א, ושתשתתפ
בת הרבנים הרב ח.ביק ח.פאלאק ,מחמודות. דנו על דבר עגונה מרת אסתר א
חיאגאלדוואסער. ואתרי החקבל גב"ע מהרבנות הראשית דקראקוב, שעדים העיד/
שראו אותו בעלה אברהם יחזקאל בן משה גאלדוואסער מת ואחר כך נשרף
על סמך זה ובצירוף עוד מכתבים שתעידו על זה החליטו להתירה לשוק.
ואם יסכימו על זה הסודרת הממשלה על פי נמוסי המדינה שתנשא לאיש אז א
אין שום מניעה מצד רת חוה"ק שתנשא לאיש כדת משה וישראל.
וניתן השורה הזאת בידה לאות ולראיה .
באתי על החתום יום ועש ק שבח נחמו שנת תש"ו
נאום הרב מרדכי שוסטמאן
מזכיר הועד לעניני עיגון ועגונות ע"י אגוה"ר דאה"ב וקנדא

The ruling of the *beit din* clearly adjudicated that my father had died, thus permitting my mother to remarry. But the *beit din* said nothing about the details of his death. Where did he die? Exactly when did he die? What was the cause of his death?

Nevertheless, the *beit din*'s determination did contain one bit of important and heretofore unknown information. According to the report received from the Chief Rabbinate of Krakow, witnesses there testified that they saw that my father's body had been burned after his death. This necessarily meant that my father had died in a place where his body could have been cremated, such as a concentration camp or a death camp – but not on a death march.

Until I started work on this book, I had always believed that my father died on a death march. This is what I recall that my mother had told me on the few occasions when she talked about my father's death.

I also had a vague recollection of being told by two or three people at a wedding in the 1950s that they had been with my father on a death march when he died. Unfortunately, I do not recall whose wedding it was, I did not keep a record of the witnesses' names, and I have been unable to locate them since. I was, however, told by researchers at Yad Vashem what I have always known as a lawyer: undocumented reports drawn from witness testimony, such as the report from Krakow, as well as verbal statements recounted anecdotally (such as the statement made some sixty years ago that I vaguely recall), may not always be accurate.

While the *beit din* did not say where, when, or how my father died, at some point, my mother determined that my father had perished on December 3, 1944, in Flossenberg and that the cause of death was typhus. She wrote several undated statements, two of which are reprinted on the following page, to this effect.

My husband ABRAHAM JECHESKEL GOLDWASSER were an arm band "Star David"

since end of 1939. In 1941 he went from Cracow,Poland to Radomysl

Wielki,then to Mielec where he did forced labor for German airplanes

in by "Henkel Flugzeug Werke". until June or July 1944.
He was transfered with other sick people to Flossenburg.
After he was sent to several Conc.Camps in Germany.He died from typhus

in Flossenburg December 3.1944 .I came here Feb.1.1940 (left Poland Dec.29.39)
I was pregnant (I have a letter from a German doctor).My son was born in
Brooklyn,May 12.1942 1940
Witness: Henryk Sperling   89 Mildred Terr. Clark,N.J/07066

Abraham Jecheskel GOLDWASSER wore
an arm band "Star David since end
of 1939. In 1941 went from Cracow
to Radomysl Wielki,then to Mielec
where he did forced labor for
Germans by airplanes. Beginning 1944
he was send to several concentr.camps
in Germany, From CC Flossenburg was
sent to Augsburg ,Bavaria. In November
1944 was transfered with a transport
of sick people back to Flossenburg.
Died December 3,1944

Unfortunately, neither the records that my mother kept, nor extensive research by the staff of Yad Vashem and by me has uncovered documentation to substantiate my mother's conclusion. As noted in the prior chapter, the October 13, 1944, list of prisoners who were supposed to be transported from Leitmeritz to Mauthausen is the last official record concerning my father. As also noted, my mother received information from a cousin that my father was in Germany during 1944 and from one of my father's friends that he had been sent to Augsburg, a sub-camp of Dachau, in November 1944. But there is no extant record that my father was ever in Mauthausen or Augsburg or Dachau or, for that matter, that he was in Flossenberg or Leitmeritz after October 13, 1944.

It is possible that the testimony and letters sent by the Chief Rabbinate of Krakow to the Agudas Harabonim might have resolved these uncertainties. But those records have apparently been lost over the many decades since then. The current administrator of the essentially inactive Agudas Harabonim has advised that in his fifty years with them, he had never come across any records or files pertaining to the *agunah beit din*.

While I do not know the basis upon which my mother concluded that my father died of typhus on December 3, 1944, in Flossenberg, I also do not have any basis upon which to question her conclusion. The Hebrew date for December 3, 1944, was the 17th of Kislev, and that is the date on which I have observed my father's *yahrzeit* for more than sixty years. In almost all of those years, I have read for the congregation, with some emotional difficulty, the Torah portion for that week, which includes the verses from Genesis, chapter 32, quoted at the beginning of this book.

May my father's memory continue to be a blessing for many years.

July 9.1973,

Women's World
1640 Rhode Island Ave, N.W.
Washington, D.C. 20036

LET'S HOPE & PRAY NEVER AGAIN

To whom it may concern:

Here are some names,ages and occupations of some of my
relatives and friends who perished in the Nazi Holocaust:

Abraham Yecheskel Goldwasser,Krakow,Jozefa 9.Poland,my husband,
born in Kracov June 17,1908 furier died in C.C.Dec.1944

Gusta Hilsprung,Krakow,Sebastjana 10,Poland my sister,born
in Kracov,Dec.30.1902 housewife, my sister

her husband
Simche Hirsprung,Sebastjana 10,Krakow,my brother in-law,
born in Krakow 1898 merchand

their two children:
Reizel Hirsprung address as above born Oct,1.1930 student(young)
Jacob Hirsprung   "   "   "   born Dec.1.1931   "   "

Feige Pessel Goldwasser,Welnica 4.Krakow my mother-in-law
housewife *widow*

her children
Chana Kahane (born Goldwasser)Welnica 4.Krakow, my sister-in-law
housewife born 1910

her husband Samuel Kahane address as above,my brother in-law
merchand died in CC Dec.1944 (together with my husband)

Joseph Goldwasser,Krakow,my brother in-law born 1912 merchand

his wife Regina Goldwasser housewife

Jacob Goldwasser,Welnica 4.Krakow,my brother in-law born 1914
Zofja Goldwasser   "   " my sister-in-law born 1916 Srudent

Helena Pinkesfeld,Krakow,Dietla 50.my aunt housewife
Abraham Pinkesfeld (her son)Dietla 50.my cousin

Lea Kernreich,Orzeszkowa 10,Krakow,housewife (my cousin
her daughter Cecilja young student

Schachne Grunfeld,ul.Kordeckiego 4,Krakow,my uncle,merchand
his wife Yetta Grunfeld   "   "   my aunt housewife
their married children with spents: *wifes*   hir wife Perla
Ignac Grunfeld,Benerowska my cousin merchand his wife Erna
Eliasz Grunfeld,Krakow   my "   "
Saul Grunfeld,Krakow Grodzka 71.merchand my uncle his wife Regina
his son Szymen Grunfeld,Krakow,lawyer and wife my cousin
his daughters :Reza,Ewa,Melanja my three cousins

Noe and Ruchla Frei,Krakow,Jozefa 9. merchands my neighbors
Amalja Feiler,widow with three children Lea,Jadwiga and L
         Krakow,Josefa 9.my neighbors

name is :Ernestine Laulicht,67-30 Clyde St.Forg
                                              U.S

In her letter to the Women's World arm of B'nai Brith, written on July 9, 1973, my mother
lists many members of our family who perished during the Holocaust. In it, she indicates
her belief that my father died in a concentration camp in December 1944. Note the
poignant handwritten message in the letter's upper right corner: LET'S HOPE AND PRAY,
NEVER AGAIN.

B'NAI B'RITH 1640 RHODE ISLAND AVENUE, NORTHWEST, WASHINGTON, D.C. 20036 · (202) 393-5284

INTERNATIONAL COUNCIL
Cabinet On Israel Affairs

October 9, 1973

Ms. Ernestine Laulicht
67-30 Clyde Street
Forest Hills, New York 11375

Dear Ms. Laulicht:

Many thanks for the information about the victims of the Holocaust
you sent Women's World for registration with Yad Vashem in Jerusalem.
This information about the members of your family who died the
death of martyrs during the Nazi terror will be preserved for
future generations. Perpetuation of their memory should inspire
all of us to greater deeds and service for our people.

Sincerely,

Hy Bornstein
Field Representative

HB/ek

The response from B'nai Brith indicates that my mother's information was being registered with Yad Vashem.

CHAPTER TWELVE

My Second Father

While my mother learned that under halachic law she was free to remarry, the question of Phillip Laulicht's status remained briefly in question. The *beit din*'s response to his petition concerning his own status arrived in September 1946. It stated:

> At a sitting of the *beit din* held on Wednesday, the 8th day of Elul 5706 (September 4, 1946), in the office of the Agudas Harabonim, in which participated Rabbi [*illegible*], Rabbi Leutman, and Rabbi Feinstein, they adjudicated the matter of Reb Feivel ben Chaim Ovadyah Laulicht, who had several letters stating that his wife was sent to places of killing. And relying on this, he is now permitted to remarry.
>
> And this is given to him as witness and proof.

A copy of the handwritten original determination is reproduced below.

Based upon the clearances received from the *beit din*, the couple proceeded with their wedding plans and on September 14, 1946, Philip Laulicht married my mother. As she faced the future, my mother was intent on building a new family in her newly adopted homeland. A key part of this process was providing a father figure for me, her young son, who had, for my first six and a half years, never known one.

Me (*far right*) at age five in orphanage. Note yarmulke on my head.

I had been brought up solely by my mother and grandmother with occasional stays in institutions during those periods when they did not have the ability to care for me at home. In my mother's eyes, I was the last remaining vestige of the husband she tragically had lost. She simply could not bear to do anything that I might find unwelcome or unpleasant. Hence, it was impossible for her to properly discipline me and, as a result, I became something of a willful and "wild" child. By the time I turned six, my mother recognized the direction I was heading and realized that our family needed a male presence – if for no other reason than to provide a stronger role model and some discipline for her rambunctious son.

Exactly when and where did Erna meet Philip? The answer is unclear. It is possible that they knew each other in Poland before the war, although I have not seen any direct evidence of this. What makes this a possibility is the fact that Philip Laulicht owned a large grocery business located on the same street in Krakow (Josefa Street) where my mother grew up and where she and my father had lived. It is safe to assume that even if my mother did not know Philip personally at the time, she was probably familiar with his business enterprise. The grocery is depicted on the cover of the December 2009 issue of *HaModia* magazine. The name F. (for Feiwel, Philip's Yiddish name) Laulicht may be clearly read on the sign (see photo).

The earliest record I have of the man whom I would come to call my second father is a photo of him with the date 1945 written on the bottom (see photo). It is not clear from this, however, whether my mother knew Philip Laulicht at that point, or whether that is merely the date that the photo was taken. In any event, my mother was introduced to Philip by Sol and Ann Gutfreund, who indeed were their "good friends."*

Like my mother, Philip Laulicht had left a spouse behind in Poland when he ran from the Germans to America. The couple had two children, and Philip managed to bring one of them, his sixteen-year-old son Victor, with him when he entered the United States in 1941. Philip left Victor's older sister, Esther, in the care and custody of his wife, Scheindel Chana (née Kanner).

---

* Gutfreund means "good friend" in German or Yiddish.

It was actually a member of Scheindel's family who made it possible for Philip and Victor to flee to America after the Germans invaded Poland.

Sam Kanner, Scheindel's brother, had immigrated to the US long before World War II and flourished. He owned a successful dressmaking company in Elizabeth, New Jersey, and somehow managed to lay his hands on two visas. Sam offered them to his sister and her four-person family, trapped inside Poland, on the eve of the Holocaust.

It was not as much of a "Sophie's choice" as one might think to determine which of the four family members would use the two visas. Scheindel did not wish to leave. She was not prepared to give up their very successful grocery business. And besides, she told Philip: "I know these Germans. They rant on and on about the Jews, the Jews, the Jews, but at the end of the day, they are an educated, civilized people and we'll manage all right, just as we did before." Tragically, she was mistaken.

My second father, Philip Laulicht (*right*) with his first family – wife Scheindel Chana, daughter Esther, and son Victor – circa 1940

My second father, Philip Laulicht, serving in the Austro-Hungarian army during World War I

Philip Laulicht's father, Ovadyah Laulicht

Philip Laulicht was born in 1895 and served in the Austro-Hungarian army during World War I. He was the only non-Chasid in an observant family of six brothers and a father, all of whom were followers of the Bobover Rebbe. Philip, coming from a less affluent background, did not share his wife's high regard for German culture and took Hitler at his word when the Fuehrer announced that he would wipe out the Jews. So it was determined that Philip would employ the visas to travel to America with Victor while their daughter, Esther, would remain behind with her mother, Scheindel. Some documents suggest that the visas did not authorize entry to the United States but rather into Santo Domingo. Thus, according to passenger manifest lists, Philip and Victor entered the United States from Santo Domingo on January 27, 1941, aboard the SS *Borinquen*.

This route would make sense given the existence of the Sosua Jewish refugee settlement at that time along the northern coast of the Dominican Republic. In 1938, to pacify the rising tide of voices urging the Roosevelt administration to take action in behalf the Jews of Europe, the US

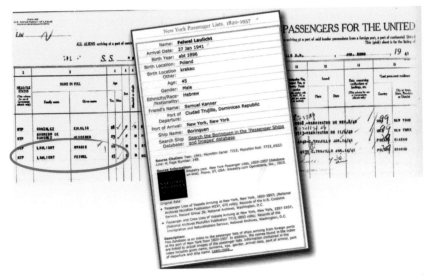

The passenger manifest for the ss *Borinquen* listing my second father, Feivel Laulicht, and his son (whose Hebrew name, Ovadyah, is listed on the manifest, spelled "Ovadie"), as well as a record from the US National Archives documenting the arrival of "Feiwel" Laulicht on January 27, 1941, from the Dominican Republic. Note the name of Philip's brother-in-law Samuel Kanner listed as "friend."

organized a conference to discuss the subject in Evian, France. Of the thirty-two countries that sent delegates to Evian, only one, the Dominican Republic, announced that it was prepared to receive Jewish refugees within its borders. Although they publicly agreed to receive 100,000, only about seven hundred Jews actually reached Dominican shores, due to the practical challenges of finding transport and getting through submarine warfare in the Atlantic.

In light of the *Borinquen* manifest, it is likely that Philip Laulicht and his son, Victor, were among them. There is, however, no doubt that Hitler was paying close attention to events in Evian. It was the indifference of the world community to the suffering being inflicted on Germany's Jews that emboldened him to raise the stakes. Within a few months the nationwide, state-sponsored pogrom known as Kristallnacht took place, marking the beginning of the Holocaust.

Just as my mother had done, Philip Laulicht arrived to America with his family torn to shreds by the Nazi onslaught. Once in the United States, it became clear that the Nazi threat was not going to pass quickly. Any thoughts Philip might have harbored of sitting things out in sanctuary in the US and then returning to Poland swiftly dissolved. For a short time, Philip no doubt did all he could to bring his wife and daughter to America. Encountering the same roadblocks and sub-rosa antisemitism at the highest levels of the US government that impeded my mother's efforts, Philip was likewise unsuccessful. He at some point learned that his wife and daughter had been killed after he had left Poland – presumably after having been taken to "killing places," as reported by the Agudas Harabonim certificate.

The forces of attraction that brought my mother and second father together are not difficult to comprehend. Philip was a respectable and resolute émigré from not only the same town, but even the same neighborhood as my mother. He had been working steadily at his brother-in-law Sam Kanner's clothing factory and exhibited a warm and embracing personality toward me. The couple also shared a powerful common wound, having both lost spouses and numerous family members in the inferno that had engulfed the Jews of Europe. As was the case with many survivors, both were ardently seeking the stability and security of family life that they had enjoyed "before."

My earliest recollections of my mother's new husband are set in our tiny apartment on Scholes Street in the Williamsburg section of Brooklyn. "Murray," she would say, "come say hello to your uncle Philip."

"Uncle" Philip was, in my eyes, a very pleasant man who, while not

Wedding photo of my mother and my second father, Erna and Philip Laulicht, New York City, September 14, 1946

really pampering me, still appeared friendly and gregarious. He and I got along well from the very start. As Uncle Philip evolved over the next few months into my second father, that affection would eventually turn to love.

After my mother and "Uncle" Philip became husband and wife in September 1946, our little family moved into Philip's small apartment in Newark, New Jersey, where we stayed for only a few weeks. In November my parents purchased a home in nearby Elizabeth, where I was enrolled in the local public elementary school. Our new home happened to be only a few blocks from the home of Rabbi Pinchas Mordechai Teitz, a prominent Latvian-born Orthodox spiritual leader and educator. Rabbi Teitz had, in 1941, founded the Jewish Educational Center in Elizabeth and was heavily involved in launching an elementary day school. Rabbi Teitz approached our family shortly after we moved into the neighborhood about enrolling me into his new yeshiva.

My parents were deliberating this change for me shortly before Chanukah as they went to visit my grandmother, who lay gravely ill in the hospital. As we stood at her bedside, my grandmother took the hands of both my mother and my new father into her own and explained: "What I'm going to say to you is not a *tzava'ah* [a last will and testament, often a deathbed command]. It is merely some advice." According to Jewish teach-

Rabbi Pinchas Mordechai Teitz

ings, a *tzava'ah* must be carried out by the issuer's heirs, whether they wish to do so or not. After making it clear that my parents were not obligated by Jewish law to act upon her advice, she told them the following in Yiddish: "If you want to have pleasure from life, give the child a Jewish education."

Fulfilling my grandmother's wish would require a pioneering act on the part of my parents. Jewish day schools were few and far between in those days, centered primarily in cities with large Jewish communities. Removing me from public school and enrolling me into a yeshiva was certainly no easy decision for my parents. Whether it was my grandmother's words, Rabbi Teitz's persuasive charm, or other factors, they decided to do so. It turned out to be the decision that had the most profound influence on my future life. This is due to the fact that everything else in my life that followed, especially my marriage to my wonderful and beloved wife, Linda Kushner, arose as a result of this basic decision regarding my Jewish education.

As fate would have it, the decision was made shortly before the beginning of Chanukah, which also happened to be a few weeks before Christmas. In those halcyon days before religion had been banished from the public schools, many of them put on Christmas pageants, student plays recounting the birth of the Christ-child. Among them was PS 12 in Elizabeth, New Jersey, where first-grader Murray Jack Goldwasser (as I was known at that time) had been rehearsing for weeks for his debut performance as a holy angel. It would have been my job to sing hosannas of praise at the birth of the newborn king.

My parents, in their infinite wisdom, understood that this transition from a public school to a Jewish yeshiva would not go smoothly unless I was in favor of it. So they devised a strategy designed to appeal to my six-year-old mind.

One evening, a few nights before the beginning of Chanukah, as my parents and I were taking a leisurely walk, we arrived at the Jewish Educational Center. As we stopped near the entrance, my father (from this point forward I will refer to my second father, Philip Laulicht, as my father) pulled a dollar from his pocket and handed it to me.

"Go inside the school and buy some Chanukah candles, Murray," he instructed. I did as he asked and came out smiling a few minutes later with the candles...and with an announcement.

"They're showing cartoons in there," I informed my parents. "I want to stay here at this school. Can I?" The only place I could ever watch cartoons in that pre-TV era was after buying a ticket at the movie theater. Seeing cartoons (for free) was a big deal.

"How will you get home?" asked my mother.

"I met a very nice man who asked me where I live and he said that he lived very close and that he would bring me home after the movies." My mother went inside and discovered that the nice man was none other than Rabbi Teitz, and so she granted permission. By the time Rabbi Teitz brought me home that night, I was ready to say farewell to all the angels and join the other Jewish children at the JEC. I had been seduced into Judaism by none other than Donald Duck and Felix the Cat.

I got off to a bit of a rough start at my new school. After having taught myself to read English by studying candy bar wrappers and milk cartons (the public schools did not start teaching reading skills until the second grade), I was capable of following the secular studies at the JEC. But the religious lessons were conducted partly in Hebrew, and that was something I did not know at all. What was most upsetting was that all my new classmates seemed to be able to read Hebrew without difficulty. This fact aggravated me, so I began acting out – throwing spitballs and disrupting the class whenever something was said that I did not understand. After a few months, my parents were called in to the office of the principal, Mr. Jack Aboff, and informed that they would have to remove me from the school.

My mother reacted at once. She pleaded and cajoled and finally convinced Mr. Aboff to give her son a second chance. As my grandmother had died only a short time earlier, my mother no doubt recounted my grandmother's deathbed advice. After hearing this, the principal relented and agreed to a two-week trial period.

"But if, after two weeks, Murray is still unable to keep up with the other children and continues to make trouble, we will have no choice." My parents agreed and began an intensive remedial Hebrew home study program. My mother began with the basics: *alef-bet*, the vowels, block and cursive letters. Fortunately, I was a quick

My second father and me, circa 1950

study in language skills and soon became fascinated with the Hebrew language. The fascination has endured through the present day.

Thanks to my mother's home tutoring, I soon stopped throwing spitballs and became integrated into my new school. Not only did I begin mastering the Hebrew language, I also began learning about the teachings and traditions of the Jewish people. This new direction of my schooling sometimes led to challenging situations at home.

My parents were not strictly observant Jews at this point. They were not *shomer Shabbos* (literally "guarders of the Sabbath"), and while we did keep a totally kosher home, they were not as rigorous when it came to other aspects of Jewish tradition such as Sabbath restrictions. My father's attitude about such matters was shaped by his tragic experiences of the Shoah. All the members of his family were observant *shomer Shabbos* Chasidim. He was the exception. Yet he alone survived the flames and they all perished. What is one to conclude from such an outcome?

So it was not surprising that when my father's brother-in-law, Sam Kanner, who also happened to be his boss at the garment factory, instructed my father to report for work every Saturday, he complied. This practice, naturally, resulted in a conflict when I began to understand that my father was violating one of the Ten Commandments. My father decided to take action and approached his boss.

"Sam, I've got a problem," he explained. "Murray is going to a day school where they teach him about Shabbos and what you can and cannot do. And then he sees me going to work every Shabbos. It's confusing the child. And so, I'm not going to work on Shabbos anymore." Sam was not pleased, but he understood and agreed to revise my father's work schedule.

From that point on, my father and I attended Shabbos services together every Saturday morning. And as we did so, I could see that each week he was being drawn closer and closer back to Judaism. I could tell from the way he fervently recited each word of the prayers and the way he would rock back and forth that he was very serious about davening (praying). He told me that he wanted me to learn to daven properly and came up with a plan that would accomplish this goal.

"Murray," he told me, "I'm going to pay you to daven. For every three days that you recite your prayers here in the house, I will give you twenty cents. Twenty cents for Sunday, Monday, and Tuesday. And another twenty cents for Wednesday, Thursday, and Friday. Shabbos you daven for free."

To my eyes, the prospect of earning a whopping forty cents per week that I could spend any way I chose was exhilarating. This "pray for pay" ploy worked perfectly and I soon became highly adept at reciting the prayers in the Siddur (prayer book).

As mentioned, during this period I went by the name Murray Jack Goldwasser, which I retained through the fifth grade. As it happened, a gentleman by the name of Murray Goldwasser also lived in Elizabeth, and one day, in 1947, his phone rang and Mr. Goldwasser's wife picked it up.

"Hello," said the caller, "is this the home of Murray Goldwasser?"

"Yes, it is," replied Mrs. Goldwasser.

"This is PS 12 and I'm calling to find out why Murray is not in school today."

"Well, it could be because he's married to me and we have two children."

Our family got to know the other Murray Goldwasser family and tried unsuccessfully to determine if there was a family relationship. None was found, but we started to feel that having two Murray Goldwassers in the same community was pretty confusing.

A few years later, in order to solidify our family unit and to end any further confusion, my father decided to formally adopt me and did so in April 1950. Thus, a month before my tenth birthday, I stopped being Murray Jack Goldwasser and became Murray Jack Laulicht. Of course my Hebrew name (Moshe Yaakov ben Avraham Yechezkel Halevi) continues to include the name of my natural father.

I recall that the judge at the adoption hearing called me into his chambers for a private chat. He wanted to know how I felt about being adopted and changing my name. I don't recall my exact response, but I know that I was enthusiastically in favor of it.

Not long after, in another display of his devotion to my Jewish education, my father retained the services of a *yeshiva bochur* (student) to teach me to read directly from the Torah. This is something of an arcane

art form, known as *leining*, and involves mastering the use of ancient dia-
critical marks called *trop* in order to properly chant any given passage. In
America in those days, education in this area was normally reserved for
boys preparing for bar mitzvah at age thirteen. But my father thought I was
ready at age ten. So every Shabbos afternoon, I would trudge the two miles
to the instructor's home and learn another note or two of the *leining*. My
skills grew rapidly to the point that by the early fall of 1951 I felt confident
enough to read from the Torah during the junior congregation's Shabbat service. When Rabbi Teitz got wind of this, he was less than pleased.
"What's that child doing reading from the Torah?!" And that was that...till
I turned thirteen. The good news is that by that time I was so familiar with
the Torah that I needed next to no preparation for my bar mitzvah.

After I graduated from the JEC following the sixth grade, I was enrolled
at the Hebrew Academy of Essex County (today known as the Joseph
Kushner Hebrew Academy) in Newark. As I prepared to move into the
eighth grade, the school underwent a change of direction. The Orthodox
rabbi who served as principal was to be replaced by a Conservative rabbi.

As a result of the Hebrew Academy's change, the outgoing principal asked me to accompany him to a Brooklyn neighborhood known as
Brownsville and there visit the Yeshiva Chaim Berlin, a Lithuanian-style
school that extended through the twelfth grade. While the tour of the
school made a positive impression on me, my most salient memory of
the visit was discovering that the school stood a mere three blocks from
the Kishke King, a kosher eatery the likes of which we could only dream
about back in Elizabeth. So, based on both spiritual and gastronomical
considerations, I switched to Chaim Berlin in the eighth grade and continued there through high school, where I sought to feed both my Jewish
body and Jewish soul.

Ironically, I soon learned that the Kishke King, which was open on
Shabbat, was off limits – except perhaps to watch the Brooklyn Dodgers
play on the store's outdoor black-and-white TV set. Just so I wouldn't feel
too guilty, I would often nosh on some ices during the games.

Although our family probably qualified for some form of financial
assistance, my parents never applied for any type of scholarship to help
bear the cost of my Jewish education. My mother worked as a bookkeeper

at Rabbi Teitz's Jewish Educational Center and my father continued to put in long hours at Sam Kanner's dress factory.

During the summer of 1957, following my senior year at Chaim Berlin, I was faced with the choice of where to carry out my higher education. I had sent my College Board scores to a number of colleges, including Yeshiva University in New York, the leading Modern Orthodox rabbinical seminary in the nation, which also included in its curriculum other fields of study. My advisor at Chaim Berlin, a decidedly right-wing institution, did not hold YU in very high regard.

"Moish," he told me, "I understand you're not going to Brooklyn College and you are contemplating Yeshiva University." I said that was true.

"I would rather see you go to St. John's than to YU. Why? Because at St. John's if they give you an orange peel to eat, they will tell you that it's an orange peel. At YU, they will give you an orange peel and tell you that you're eating an orange."

I came to understand the intent behind the metaphor over the ensuing summer, thanks to an opportune encounter at a Food Fair supermarket in Elizabeth between my mother and a Mrs. Kanovsky, a respected Jewish educator.

"I see your son, Murray, is graduating this year," said Mrs. Kanovsky. "Does he have a job for the summer?" My mother confirmed that I did not.

"There is an outstanding summer camp in New York called Camp Galila and they are looking for counselors." My mother came home from the Food Fair and delivered the news to me. I phoned up the camp immediately and, based on my prior summer's camp counseling experience, they offered me the job. It turned out to be an amazing summer that had a huge impact on the course of my life.

Camp Galila's counseling staff was made up mostly of very bright Yeshiva University students and alumni. At first, my reaction to this crowd was one of arrogance and cynicism. These were college boys who knew less about Judaism than did a yeshiva high school graduate like me. But then I met someone who caused my attitude to adjust dramatically. His name was Nathan Lewin and he was the twenty-one-year-old charismatic drama counselor at Camp Galila. He had just graduated from YU as the valedictorian of his class and was about to start studying at Harvard Law

School. Nat would go on to enjoy an illustrious career as one of America's foremost
constitutional attorneys, having argued
twenty-seven cases before the Supreme
Court as of April 2015.

During that languorous summer of 1957,
Nat and I spoke often about life on campus
and the more I listened, the more interested
I became. By the end of the summer, Nat
had convinced me that, given the intellectual ability of its students, YU might not
be such a bad choice after all. Ironically, as
soon as I returned home I found a letter

Nathan Lewin, 2010

waiting for me from Yeshiva University. I was informed that, based solely
upon my College Board scores, I had been granted a full scholarship and
could attend tuition-free. This astounded me because I had not even submitted an application for admission!

A few days later, on Labor Day 1957, the counselors from Camp Galila
embarked on a boat ride to a popular park known as Bear Mountain in
upstate New York. Fortunately, Nat Lewin was there and I immediately
showed him the letter from YU.

"Is this normal?" I asked Nat. "Do they normally grant full tuition schol-
arships to people who have not even applied for admission?"

"You must have really impressed them with your test scores and they
probably did some checking up on you. It's a small Jewish world, Murray."

"Maybe this is some kind of sign. What do you think I should do?" I
asked.

"Look," Nat responded, "a YU education might not be everything you
could get if you studied Torah full-time somewhere else, but you will be
receiving an excellent college education in a Jewish atmosphere. You'll be
in the company of professors and rabbis to whom you will be able to turn
with questions. Really, would it be so terrible to be like one of us?" I knew
that among the seven other Galila boys' counselors educated at YU, two
had been accepted to Harvard Law School, another had been admitted to
the Albert Einstein Medical School, yet another to a dental school, one

was studying to become a rabbi, and two others came from prominent rabbinic families. Rather impressive, I thought. In the end, I had to agree that YU was the best choice.

"Okay," I said. "If they'll take me, I'll go."

As it turned out, YU did accept me and I went on to spend four of the best years of my life there. For their part, my parents supported my decision to attend YU and felt, correctly, that doing so would provide me with both the Judaic and secular education that I needed to succeed in the modern world while remaining an observant and knowledgeable Jew.

Sadly our family unit was not destined to remain intact much longer. I grew up knowing that my natural father had been killed by the Germans and believing that no such misfortune could now befall us here in the safety of America. This turned out to be a naive notion.

As has been stated, my father worked in a garment factory owned by his first wife's brother, Sam Kanner. It was backbreaking, physical work that required my father to tote large bolts of fabric and put them into place for use by the cutting machines. Like most factories in the 1940s and '50s, Mr. Kanner's factory had no air-conditioning available during the grueling summer months. I recall how my father would return home at the end of the day so exhausted he could barely move from his chair.

My parents, Erna and Philip Laulicht, 1958

In 1948, at age fifty-three, my father suffered his first heart attack. He recovered quickly, but in 1952 he succumbed again. At that point, my father was placed on medication, and over the ensuing five or six years, it appeared that my father's health was in good shape.

In 1958, I was a sophomore at Yeshiva University, where I lived in a dormitory during the week. I would travel home to Elizabeth for Shabbos just about every weekend. This particular week I had brought a friend home with me from school, Bobby Asch, to spend Shabbos with our family. I recall, with some pain and regret, that as we both departed to return to the dormitory on Saturday night, I was too embarrassed to kiss my father good-bye in front of my friend. Fortunately, my father called me over and told me that I should never be embarrassed to kiss him. And that's just what I did.

The following Monday, October 20, 1958, I was called out of class and told to meet my dorm supervisor. He brought me into his office and asked me to take a seat. I could tell from his pained expression that he was about to convey some bad news.

"Murray, I don't know any other way to tell you this, but your father died today." To say I was stunned would be an extreme understatement. How could this be? I had already lost one father without ever having met him.

My mother and second father in 1958, shortly before his death

Wasn't that enough? My second father had not been sick. He and my mother had traveled to Israel over the past summer. "What could have happened?" I implored.

"I don't have all the details, but I understand he had a heart attack at work and died immediately. I am so very sorry. I'll help you make arrangements to go home." I thanked him weakly and left without saying another word. As it turned out, my roommate and lifelong friend, Bobby Asch, drove me home. We both sat in stunned silence during the entire one-hour drive from YU to Elizabeth.

The death of my second father could only be described as a traumatic event. As I went through the Jewish mourning periods associated with the death of a family member (shivah, *shloshim*, the year of mourning), I recall how Rabbi Teitz consoled me with these words: "The Talmud says that he who raises someone else's son is regarded as if he had actually given birth to him." Somehow, perhaps in an odd way, the grief I experienced for my second father spilled over and allowed me to fully grieve – for the first time – for my first.

Losing my second father also marked a turning point in my life on a number of levels. It prompted me to become more serious about the direction of my life. Shortly before my second father's death, I began studying under the brilliant Talmudic scholar Rabbi Joseph Soloveitchik. I recall how proud my father was when he learned that I had been invited to attend

Rabbi Joseph Soloveitchik

Rabbi Soloveitchik's class. Rabbi Soloveitchik emphasized the singular importance of applying Jewish knowledge to secular knowledge and vice versa. Rabbi Soloveitchik's approach has continued to guide me throughout my personal, professional, and communal life.

It was during this time that I also realized that I was now my mother's only immediate family member and began feeling responsible for her welfare. It was this sense of responsibility that prompted me to suggest to my mother, after the shivah period for my father had ended, that I should quit YU, get a daytime job, and attend college at night. My mother adamantly disagreed. "You have a good head, Murray," she said. "It should not go to waste. Somehow we will manage." And, thanks to my mother's continued hard work and support, somehow we did. I continued my studies, deciding to major in chemistry.

The reason for my decision to study chemistry was essentially a financial one. With my second father gone, our family could not easily afford the expense of a law school education. As a trained chemist, I envisioned myself obtaining a fellowship that would underwrite my postgraduate education.

Of course, after my second father's death, both my mother and I maintained our relationship with his son from his first marriage. Victor was a sixteen-year-old student when he arrived to America with his father in 1941. By the time my parents wed in 1946, Victor was living on his own and never became part of our household. In between, Victor joined the US Army and was part of the D-Day invasion in Normandy on June 6, 1944, where he was injured. The experience had left its mark on him, both physically and emotionally, and, as a result, he was required to undergo electric shock therapy treatments from time to time. I recall that if Victor failed to undergo these treatments he would behave in a bizarre and often belligerent manner.

I prefer to remember Victor as he was in his more lucid moments, during which he and I enjoyed an outstanding relationship. He was an avid chess player and a passionate baseball fan just as I was, and, in a way, he fulfilled the role of an older brother in my life at that time. Victor Laulicht eventually married and sadly suffered a fate similar to that of our father by succumbing to a fatal heart attack in 1968 at the age of forty-three. Ironically, in the days after Victor's death, we received the results of an EKG that had been conducted just a few days before his death. It showed that his heart was in fine shape.

My step-brother, Victor Laulicht, circa 1943. Victor, the son of my second father, Philip, died in 1968.

After my second father's death, I became more interested in trying to learn what had happened to my first father. I recall my mother telling me repeatedly that she had saved the letters my father had written to her. She said that someday she would show them to me and then I would understand. She never did so. Nor did my mother discuss the circumstances of my natural father's death. For many years I continued to believe that my father died in the winter of 1944, on the 17th of Kislev, while on a death march.

Like many Holocaust survivors, my mother was reluctant to talk about her family's experiences. It was not until late 1987 when my mother was in the hospital during the last stages of her life that my wife, Linda, discovered the letters on the top shelves of a small closet in my mother's apartment. It is this collection of correspondence that has formed the core of this book.

There are numerous studies that indicate that people who wish to communicate their tragic experiences to their heirs – experiences too painful to discuss face-to-face – will leave clues and written accounts to be found after they have died. I suspect that this was the case with my mother. She wanted me to know what had happened to my first father, but she did not have the heart to go through the painful memories that such an account would stir up. I understand this and I owe her a debt of gratitude for allowing me to learn of my natural father's fate by leaving behind a written account. By sharing this account with others, via this book, I feel that I am perhaps repaying that debt in some small way.

But being on the receiving end of such a legacy is not without its own set of challenges. Dealing with such emotionally charged information about my parents in a dispassionate manner and without succumbing to despair has taken time and has exacted a heavy toll. It has been more than twenty-five years since I first encountered this material, shortly before my mother's death on November 2, 1987. It is only now that I find myself able to tell their tale without a flood of tears.

My cousins Mala and Henry Sperling, 1947. Mala translated the Polish and German letters reproduced in this book into English.

In the years and decades that followed, as I married and began raising my own family, I have attempted to keep alive the memories of both of my fathers. Not only via the traditional Jewish rituals of Yizkor and *yahrzeit* but in a more tangible way by sharing glimpses of their lives with my children and grandchildren and by being actively involved in Holocaust education and the broader Jewish community.

As explained earlier, it was shortly before my mother's death in November 1987 that I first encountered the correspondence between her and my first father, Chaskel Goldwasser. I enlisted my cousin Mala to translate the letters into English and then asked my oldest daughter, Laurie, to type up Mala's translations. This experience afforded Laurie the opportunity to learn the details of a world she had only heard about vaguely as she was growing up. It had a profound effect upon her and she shared her feelings with me in a letter when she presented the typed transcriptions to me on my fifty-first birthday, May 12, 1991. The letter is reproduced on the following pages. It was Laurie's comments – and similar urgings by my wife and our other children – about preserving the memories of our lost family members that motivated the research and production of this book. It is my hope that even after I am gone, this book will serve to keep those memories alive.

Dear Daddy,   5-12-91

    Happy Birthday!!

As you have frequently reminded me, you were born on Mother's Day. Therefore, I find it particularly appropriate to present you with the letters from your father and other relatives on the exact day on which you were born 51 years ago.

Dad, your birth represented hope and continuity to our family in Europe. Your father, aunts, uncles and cousins were so excited when you were born in America, away from the Nazi atrocities, because they knew that you and grandma would survive and remember them if they were killed. As is written many times, your photographs and grandma's letters gave them a will to live. You were their link to a world that many would like to forget.

Although this places a very hefty burden on you and your children, as I am sure you frequently feel, I am confident that your father and other relatives would be very proud of you today. On the personal level, you have raised children who are ~~knowledge~~ knowledgeable in Torah and maintain פאר שנלי homes. On the communal level, you are involved in many Jewish organizations but I think, that the Holocaust programming that you participate in gives you the most satisfaction because it enables you to set aside the time to remember our family too.

Dad, as I proof read these letters (the computer can't pick up all mistakes even it is not perfect), I was able to relate to two important messages that they contain. First, there is a constant and unconditional belief in God even in the bleakest of times. There is always hope that God will not forget his People and that somehow He would reconcile the situation faced by European Jewry and they would all be saved.

Also, dedication and devotion to family is represented throughout the letters. For example, your father writes, in an almost matter of fact manner, how he sends Gusta supplies and money whenever possible. In a time when people needed to be selfish to survive, your father came to his sister-in-law. Also, Leah (my great grandmother) did not want to leave Europe until your father could leave with her. Because she felt he had a better chance of leaving if accompanied by an American citizen, Leah stayed until the last moment. Even in the last letter before her departure, Leah is unsure of if she is doing the right thing by leaving Haskel behind. Many others would have left and tried their best from America. But, your grandmother stayed, essentially risking her life, to see if she could help your father.

Dad, as I typed these letters into the computer, I was finally able to feel a sense of loss for people I never knew. Although neither of us had ever met your father, he is no longer unknown to us. He is no longer only a part of the Holocaust atrocities but, he is a part of us. Thank you for giving me the opportunity to meet him in the only way possible - through his writings. I am sure that I would have loved him a lot.

I love you,
Laurie

CHAPTER THIRTEEN

The Results of Their Sacrifices

While my mother ultimately and tragically failed to liberate my natural father, Chaskel Goldwasser, from the ravages of the Holocaust, and thereby was never able to satisfy his "yearning to breathe free," she did clearly succeed on so many other levels. My mother tied the ragged threads of our lives together after the war and fashioned a strong new family fabric – here in the shadow of the New Colossus. Even with all of her dogged tenacity, she was unable to categorically determine my natural father's final fate. Perhaps that is why I have felt compelled to pick up the mantle and pursue this mystery as I have chronicled in the pages of this book. But it was that same strong-willed stance that enabled my mother to pave the way not only for my own successful pursuits, but also for those of my children and grandchildren.

In this chapter, I would like to acquaint the reader with the results of my mother's incredible bravery in coming to the United States in 1940, alone and pregnant, and of my natural father's supreme sacrifice in letting her go.

As mentioned previously, upon the death of my second father, I had suggested to my mother that I quit YU. She insisted that I continue my studies there, and I did so. At the time, I was majoring in chemistry. However, by my junior year, I realized that I was not as enamored with chemistry as I had anticipated, and I began to explore the possibility of fulfilling my boyhood dream of going to law school and becoming a lawyer. I did surprisingly well on the Law School Admission Test and, as a result, by the end of my junior year, Columbia Law School had accepted me and offered me a full scholarship. Once again, my mother rejected my suggestion that I forgo this opportunity and start earning a living. Like her own mother, she wanted to provide her child with the best possible education.

When I started at Columbia I was greatly concerned that I would be unable to compete academically against my classmates. Most of them had studied at the finest colleges in the United States and had majored in subjects such as political science, English history, American history, literature, psychology, business, and economics. Their studies seemed far more closely related to law than did my background in chemistry, in which I had majored at YU. I had taken very few liberal arts courses and as a result felt unprepared and a bit intimidated.

Despite such misgivings, I realized during my first semester at Columbia that YU had given me two tremendous advantages over my classmates. First, as a result of my Talmudic study, I had been fully exposed to numerous disputations in which we were repeatedly challenged to explain why one rabbi put forward a certain idea and another rabbi promoted the exact opposite. My classmates had never been required to grapple with this type of dialectic. As a result, and much to my surprise, they exhibited considerable difficulty in comprehending why the majority of a court took one position and the dissent took the opposite.

My graduation photo from Yeshiva University, June 1961

Secondly, as part of my Talmudic studies, I had analyzed many of the same questions that arose in law school, such as what proof is necessary to sustain a criminal conviction? How do you prove the validity and meaning of a contract? Is tort liability based on fault or no fault? What relief should be given to someone who has been injured by the wrongdoing of another? Moreover, the process I had learned at YU, and particularly from Rabbi Soloveitchik, of delving into how and why, in many cases,

divinely inspired Jewish law deviated from the system of secular common law – a system produced by eight hundred years of the finest minds
of Western civilization – increased my skills and understanding of both
systems. The result of these advantages from my YU education was that I
did extremely well at Columbia Law School, finishing first in my class. My
grandmother's advice about the pleasures derived from a Jewish education
rang true once again, this time in a most unexpected way.

Throughout my undergraduate and law school years. I continued to
attend Shabbat services at the JEC, where I sat directly behind a very sweet
and friendly gentleman, a Holocaust survivor named Joseph Kushner.
Over time, Mr. Kushner grew fond of me, and in particular, he seemed to
like the way I chanted from the Torah. My chanting ability had been developed as the result of the emphasis placed on this skill by my second father.
Little did I know, when trudging to my teacher's home and studying the
trop all those years earlier, that I was learning a skill that would someday
lead me down the aisle.

In late 1963, my mother was visited by a friend of Mr. Kushner named
Joseph Graff, also a Holocaust survivor, who politely explained that he was
something of a *shadchan* (matchmaker). He wanted my mother to know
that Mr. Kushner would have no objections if her son Murray were to call
upon his daughter Linda. When my mother broached the subject to me, I
expressed concern about the difference in our ages – I was in my last year
of law school and Linda was a senior in high school.

In Rabbi Teitz's shul at the JEC, all the women were seated in upstairs
open balconies. This arrangement allowed the men and women to view
one another during services and allowed me to steal an occasional quick
glimpse of Linda Kushner. I thought that she was very pretty and eventually approached her, offering to walk her home after Shabbat services.
She agreed and after a bit of walking and a lot of talking, I discovered that
I really liked her and that she seemed to like me as well.

In February 1964, I hosted an Oneg Shabbat (Sabbath gathering) at
our home for the younger members of our congregation. That Friday night
the house was filled with energetic teenagers. I was somewhat surprised
to spot Linda Kushner among them. Linda explained that she had been

planning on going straight to bed that night, but was urged by one of her friends to attend the Oneg at my home instead.

By 10 P.M. everyone was beginning to filter out, and I asked Linda if I could accompany her for her thirty-minute walk home. She agreed. I don't know if it was the moonlight or the kosher wine, or simply Linda's resplendent charms, but by the end of our stroll I was smitten. I was impressed not only with Linda's beauty and poise, but even more with her intellect. She was not the least bit intimidated by my expounding about every subject, from my legal studies to the importance of a Jewish education and why Linda should consider going to Stern College, YU's women's college, which in fact she did upon graduating from high school.

Linda's parents, Joseph and Rae Kushner, were Holocaust survivors from eastern Poland/Belarus. After the Germans invaded the area in 1941, Rae and her family were interned in the Novogrudok ghetto. Of the thirty thousand Jews sent to Novogrudok in the ensuing years, only 250 survived. Rae, her father, and her sister Lisa managed to survive by tunneling out of the ghetto into a forest in the summer of 1943. There they joined the partisans and eventually became part of the famed Bielski Brigade. Rae's mother, another sister, and a brother were murdered in the Holocaust.

Linda's father came from a small nearby shtetl, Korelicze. The youngest of eight children (six of whom were girls), Joseph lost his father at age nine. He was forced to learn a trade and begin working, forgoing any sort of formal education. During the war, Joseph survived somehow in the forests of eastern Poland. His mother and three of his sisters were all murdered in the Holocaust.

After the war, Joseph met Rae through his older brother Chaim. After seeing her only three times, he gave Rae a pack of American cigarettes, a red dress, and a ring, and asked her to marry him. Rae accepted the proposal and they were married in August 1945 in Budapest, at the famed Dohany utca Synagogue, the largest such structure left standing in post-Holocaust Europe.

The couple made their way to Italy, landing in a DP camp in Cremona, where, in April 1947, their daughter Linda was born. President Truman, responding to the Earl G. Harrison Report, which revealed that Holocaust survivors were living in deplorable conditions in DP camps across Europe, raised the immigration quotas via executive order and authorized entry visas to thousands of Jewish Holocaust survivors. Finally, the golden door of Emma Lazarus's poem was opening a bit to the huddled masses yearning to breathe free.

Joseph and Rae Kushner, Budapest, 1945

Sponsored by Rae's American aunt, the family was able to immigrate to the United States, arriving in New York Harbor in 1949. Settling first in the Crown Heights section of Brooklyn, Joseph Kushner immediately rolled up his sleeves and went to work as a carpenter. Two years later, he started to build homes in Union, New Jersey. Working from early in the morning till late at night, Joseph slept at the job site during the week, returning only to spend Friday night and Saturday with his family in Brooklyn.

In the mid-1950s, the Kushners moved to nearby Elizabeth. As a traditional Jew, Mr. Kushner became a member of the JEC synagogue, where his seat was located right in front of mine. We soon got to know, like, and respect one another. And the rest is matrimonial history.

Whenever I think of the long series of fortuitous events that had to transpire in order to enable Linda's path to cross mine – any one of which, had it not taken place, would have meant that she and I would never have met – I can only marvel at the workings of destiny and the divine hand that brought us together.

In the weeks that followed the Friday night that I walked Linda home after the Oneg at my house, we saw each other often. I escorted Linda to the reading of the Megillah at Columbia on Purim. We "made *aliyah*" together to the top of the Empire State Building. I was totally smitten – *farchlobet*, as Mrs. Kushner would say. After three weeks of courtship I gave Linda my Yeshiva College ring. I told her that she already had my heart, so I wanted her to have my ring as well. Soon thereafter we were engaged, but Linda insisted that we wait to be married until the following April, when she would be eighteen and could sign all of the necessary marriage documents herself.

Because of Linda's determination that we delay our wedding until she reached legal majority, we enjoyed a rather lengthy engagement. This period, lasting a little more than a year, turned out to be a very eventful one for me. Not only did I graduate from law school, I also found myself immediately swept up in one of the key moments in our nation's history.

On the day that I completed my last final exam in May 1964, I received a call from my friend, Nat Lewin, who had earlier convinced me to enroll at Yeshiva University. The question that he posed stunned me.

"Murray," he asked. "Would you be interested in working as part of the legal staff of the Warren Commission?"

The commission, appointed by President Lyndon Johnson mere days after John F. Kennedy was assassinated in Dallas on November 22, 1963, was headed by Supreme Court Chief Justice Earl Warren and charged with the task of investigating the crime and reporting its findings to the president and the public. Johnson, forced to contend with a rising tide of conspiracy theories that sought to pin the blame on everyone from the Kremlin to the Mafia to the Teamsters Union, felt that it was crucial to set the nation's mind at ease as to what actually happened. He felt so strongly about this that in order to convince certain individuals, such as Senator Russell Long, future president Gerald Ford, and Warren himself to join the commission, Johnson explained that failure to suppress the rampant conspiracy theories ran the risk of igniting a wave of anti-Soviet hysteria that could lead to a nuclear war.

I asked Nat how he had come to select me for this opportunity. I knew that he had recently clerked for Supreme Court Justice John Marshall Harlan and was now working in the Solicitor General's Office in Washington. There, Nat explained, he was approached by Howard Willens, a fellow lawyer in the Solicitor General's Office who was one of the chief legal administrators at the Warren Commission. Willens had asked Nat if he knew of any bright young lawyers whom he could enlist to serve on the commission's staff, and Nat had recommended me.

I immediately arranged to fly to Washington, where I was interviewed by the former US solicitor general, J. Lee Rankin, who had represented the

Eisenhower administration in the landmark Supreme Court case Brown v. Board of Education. Rankin, a modest and self-effacing gentleman, was at this time serving as general counsel for the Warren Commission.

During the interview, Mr. Rankin presented a caveat: "You know we have a deadline on this thing, Murray," Rankin explained. "The chief justice has promised to hand in our report to the president by the end of June. So we work like beavers around here, and that includes evenings and weekends. I hope that's no problem."

Actually, it was.

"I suppose that one of the things that Nat Lewin told you about me, sir, is that I'm Jewish and that I observe the Sabbath from Friday sunset to Saturday sunset each week." Mr. Rankin responded with a wry smile indicating that this was precisely the reason he had brought up the subject.

"The rest of the week, I will be available around the clock, but I cannot perform any work on the Sabbath. I'll be your man 24/6," I said with a slight smile of my own.

I could sense that Mr. Rankin respected my dedication to my faith as he stood and shook my hand. "That sounds fine to me. See you next week."

I returned to New York to attend my graduation exercises. With me were my mother, Linda, and her parents. The most memorable moments occurred when my favorite professor, Harry W. Jones, who was the Benjamin Cardozo Professor of Jurisprudence at Columbia, was called up to the stage to present the John Ordronaux Prize. This was to be awarded to me as the graduate with the highest grades in the class. Professor Jones said that instead of giving the prize to me, however, he was going to give it to my mother to recognize her extraordinary bravery and determination. He walked down from the stage, presented the prize to my mother and planted a heartfelt kiss on her blushing cheek. Somehow this most illustrious non-Jewish professor of law had learned of my mother's travails and accomplishments, and had found a most appropriate way to demonstrate his respect for her and what she had accomplished. My mother was deeply touched by the gesture, as was I.

I began working for Mr. Rankin as his law clerk, conducting research and preparing memos about various legal questions that arose during the course of the investigation. In short order, however, Mr. Rankin informed me that the lead attorney on the Jack Ruby team was leaving to go back to his New Orleans law practice and this had created an opening. He invited me to become part of the Ruby team.

I agreed and was called upon to draft the chapter dealing with Ruby's motives for killing Oswald. Once on board, I began poring over trial and deposition transcripts, FBI interview reports, and other key evidence. I soon discovered that Ruby was a highly unstable individual who had come to Dallas from Chicago and had spent his life trying to become a "somebody." While Ruby was frequently quoted as saying that he killed Oswald to spare Jackie Kennedy from the ordeal of testifying at a trial in Dallas of her husband's murderer, a Dallas police officer testified that Ruby had said that he killed Oswald "to show the world that Jews have guts."

Just as I had completed my research and was preparing to draft my preliminary report about Ruby's motives, Mr. Rankin presented me with some highly disappointing news. This is what he said: "The chief justice is concerned because Mr. Ruby's lawyers have announced that they intend to appeal his murder conviction. Because there is a chance that the case may eventually reach the Supreme Court, it would be prejudicial for the commission to speculate and write about Mr. Ruby's motives when those motives may become a material issue in a future appellate proceeding."

I was sorely disappointed by the news that I was being pulled off the very challenging assignment I had been working on with so much enthusiasm. But I quickly realized that, of course, the chief justice was correct. A chapter in the final commission report laying out Ruby's motive could serve to compromise the chief justice's impartiality and thereby his ability to preside in a potentially historic case.

I was reassigned to draft a biography of Jack Ruby and when that was completed, I worked with the remaining lawyers and staff members on reviewing and fact-checking the final draft of the report. To say the least, it was fascinating work. I also had the opportunity to work closely with top lawyers from all over the United States.

The June deadline for submitting the report came and went, but when the Warren Commission finished its work in September 1964, I returned to New York to work as the law clerk for Harold R. Medina, a highly respected federal appeals court judge. Judge Medina, who had won the

Ordronaux Prize in 1912, was a phenomenal teacher. Indeed, for more than twenty-five years he had single-handedly presented his bar review course to almost forty thousand aspiring lawyers studying for the New York bar exam. He also had a remarkable writing style – breezy but clear – that I quickly tried to emulate.

In early 1965, Linda and I began to plan our wedding. We selected the date of Sunday, April 4. We were married at the Biltmore Hotel, which coincidentally was the site of a famous Zionist conference in May 1942 that attracted nearly six hundred delegates, including Chaim Weizmann and David Ben-Gurion. The conference urged that the gates of Palestine be opened and that Palestine be established as a Jewish commonwealth. This statement marked the first time that non-Zionist organizations joined the Zionists in advocating the establishment of an independent Jewish state.

The Kushners made a beautiful and elegant wedding for us. Rabbi Teitz presided, and virtually every member of our families walked down the aisle. More than four hundred people attended. After the ceremony, Linda asked her parents whether marrying me was a good idea if so many peo-

ple were crying when she and her parents walked down the aisle. Her parents replied that these were tears of joy and amazement. "Who could believe that less than twenty years after the end of World War II, the child of two Jewish survivors who were married after the war would now be a bride? We are rebuilding a Jewish world that we thought would never exist."

As I write these words in April 2015, we are preparing for the Passover holiday. This year's Seder will be an especially meaningful one for Linda and me because the first day of Passover will mark our fiftieth wedding anniversary. We will certainly not be ask-

Our wedding photo, April 4, 1965

ing "Why is this night different from all other nights?" as we look back on how our family saga in America has stretched from the golden door to our golden anniversary.

After the wedding, I returned to working for Judge Medina. We postponed our honeymoon until August so that I could finish drafting several major opinions. On our honeymoon, we visited Israel for two weeks, spent a few days in Rome, and then toured Paris and London for about one week each.

Israel in August 1965 was simply spectacular. We stayed first in the Dan Hotel in Tel Aviv. We were so excited to be in Israel that we awoke at the crack of dawn so that we could immediately walk the streets of this modern metropolis. We also met with family members, many of whom had gone to Israel after World War II.

In Jerusalem, we stayed at the Kings Hotel on King George Street, about one kilometer (a little over half a mile) from the unpaved no-man's land separating Israeli and Arab-controlled areas. As this was before the Six-Day War, we could not go to the Old City of Jerusalem, which contains many of Judaism's most important sites, even though we had American passports. This was a bitter disappointment, even though we were informed that the Jordanians were using the Kotel (the Western Wall, Judaism's holiest site) as a garbage dumpsite. It was not until after the Six-Day War in June 1967 that Jews could go freely into the Old City, an area from which Jews had been barred since 1948 while it was under Jordanian control.

Despite this limitation, we still had a wonderful time in Israel. We saw as much of Jerusalem as we could. In the north, we visited Kibbutz Ayelet Hashachar, the bustling port and refineries in the city of Haifa, and the lush farmlands of the Galilee near Lake Tiberias.

On Tisha b'Av, the day that marks the destruction of both the First and Second Temples, Jerusalem was essentially shut down. At night, restaurants, shops, and movie theaters were closed and traffic was light and very quiet. On the afternoon of Tisha b'Av we visited the community of Rishon LeZion (literally First to Zion), established in 1882 as the second Jewish settlement in what was then Palestine. We discovered that it had an excellent winery. So even though it was a fast day and although drinking wine is forbidden during the nine days of mourning culminating in Tisha b'Av, we shared a glass of local wine and recited the *shehecheyanu* blessing thanking God for keeping us alive, preserving us, and allowing us to reach this time, and, we added, allowing us to reach this very special place.

After a brief stay in Rome, of which I remember very little, except tiny Fiats whizzing around dangerous curves at high speeds, we arrived to Paris. We stayed at the Hotel Claridge, a block away from the Champs Elysees, a famous tourist location. When we got into a cab and asked to be taken to the Eiffel Tower, the driver pretended not to understand. Asking for a glass of water or some bread in a local restaurant produced similarly feigned ignorance. The arrogant Parisians insisted that we speak to them only in French.

Paris was and remains an unquestionably beautiful city. None of its churches, museums, or parks and gardens had been attacked during World War II because France surrendered within six weeks after the Germans invaded. The price that Paris paid to save its beauty disfigured it in our view. With one notable exception, our trip to Paris was a downer.

Linda, in particular, felt miserable in Paris. She kept on saying that she didn't feel right. Knowing even then that Linda never complained about aches or pains, I set out to find a doctor who would come to the hotel and who would speak to us in English. The concierge found us someone who would charge us a small fortune to do so. The doctor examined Linda briefly, and then started laughing.

"What is so funny?" I asked angrily.

"Don't you know what is wrong with your wife?" he asked.

"Why would I have agreed to pay your exorbitant fee if I knew what was wrong?" I responded.

"Well," he said, "there is nothing wrong. You are going to have a baby."

London was the final stop on our honeymoon tour. Although Linda continued to feel sick, her mood had brightened considerably since she learned that she would soon be a mother. Remembering how delighted Linda's younger cousins were to see her at the JEC, it was obvious to me that Linda would be a loving and caring mother. In addition, having a baby would be our next step toward rebuilding a Jewish world, as her parents had spoken of at our wedding.

We toured London extensively and were amazed at how much of the city was still filled with rubble and ruins more than twenty years after the war had ended. Many buildings still had bomb markings on them. Most notably, it was clear from the rubble that the Germans had bombed areas adjacent to many of London's most historic sites: the Houses of Parliament, Westminster Abbey, and St. Paul's Cathedral among them. For all this, in sharp contrast to the Parisians, the Londoners were modest and friendly and repeatedly expressed their thankfulness for America's help during the war.

Following our honeymoon, I began working at Kaye, Scholer, Fierman, Hays & Handler, one of the very few major law firms that employed Sabbath-observant Jews. Milton Handler, my antitrust law professor at Columbia, was a name partner and I worked in his department. I also joined a newly formed organization called the National Jewish Commission on Law and Public Affairs, which sought to protect the legal rights of Orthodox Jews on issues such as Sabbath observance, *gittin* (divorce legislation), ritual slaughter, and state aid to non-public schools.

On Saturday night, April 23, 1966, the Kushners were attending a Yom Ha'atzmaut (Israel Independence Day) party in Brooklyn. Before and after the party, they stopped at our apartment in the Flatbush section of Brooklyn. On their second visit, at about midnight, Mrs. Kushner announced that she was staying with us because she thought that Linda was about to give birth. She told Mr. Kushner to go back to New Jersey and that he could pick her up at the hospital after the baby had arrived.

After repeated calls to Linda's obstetrician, he finally told us, at about 6 A.M., to come to Brooklyn Jewish Hospital, where I had been born almost twenty-six years earlier. In those days, no one accompanied delivering mothers to the labor or delivery rooms. Thus, my mother-in-law waited downstairs with me, while Linda was wheeled to the labor room. After about an hour, I was told that the doctor wanted to see me upstairs. When I got there, the doctor told me that there were some complications that could result, God forbid, in our baby's death. The doctor recommended a Caesarian section, which required the patient's consent. As Linda was only nineteen and the age of consent then was twenty-one, I needed to sign for her. I asked Linda what she thought and she said that she wanted "my baby" and that I should sign, which I did. As I was leaving her room, Linda whispered, "Don't tell my mother."

I was stunned. Here Linda had just received this awful news and she still had the presence of mind and the selflessness to worry about her mother's sensitivities. Fortunately, the operation was a success and we welcomed our first child, a beautiful daughter we named Laurie in English and Leah in Hebrew, in memory of my grandmother, Leah Grunfeld. Laurie's Hebrew birthday is the 4th of Iyar, the same as mine. In 1963, three years before Laurie's birth, the date had been established as Yom Hazikaron, Israel's official memorial day commemorating fallen soldiers and victims of terror.

In 1968, two years later, Linda gave me the wonderful news that she was pregnant again. Linda also said that even though the standard procedure then was "once a Caesarian, always a Caesarian," she wanted to try to have a natural delivery. Linda found a doctor named Francis Ryan of New York Hospital, who said that he thought he could help us.

At the time, we were living in a relatively small apartment in Flatbush. After Laurie's birth, we converted our small dining room into her bedroom. But we felt that the addition of a newborn infant would render our apartment a bit overcrowded. At about the same time, in the spring of 1968, I had joined a firm in New Jersey then known as Lowenstein & Spicer (now Lowenstein Sandler) which did not have an antitrust lawyer and offered to give me full responsibility for a major price-fixing case and an FTC merger investigation, each involving a major client of the firm. Thus, when Linda's father told us that he was planning to construct some houses in West Orange, New Jersey, in a community that included a Modern Orthodox synagogue and several nearby day schools, we decided to move there.

Our second daughter was delivered naturally by Dr. Ryan on Friday evening, September 27, 1968, the Shabbos between Rosh Hashanah and Yom Kippur. We named her Shira Tova (literally "good song"), in memory of my second father (Shraga Feivel) and my mother's sister Gusta, whose Yiddish name was Gittel, which means good. Our baby's English name was Pamela (keeping alive the P in Philip) Terry (a reminder of Tova or Gittel).

After we moved to our new home in West Orange in January 1969, Linda and I became involved in the local Orthodox synagogue, Congregation Ahawas Achim B'nai Jacob and David (AABJ&D), and the local Jewish Federation. Two years later, Dr. Ryan delivered our third daughter, Shellie, named for one of my father-in-law's sisters, Shimke, who had been killed in the Holocaust.

On Saturday, October 6, 1973, which, not coincidentally, happened to be Yom Kippur, the holiest day in the Jewish calendar, Egypt and Syria, assisted by Iraq, Jordan, and Algeria, launched massive surprise attacks against Israel's northern and southern borders. For the first few days of the war, the situation looked very bleak for Israel. However, after a week of war, the Israel Defense Forces began to turn the tide.

I was invited to attend a meeting of the national UJA (United Jewish Appeal) to be held a few days hence at the Plaza Hotel in New York City. I had not previously attended this type of meeting and did not know what to expect. What I recall most vividly was that at some point Israel's casualty figures were announced. More than 650 Israeli soldiers had been killed in the first week of the war. This was an enormous loss for Israel, far more than anyone had expected. The point was made repeatedly that Israelis were losing their lives and sacrificing their sons while we American Jews were being asked only to give up some money in order to provide vitally needed humanitarian relief. Without having discussed this previously with Linda, I agreed that we would double our previous commitment to the UJA.

When I got home, I told Linda what I had done. She said that she was very happy that I had raised our gift. A few weeks later, I told her that the UJA was going to conduct a mission to Israel in March and suggested that we should go on it. Linda immediately agreed.

The UJA mission was scheduled to take place in March 1974. By then we knew that Linda was pregnant with our fourth child. Nevertheless, we decided that we should go on the mission to provide support for our Israeli brethren and to observe firsthand the effects of the Yom Kippur War. For many reasons, this trip was vastly different from our first trip in 1965. First and foremost, as a result of the Six-Day War of 1967, all of Jerusalem was now controlled by Israel (although for political and religious reasons, it ceded control of the Temple Mount to the Arab authorities). This meant that we could now enter the Old City and view the religious heart of the Holy Land.

I remember the emotions that I felt the first time that I saw the Kotel (the Western Wall). The Kotel represented a very small part of the Temple, almost all of which had been destroyed by the Babylonians and then the

Romans. For almost nineteen hundred years, the Kotel had been in the hands of our enemies, who could have destroyed it whenever they wanted to. Yet, despite this, the Kotel remains. These parallels between the Kotel and the Jewish people were and are obvious to me. The Kotel symbolizes the miraculous survival of the Jewish people.

In addition, the mission gave us the chance to meet Israel's leaders, including Moshe Dayan, and the national and local leaders of the UJA. We traveled to Kilometer 103, where we saw the ceasefire line in the Sinai. We traced the battles of the Yom Kippur War, from a helicopter strip near Kilometer 103 to an air field and temporary hospital at a military base at Refidim (previously named Bir Gifgafa when the Egyptians controlled it) in the middle of the Negev. We also visited a modern hospital in Be'er Sheva and a military rehabilitation center further north.

At the rehabilitation center we met injured soldiers who had been treated in each of the places we had visited. They had been evacuated by helicopter from the Suez Canal to the hospitals at Bir Gafgafa or Be'er Sheva. Some had even been treated in hospital tents after landing at the helicopter strip in the middle of the desert. I remember one soldier in particular who was in a cast covering his entire body – from his ankles to his neck. When I asked him, in Hebrew, how he felt, he replied, "*Meah achuz*" (one hundred percent). When I asked whether that meant very good or very bad, he smiled and replied, "*Meah achuz tov*" (one hundred percent good). Here was Zionism at its very best.

Linda and I were profoundly moved by this trip to Israel. Remembering the many members of our families who had been killed during the Holocaust, we realized that most of them could have been saved had there been a Jewish State of Israel to which they could have fled. We saw Israel as our best hope to assure that the words my mother had written on her 1973 list of Holocaust victims, "Never Again!" would be fulfilled. As a result, we doubled and redoubled our efforts on behalf of our Jewish state.

On October 1, 1974, the first day of Sukkot, Linda gave birth to our fourth daughter. As we were considering what to name our new baby, Linda told me that unless I could guarantee that our next baby would be a boy, this would be my last chance to name a child in memory of my father, Avraham Yechezkel. As I could offer no such guarantee, we named

our new baby Avigayil Yehudit (the joy of my father is a female Jew) and
gave her the English name Abigail Judith.

During the ensuing years I continued to engage in a variety of community activities. Following our 1974 trip to Israel, I chaired the Young Leadership Division and the Lawyers Division of the Essex County UJA. In
1978, I became president of our synagogue, AABJ&D. In 1979, I switched
law firms and became a partner in a firm now known as Day Pitney. The
following year I became president of the Jewish Education Association
of Essex County. I also continued to be active in our local Jewish Federation. In all of these endeavors, I was mindful of my mother's devotion to
Jewish education, prayer and synagogue life, and acts of loving kindness.
Not coincidentally, these are the three pillars upon which the world stands,
according to a famous Rabbinic statement at the beginning of the ancient
text Pirkei Avot (Ethics of Our Fathers).

Beginning in the mid-1980s, I began my active involvement with Holocaust education and remembrance. The mayor of West Orange, Samuel
Spina, appointed me the township's representative to the United States
Holocaust Memorial Council. For several years, Mayor Spina and I spoke
about the Holocaust at Yom Hashoah (Holocaust Memorial Day) programs to the students of West Orange High School and Seton Hall Prep
(a Catholic school). My aim was to share my parents' story and to teach
the students about the terrible consequences of hatred and intolerance.
The mayor's goal was to talk to the students about what they should do if
they saw acts of bigotry, discrimination, or bullying.

After a few years of these programs, we started to invite guest speakers.
Our guests included Sister Rose Thering, a professor at Seton Hall University and a leader at Vatican Council II, where she was instrumental in the
removal of anti-Jewish portions of the Catholic catechism. She and I developed a very close relationship. We also invited my cousin Mala Sperling,
who told the students about her terrible ordeals during the Holocaust, as
well as a West Orange resident named Cliff Barrett, who, as an American
soldier, had been one of the liberators of Dachau. Mr. Barrett was a quiet
but very effective speaker, whose harrowing tale was corroborated by US
Army videos of the liberation, which we also showed to the students.

In 1982, Governor Thomas Kean, whose father had, in 1942, been the first in the US Congress to denounce the killing of Jews, issued an executive order establishing the Governor's Advisory Council on Holocaust Education. The council had to be reauthorized every few years by executive order. Finally, in 1991, the council became a permanent state agency, known as the New Jersey Commission on Holocaust Education. I was appointed to the commission in 1992 and became its chairman in 1993.

From its inception, the commission debated whether it should seek legislation to mandate Holocaust education in the schools of New Jersey. Interestingly, most of the educators on the commission were against the mandate, because they did not want to establish a precedent for legislative interference in the curriculum. The non-educator commission members, including survivors, legislators, and lay leaders such as me all favored the mandate. Sister Rose cast a vital vote supporting the mandate, stating that the need for Holocaust education required drastic action, including setting a precedent that she, as an educator, might have otherwise opposed.

In May 1993, a few weeks after the dedication of the United States Holocaust Memorial Museum in Washington, DC, and the commemoration of the fiftieth anniversary of the Warsaw ghetto uprising, the commission adopted a resolution stating that Holocaust education should be mandated in the secondary schools of New Jersey and approving newly revised Holocaust curriculum objectives. In support of the mandate, the commission noted that very few New Jersey high schools had a course on the Holocaust or devoted more than ten hours during the four years of high school to the subject. The commission also noted the very limited coverage of the Holocaust in textbooks and the need to reduce bias crime in New Jersey, which has an extremely diverse population.

The speaker of the assembly, Chuck Haytaian, appeared at the commission's September 1993 meeting to urge the inclusion of "the events in Armenia and Cambodia" in the commission's curriculum guidelines. Following the speaker's dramatic description of the murders of many members of his family in the Armenian genocide at the hands of the Turks, the commission approved a resolution supporting proposed legislation requiring instruction "on the Holocaust and genocide, including the events in Armenia and Cambodia." Although we knew that the issue of the Armenian genocide had plagued the prior efforts of the Holocaust Council, we decided to include material about Armenia because of Hitler's remark a week before he started World War II in which he asked, "Who, after all, speaks today of the annihilation of the Armenians?"

Understanding the sensitivity of the issue, and after having been told by several national Jewish leaders to keep in mind that Turkey had long been a friend of the State of Israel, I verified with Dr. Michael Berenbaum, then the director of the United States Holocaust Memorial Museum, both that there was an Armenian genocide and that the quotation attributed to Hitler was accurate. The commission also believed that it was important to warn our students about the budding movement toward Holocaust denial. If the Turks in 1993 were still denying the Armenian genocide almost eight decades after it happened, we wanted the students to be prepared to counter efforts to deny the Holocaust. We also wanted to include references to the Cambodian genocide to teach our students that genocide was not something that happened only in the past. To the contrary, Cambodia, like the "ethnic cleansing" then taking place in Bosnia, showed that genocide was a current and very relevant issue.

During the rest of 1993 and for the first three months of 1994, Sister Rose and I traveled together several times a month to the state capital in Trenton to testify in support of the mandate. We did so before several different New Jersey legislative committees. We were a highly unusual but ultimately effective team – a Roman Catholic nun and a lawyer wearing a knitted yarmulke. We were accompanied at many of the legislative sessions by Dr. Paul Winkler, the commission's executive director, who had led the governor's council and the commission since their inceptions. The legislators proved highly responsive. Indeed, believing that even young children should be taught about the evils of hatred and bigotry, they expanded the mandate to include students in New Jersey's elementary schools as well as its high schools.

The mandate law requiring "instruction on the Holocaust and genocides in an appropriate place in the curriculum of all elementary and secondary school pupils" was approved by both houses of the New Jersey Legislature in March 1994 and signed into law by Governor Christine Whitman at the commission's Yom Hashoah program in the assembly chamber on April 7, 1994. For the next eighteen months, I devoted a substantial amount of time to working with Sister Rose, Dr. Winkler, and Richard Flaim, coauthor of the original New Jersey Holocaust curriculum, on a completely revised high school course of study. Peppy Margolis, an experienced Holocaust educator, prepared a new elementary school curriculum. Both were approved by the commission in late 1995.

In October 1994, Linda and I participated in a national UJA mission to Poland, Israel, and Jordan. The first Oslo Accord had been signed in Washington, DC, on October 13, 1993, thus enabling us to go to Jordan. We dubbed this the mission of the past, the present, and the future. Because the mission left on the same day as the bat mitzvah of one of Linda's nieces, she did not accompany me to Poland and joined me later in Israel.

Governor Whitman presenting me with a signed copy of the Holocaust Mandate Law, April 7, 1994

Our mission began in Warsaw, which was basically destroyed by the Germans during World War II and then rebuilt by the Soviets. We visited the site of the Warsaw ghetto and the

Speaking at a Jewish War Veterans Holocaust program in front of the Liberators' Monument in Liberty Park, with the Statue of Liberty in the background

powerful sculpture by Nathan Rapoport. We also saw the *Umschlagplatz*, the square where many tens of thousands of Jews were gathered for deportation to Treblinka. Our group visited the huge Jewish cemetery of Warsaw, covering acres and acres of land, where many of the outstanding rabbis and intellectuals of the past two centuries had been buried.

From Warsaw our group traveled by bus to Krakow, where I immediately visited the home of my parents and grandparents at 9 Josefa Street. I wanted to make it to the site that my mother had left in December 1939 with me in her womb, prior to the fiftieth anniversary of my father's death. I wanted to be able to tell the people of Krakow that the Germans had not succeeded in destroying this man's family.

The building turned out to be an old, multistory apartment building with a stone inner courtyard. An elderly lady stuck her head out of one of the apartments on the second floor. I requested that our Polish guide ask her how long she had lived in the building. She replied that she had been there for many, many years. I asked the guide to ask her whether she had been there fifty years ago. She shook her head no and said that all of the people from fifty years ago were gone. When I asked her where they were, she closed the window and disappeared. Walking the streets of my parents' neighborhood, we saw the remains of five or six old synagogues, including the Rema cemetery and synagogue, named after Rabbi Moshe Isserles (1520–1572), compiler of the Code of Jewish Law on which Ashkenazi Jews base our religious lives.

Our mission then traveled from Krakow to Auschwitz, about forty miles away. There we spent the better part of a day. We walked through many of the more than two hundred barrack buildings, filled with the wooden frames of triple decker bunk beds crowded together. When we arrived at the crematorium, our scholar-in-residence, Rabbi J.J. Schachter,

A brick from Auschwitz: a tangible reminder

suggested that we all say Kaddish together and that I take one of the broken red bricks lying on the ground near the crematorium as a tangible reminder of our visit.

In the museum building, we saw exhibit areas filled with suitcases, eyeglasses, prosthetic devices, shoes, and mounds of hair taken from the victims. We also saw some of the numerous lists, books, and other records documenting a small part of the Germans' murderous atrocities.

We next journeyed to Lodz, the city with the second largest prewar Jewish population in Poland, numbering more than 200,000 souls. I distinctly remember our visit to the Poznanski Mansion, a magnificent building constructed at the beginning of the twentieth century, which had been converted to a large museum, half of which held an exhibit about the pianist Arthur Rubinstein, and the other half of which was the Museum of History of the City of Lodz. A group of Polish high school students was visiting the museum at the same time that we were there. They were absolutely amazed when Sister Rose, who was part of our mission, told them that she was a Roman Catholic nun and that the rest of the people in our group were her Jewish friends. Our wonderful Polish guide Pawel reassured the students that everything that Sister Rose said was true, and they shook their heads in continued utter amazement.

By this point, our group was very tired and was not looking forward to the lengthy bus ride over narrow and bumpy roads into Lublin. However, I had been told by our two youngest daughters, Shellie and Abigail, who had gone on the first two March of the Living tours in 1988 and 1990, that the most important part of their trips to Poland was Majdanek, a Nazi death camp located within the city of Lublin. We had traveled so far, I urged the group, it would be a shame to leave now. Fortunately, they agreed.

Lublin was the site of a very famous yeshiva called Chachmei Lublin (the wise men of Lublin), founded by Rabbi Meir Shapiro in the 1920s. Its seven-story structure had housed the first yeshiva in the world with a dormitory. During the war the building was vandalized. But by the time we saw the building, it was being used as a medical school, and the synagogue on the first floor had been rebuilt.

After visiting the yeshiva, we went to Majdanek. There we saw a camp from which the Germans had fled hastily before the advancing Red Army. They had abandoned the camp too quickly to destroy the evidence of their massive crimes. At the time that we visited Majdanek, it looked as though it could have been reopened as a death camp within twenty-four to forty-eight hours. It had gas chambers, crematoria, torture rooms, and a huge open mausoleum containing human hair and ashes.

What most amazed me about the site was that it was surrounded by numerous multistory apartment buildings, many of which had terraces directly overlooking the death camp. It seemed to me that the last place that any civilized person would want to live would be in a place that had a terrace with a full view of a death camp. Our Polish guide suggested that the Communists had made people live there, but we were in Majdanek five years after the fall of Communism, when no one was forced to live where they did not want to. My conclusion was that the murder of a then-estimated 250,000 people did not bother these many apartment dwellers in the least.

That afternoon, a Thursday in mid-October, we flew from Poland to Israel. We arrived at Ben-Gurion Airport in Tel Aviv and headed straight for Jerusalem. We were very surprised that as we traveled eastward there was a tremendous amount of traffic. What would normally have been a one-hour drive was taking more than two. When I finally got to our hotel in Jerusalem and connected with Linda, I asked her why there was such a delay. She reminded me that a few days earlier a Jewish soldier named Nachshon Wachsman had been kidnapped by a group of Hamas terrorists. She told me that on that Thursday evening there was going to be a prayer vigil at the Kotel and that more than twenty thousand people were expected. That had caused the huge traffic backup.

I marveled to myself. Here we had just been in a place where hundreds if not thousands of Polish apartment dwellers did not care about the murder of 250,000 people. But when we arrived in Israel, we found that thousands of Jews were negotiating massive traffic jams trying to get to the Kotel to pray for just one person. The contrast was stark and overpowering.

As luck would have it, the Torah portion for that coming Shabbat included Genesis, chapter 14, which tells the story of an ancient battle between Canaanite kings in which Lot, the nephew of our forefather Abraham, is captured. A refugee tells Abraham of the capture of Lot. Genesis 14:14 records Abraham's response: "When [Abraham] heard that his kinsman was taken captive, he led forth his trained men, born in his house, three hundred and eighteen, and pursued as far as Dan." Verse 15 continues that Abraham then pursued the captors to a town to the north of Damascus. At the time, Abraham was living in southern Israel. Damascus is quite a distance away. Yet, to save the life of one hostage, he traveled with his soldiers all the way to Damascus and beyond.

Thus, for thirty-five centuries, Jewish tradition has taught of the extremes to which one must go to save a single life. It is no wonder that Israel will trade more than a thousand enemy prisoners in exchange for a single hostage. And that is why Israel is there, with doctors and equipment and field hospitals, if there is a mass disaster anywhere in the world, from Haiti to Japan to the Philippines, to the Syrian border, or to Nepal.

Following our very emotional trip to Israel, we crossed the border and entered Jordan. We stayed overnight at the Intercontinental Hotel in Amman, where we learned that representatives of Israel and Jordan had initialed a peace agreement in Washington. The treaty itself was to be signed a few days later on October 26, 1994. As we traveled the streets of Amman, we saw no indication that the Jordanian people were celebrating the new accord. However, the folks in the hotel were certainly very friendly and professional, which we took as a positive sign.

With Linda as we met with King Hussein of Jordan, October 16, 1994

Our group was also privileged to meet with King Hussein, who spoke very warmly of the prospects for peace and of his relationship with Yitzhak Rabin. We visited the ruins of a coliseum, built two millennia ago by the Romans, which reminded us of similar structures in Rome and in Caesarea. Seeing Amman's connection to antiquity reminded me of Amon, a biblical nation named for Lot's son.

After a very interesting visit to the colorful excavations of Petra, we went to the airport in Aqaba. Workers were extending the landing strip there so that it could accommodate Air Force One, which would bring President Clinton there the following week for the signing of the Israel-Jordan peace treaty.

As we left Jordan to return to Israel we felt very optimistic about the prospects for peace. Little did we know what the future would bring to diminish those prospects.

One day, during the summer of 1995, I was invited to have lunch with Stanley Strauss, the president of the United Jewish Federation of MetroWest (which included Essex, Morris, Sussex, and Warren Counties in New Jersey). As I knew that the Federation's annual UJA campaign would begin shortly, I expected that Stanley would want to solicit my next gift to the UJA. Instead, Stanley made a totally unexpected offer. He said that the past presidents of the MetroWest Federation wanted to nominate me to be its next president.

I was totally stunned. Although I had been active in the Federation for many years, I was not on a presidential track, never having served as chairman of the UJA campaign. I told Stanley that I would have to discuss this with Linda. In particular, I was very concerned about the time commitment that would be needed. Linda was very supportive and encouraged me to assume this new role, because it presented a wonderful opportunity for me to accomplish a great deal of good. Having heard Linda's opinion, I told Stanley that if I was nominated and elected, I would accept the job.

During the latter part of 1995, Israelis and Jews around the world were vigorously debating the Middle East peace process. The second Oslo Accord agreement was signed on September 28, 1995. Among other things, it required Israel to withdraw from densely populated areas in the West Bank and the Palestinians to annul the clauses in their covenant denying Israel's right to exist. There were fierce debates about the wisdom of trading land for paper and about whether the Oslo process should be continued as the best hope for peace or abandoned as hopeless.

Five weeks after Oslo II, I was observing the *yahrzeit* of my mother on Saturday, November 4, corresponding to the 11th day of Cheshvan. During the evening services, someone mentioned that there had been a shooting in Tel Aviv and that Prime Minister Yitzhak Rabin might have been shot. I came home and turned on the television, where I learned that indeed, the prime minister had been shot and killed, and that a Modern Orthodox religious Zionist had been arrested in connection with his murder.

At about ten or eleven o'clock that night, I received a phone call from Amir Shacham, MetroWest's Israel representative, asking me if I would go to Israel to represent MetroWest at Rabin's funeral on Sunday. I immediately said yes and made the necessary arrangements. I did so not only because I was the president-designate of our Federation, but specifically to show that there were Modern Orthodox Jews who were completely aghast at, and totally opposed to, the assassination of the duly elected prime minister of the State of Israel. Before I left on Sunday morning, I also wrote out a message to be read at that evening's MetroWest memorial service in which I specifically condemned the assassination as totally contrary to everything that Modern Orthodoxy stands for. I urged that Jews of all types step away from hatred and violence and live by the biblical precept of loving our neighbors as ourselves.

The funeral service on Mount Herzl in Jerusalem was a truly unforgettable event. I distinctly remember the powerful-looking, stiff and erect president of Egypt, Hosni Mubarak, delivering a short, relatively cold eulogy. By sharp contrast, Jordan's King Hussein delivered an extraordinarily eloquent eulogy in which he compared Yitzhak Rabin to his own father, noting that both had been killed in the pursuit of peace and praying emotionally that he too die a similarly noble death. The next speaker was President Clinton. I recall feeling very sorry for him because he was following such a magnificent speech by King Hussein. Once again the weekly Torah reading came to the rescue. As President Clinton began, he noted that the following Shabbat we would be reading about the sacrifice of Yitzchak (our forefather Isaac). President Clinton then spoke beautifully about the sacrifice that Yitzhak Rabin, one of Israel's greatest soldiers, had made for the sake of peace. The president closed with his famous comment, a deeply felt *"Shalom, chaver"* (Good-bye, friend).

Years later, I had the opportunity to chat briefly with President Clinton. I told him how moving his eulogy had been, calling it perhaps the greatest speech that I had ever heard. Tears welled up in President Clinton's eyes as he said that he really loved and missed Yitzhak Rabin.

With Linda and President Bill Clinton

Within a few months after the Rabin assassination, elections were scheduled to select a new Israeli government. Recriminations flew fast and furious during the election campaign. Likud, the opposition party, and its leader, Benjamin Netanyahu, were blamed for the assassination of Yitzhak Rabin, a hard charge to refute given the assassin's affiliations. It was also difficult to deny that a Likud victory would reward the assassin.

It seemed, therefore, almost certain that Shimon Peres, who took over as prime minister after the assassination, would easily defeat the right-wing Likud party. However, during the first few months of 1996, the Arabs unleashed a vicious barrage of terrorist acts, including the bombing of many buses, causing huge casualties among Israel's population. As a consequence of this wave of terrorism, Likud and Netanyahu were elected to lead the next government.

In order to form a government, Netanyahu called upon the right-wing Charedi (ultra-Orthodox) parties to become part of his ruling coalition. That move caused a great deal of consternation in MetroWest, which for many years had been concerned about Orthodox control of Israeli life, particularly in the areas of conversion, marriage, divorce, and burial. I remember speaking to a large group of major MetroWest donors in June 1996, just before I was to assume the presidency. I told them that while most people in MetroWest were concerned about where Prime Minister Netanyahu would take the peace process, I was much more concerned about the coalition that he would build, which would include Charedi parties, and how Jewish unity would suffer greatly unless the situation was handled properly.

During the summer of 1996, terrible remarks by both Charedi and secular leaders were unleashed. The level of hatred in Israel was corrosive and threatened to destroy Jewish unity not only in Israel but in MetroWest as well. Accordingly, one of the first things that I did as president was to create a Committee on Religious Pluralism with a threefold mission: first, to reduce the level of hateful speech and conduct in order to promote tolerance and respect by both sides of the religious divide; second, to persuade governmental bodies to provide funding for non-Orthodox synagogues and groups in Israel, just as they had done for many years for Orthodox institutions; third, to work toward increasing the level of Jewish knowledge among all of Israel's citizens, emphasizing our common heritage and common destiny. In the nineteen years since its formation, the MetroWest Committee on Religious Pluralism has been an amazing success in all three of its original areas of focus.

One of my most memorable experiences was the dedication of a new Progressive/Reform synagogue in Ra'anana, a city that MetroWest had long supported. Ra'anana has a large English-speaking population and is more familiar than most Israeli communities with non-Orthodox synagogues. At the dedication ceremony I affixed the mezuzah at the front of the building together with Jerry Waldor, Stanley Strauss's predecessor as president of the MetroWest Federation and one of the most wonderful people I have ever known. It was truly a symbolic act to have a member of a Reform synagogue and a member of the Orthodox community working together jointly to establish this new synagogue.

In addition to promoting religious pluralism, I also devoted a great deal of time to assuring that MetroWest continued to support Israel financially and diplomatically as it wrestled with the ramifications of Oslo II and an increasingly hostile world. We also worked to effect necessary changes in the Israeli conversion process to enable as many as possible of the hundreds of thousands of non-Jewish Russian immigrants to become Jews. Unfortunately, these efforts, though supported widely in Israel and the United States, have not yet achieved success.

After my term as president expired in 1999, I continue to be actively involved in the MetroWest Federation and I also joined the boards of such institutions as the Jewish Agency for Israel, the Joint Distribution Committee, Stern College for Women, Ohr Torah Stone (a major educational operation with a huge worldwide impact), and the American Committee for Shaare Zedek Medical Center in Jerusalem, of which I became president in 2012. Since becoming a Florida resident, I have joined the boards of the Miami Federation and the Miami Center for the Advancement of Jewish Education.

In all of these activities I have tried to live by the standards and goals set by my mother of promoting Jewish education, religious life, and philanthropy. It has been a most rewarding experience demonstrating the truism that to give charity is to receive. I have also tried to live up to the hopes and expectations that my father must have had when he let my mother go to the United States while he remained in Krakow, that I grow up to be "a good man." And perhaps most importantly, I have wanted to live my life in a way that demonstrates that his and my mother's sacrifices were not in vain. In order to demonstrate this fact, we need only look at the activities of our children and grandchildren in the epilogue that follows.

Linda and I gather with our children and grandchildren at the April 20, 2011, dedication of the Linda and Murray Laulicht Center for Children and Youth in the Negev town of Ofakim

Linda and Murray Laulicht, 2011

The Next Generations

In this section I present a brief profile of each of our four daughters, their husbands, and our grandchildren. It is their lives that constitute the true legacy for which my parents sacrificed and strived. In order to collect this information, I sent out the following letter to each of my daughters:

My dear daughters,

I am in the process of writing an epilogue to the book about my parents in which I would like to describe the long-term results of my parents' incredibly courageous decisions that brought my mother to the United States in early 1940. As you know, she made the trip alone and pregnant with me. Each one of you, and your families, are very important parts of what my parents ultimately accomplished, and I am proud to say that you all have followed in Grandma's footsteps.

Jewish education was of primary importance to my mother, Ernestyna, as well as to her mother, Leah. My mother went to Bais Yaakov in the 1920s and she sent me to the JEC beginning in 1946. Grandma was an ardent Zionist and supporter of the State of Israel. She was also very involved in shul life in Elizabeth and Forest Hills and in acts of chesed [giving]. I still recall the packages of clothing that she gathered and sent to Jews in Israel and the USSR, as well as the many checks she sent to almost anyone who asked.

Grandma would have loved to know about your many accomplishments and those of your families, in each of these areas that characterized and ennobled her life. It would be a wonderful tribute to Grandma if each of you would write a description of your involvement and that of your husbands and children in these areas.

Thank you so much.

– Dad

From left: Samantha, Joseph, Laurie, Bernard, Hannah, Erica, and Zev

The Hasten Family
Chicago, Illinois

Our daughter Laurie was married to Bernard Hasten on February 1, 1987. Theirs was the only one of her grandchildren's weddings that my mother attended.

Bernard is currently the president of Congregation Kehilath Jacob Beth Samuel in Chicago, Illinois. He is also on the Yeshiva College board. He is the past president of Congregation B'nai Torah and the Hasten Hebrew Academy, both in Indianapolis, Indiana. Bernard is also actively involved in AIPAC, a pro-Israel advocacy group.

Laurie is currently the president of the board of Hillel Torah North Suburban Day School in Skokie, Illinois. She works as a docent at the Illinois Holocaust Museum and is a coordinator of the "Names, Not Numbers" Holocaust oral history project at Hillel Torah.

Their daughter Erica is a PhD candidate at Albert Einstein Medical School. She is researching genetic heart defects. She is involved in "Project START," a science outreach program designed to educate underprivileged elementary and middle-school students. She also helps coordinate Shabbat meals for Einstein students. Erica is married to Zev Dlott, a graduate of Sy Syms School of Business at Yeshiva University. Zev is currently studying for his MBA.

Their son Joseph is a graduate of Sy Syms School of Business at Yeshiva University. He was involved in the Shaare Zedek Hospital College Board. He was also president of the Yeshiva College Republicans.

Their daughter Samantha is a student at Hunter College. She is an intern at Goods for Good, an organization that provides economic opportunities by promoting local businesses in southern Africa. She also volunteers regularly at the National Eating Disorder Association. She is on the college board of Shaare Zedek Hospital and attends NYU Chabad activities.

Their daughter Hannah just graduated from Ida Crown Jewish Academy. She will be studying at Midreshet Moriah in Jerusalem in 2015–16 and then plans to attend Stern College. Every Friday she delivers candlesticks to Jewish patients at Swedish Covenant Hospital in Chicago. She is also a leader in B'nei Akiva and helps coordinate activities for ninth-grade students.

From left: Evan, Estie, Jordana, Ari, Pamela, Michael, and Avi

The Hirt Family
Bergenfield, New Jersey

Our daughter Pamela married Ari Hirt on March 26, 1989.

Ari and Pamela are involved locally and nationally in lobbying elected officials in behalf of a strong US-Israel relationship. They also support Jewish education.

Ari is a member of AIPAC's New Leadership Network and serves on AIPAC's National Council. He is an alumnus of the Berrie Fellows Leadership Program, sponsored by the Jewish Federation of Northern New Jersey and the Russell Berrie Foundation. Together with two other Berrie Foundation alumni, Ari cofounded Unite4Unity, an organization that runs programs in Bergen County that bring together Jews of all backgrounds. Ari also serves as a member of the board of trustees of the Jewish Community Relations Council and is a member of Yeshiva University's alumni advisory.

Pamela serves as a member of the board of trustees of Yeshiva University's Stern College for Women. She has also served as a member of the board of trustees of the Yavneh Academy and is a past president of the Bergen County chapter of Amit. Pamela has been involved in all of her children's schools' parent associations and has cochaired many of these schools' fund-raising dinners and special events.

Estie and her husband Evan Rottenstreich are both graduates of Yeshiva University. Estie recently received a master's in social work from Yeshiva University's Wurzweiler School of Social Work, where she was a member of Phi Alpha Honor Society. Estie is currently doing her field placement, serving at-risk NYC adolescents by providing counseling and supportive services. Estie has also been involved in Yachad and HASC, serving people with special needs.

Evan graduated from Yeshiva University's Sy Syms School of Business and is currently studying for a master's in taxation at City University's Baruch College. He will be working as a tax accountant at Deloitte.

Avi, is a junior at Yeshiva University's Sy Syms School of Business, majoring in accounting and minoring in finance. He serves as a group leader for Music Vs, an organization that provides entertainment for the elderly in Washington Heights. He serves as a leader at both MTA High School and the Torah Academy of Bergen County (TABC). Avi started a program in which he learns with boys in sixth to eighth grades on Shabbat afternoons. He has represented Yeshiva University on vacations and holidays and has been to Cleveland, Detroit, Columbus, Toledo, and several cities in California. Avi will be working as a tax accountant at Deloitte.

Michael is currently studying at Yeshivat Sha'alvim in Israel. He is a member of the board of Yachad Israel, which serves individuals with special needs. Michael is the former Friendship Circle president for TABC and served as treasurer of the TABC student council. He gave the local Israel reports while at TABC and was the lead broadcaster for most of the school's athletic events. He was also the captain of the TABC hockey team. Michael plans to attend Yeshiva University.

Jordana attends Ma'ayanot Yeshiva High School. She is involved in planning the Yom Hashoah programming there. She was selected to speak at the annual community-wide Holocaust Memorial Program. Jordana is involved in an after-school program called "Pay It Forward," which involves tutoring on a weekly basis.

From left: Joy, Elizabeth, Shellie, Eric, Samson, Isaac, and Max

The Davis Family
Efrat, Israel

Our daughter Shellie married Eric Davis on June 28, 1992. When I asked Shellie to contribute to the book, she responded in the form of a letter addressed to my mother.

Dear Grandma,

It has been a long time since I have seen or touched you, but I have a clear vision of you in my mind and heart. Your gentle touch and smile always made me know how much you loved me.

I have decided to write to you in the form of a letter because that is the link that brought my father closer to his father – through letters.

I am married to Eric and we live in Efrat, Israel. We have been living in Israel for 16 years. I know that you always felt a strong connection to the Land. We have made a really nice life for ourselves – there are so many good people here and the feeling of being a Jew always surrounds us.

Elizabeth is our oldest daughter and is named Esther Chaya after you. She just completed her National Service, where she worked for two years in a children's home in Netanya, Israel, called Beit Elezraki. Her job was to serve as a "mother" to fifth- and sixth-grade children by giving them love and support, virtually 24/7. Elizabeth still keeps in touch with many of the girls and unquestionably altered their lives. Elizabeth will be going to Bar-Ilan University to study social work next year.

Joy is 18, and just graduated from the Neve Chana high school in Alon Shvut. She has been volunteering for the past three years at the Shalva Center, an organization that serves children with special needs. Joy thinks outside the box and develops ways to teach them and encourage them to understand how special they are. The kids love her. Joy plans to go to a midrashah [advanced Jewish studies for young women] next year, and then to the Israeli army.

Max attends Derech Avot High School in Efrat. He is a leader and likes to help out with everything. Max was a big help over the summer of 2014 when we had 450 soldiers stationed in Efrat. Our responsibilities were to help prepare meals, and Max was always willing to serve and give of his time with a smile.

Isaac finished the sixth grade in Orot Etzion in Efrat. There were kids in Isaac's school whose parents were unable to provide them with lunch, so Isaac helped me prepare sandwiches in the morning to bring them to school. Isaac did not want anyone to be embarrassed, so he brought the sandwiches directly to the school office early, so none of the recipients would see him.

Samson is going into the fourth grade in Aseh Chayil in Efrat. He plays a lot of sports and is a team player. Even though he is young, you can tell that he is a leader who knows right from wrong.

Grandma, the reason I am writing to you about my kids is because that will show you who I am. I try to teach them by example with everything that I do. But before that I had as examples my parents and grandparents, who taught me to always give with a full heart.

Love,
Shellie

P.S. Grandma, on a personal note, Holocaust Remembrance Day just passed. As the siren goes off in Israel I think about you and how brave you were for leaving and going to America. It's because of you that we are all here today. My head bows down and tears fill my eyes for the six million people who were killed just because they were Jews.

A few days later is Yom Hazikaron, which is a very difficult day. Sadness fills the air for the families that have lost loved ones and for all the heroes in this country who fight for its existence every day.

In the evening it becomes Yom Ha'atzmaut, which is a day of celebration. The mood changes drastically and there is hope for a peaceful year.

So Grandma, my life surrounds me with emotion and I care about everyone around me as a Jew. I really try to help, give tzedakah, and give of myself any way possible. I do my best to live by example and be the best role model I can be for my family.

Grandma, you will always have a special place in my heart. I hope that as you look down on us, you are proud.

From left: Emily, Julia, Scott, Rae, Abigail, and Sara

The Herschmann Family
Englewood, New Jersey

Our daughter Abigail married Scott Herschmann on June 9, 1996.

Scott is a managing partner of the hedge fund Pentsao Fund. He is on the board of NORPAC, a non-partisan political action committee focused on promoting the US-Israel relationship. In behalf of NORPAC, Scott has hosted and raised significant sums for the successful election campaigns of Senators Mark Kirk (Illinois), Tim Scott (South Carolina), and James Lankford (Oklahoma). Scott is also head of the Young Wall Street Division of AIPAC and is a member of AIPAC's Congressional Club. In addition, Scott is a member of Partners in Torah, where he learns and mentors individual Russian immigrants on the weekly Torah portion. He is a member of the board and is on the finance committee of the Moriah School. Scott cofounded the Israel advocacy program at Frisch High School, which teaches students Israel's history as well as how to properly respond to antisemitism on college campuses. He is on the religious services committee at Congregation Ahavath Torah. Scott is also involved with Chabad, Shaare Zedek, Sinai, and Panim el Panim, an organization that teaches IDF soldiers about Jewish history and Torah prior to their going into combat.

Abby brought the "Names, Not Numbers" project to the Moriah School and works with the eighth-grade class on this year-long project.

She is currently a board member of the Moriah Parents' Association. Abby has cochaired numerous events and fundraising dinners at both the Moriah School and Ahavath Torah. She is the past president of the Englewood chapter of Amit and Emunah. She is a past board member of Ahavath Torah.

Emily is in the high honors program for all of her classes at Frisch High School, where she plays on the varsity basketball team and is working to integrate Israel advocacy classes into the curriculum. She has attended AIPAC's Policy Conference for the last two years and has attended NOR-PAC's missions to Washington, DC, where she met with US senators and congressman to advocate in support of a strong US-Israel relationship.

Julia graduated from the Moriah School this year and will be attending Frisch High School next year.

Sara is a student at the Moriah School and will celebrate her bat mitzvah in December.

Rae's teachers agree that she is a gifted student and report that she is a treat to have in their classes.

With Linda and our grandchildren in Naples, Florida, celebrating our fiftieth wedding anniversary, April 2015

Index